RADIO CANADA
INTERNATIONAL

RADIO CANADA INTERNATIONAL

VOICE OF A MIDDLE POWER

JAMES L. HALL

Michigan State University Press

East Lansing

All Michigan State University Press books are produced on paper which meets
the requirements of American National Standard of Information Sciences—
Permanence of paper for printed materials ANSI Z23.48-1984.

Michigan State University Press
East Lansing, MI 48823-5202

Printed in the United States of America

03 02 01 00 99 98 97 1 2 3 4 5 6 7 8 9 10

Library of Congress Cataloging-in-Publication Data

Hall, James L., 1938-
  Radio Canada International: voice of a middle power / James L. Hall.
      p. cm.
  Includes bibliographical references and index.
    ISBN 0-87013-420-5
    1. Radio Canada International.   I. Title.
  HE8697.45.C2H35   1996
  384.54'06'571--dc20   96-6094
                                                                  CIP

CONTENTS

Preface vii

1   Entering the International Arena 1

2   This Is Canada Calling 27

3   The Cold War Intensifies .53

4   Consolidation, Integration, and Stability,
       1960-70 97

5   Achieving Stability, 1967-70 123

6   Transitions, 1971-74 137

7   Introspection 157

8   Messages from the Past .181

    Appendix A 189

    Appendix B 193

    Appendix C 209

    Bibliography 281

    Index 291

PREFACE

INTERNATIONAL SHORTWAVE RADIO broadcasting is a uniquely important communications medium. The high frequency (HF) bands allocated for this special form of broadcasting are filled with more than 150 international shortwave broadcasting services transmitting a cacophony of languages and a variety of dialects to a world audience. In many parts of the globe, radio remains the primary communications medium. Television set penetration is growing, but in many areas radio is the only means by which a mass audience can receive news, information, and entertainment beamed from another nation. Although international shortwave radio broadcasting is well-known for fading signals, static, and the occasional pitched shrill of heterodyne interference, listeners disregard such inconveniences to hear, firsthand, news and information broadcast from other countries.

With such troubling imperfections, what is the attraction of international shortwave radio broadcasting? From the vantage point of the audience, there is, of course, the immediate appeal of instantaneous communication coming from a foreign shortwave radio service. To the hobbyist, there is the perpetual excitement associated with stringing an antenna between two trees, fine-tuning a highly sensitive receiver, and listening to Radio Moscow, Radio Budapest, or the World Service of the British Broadcasting Corporation (BBC). Hobbyists, known as shortwave listeners (SWLs), account for a significant segment of the radio audience, particularly in North America, where radio has lost much of its instantaneous appeal to live television news coverage which is virtually round-the-clock on cable services such as Cable News Network and its subsidiary, Headline News. In other areas of the world, television broadcasting is not as widespread as in North America and radio broadcasting remains an important, and in some cases, the essential communications medium.

International communication scholars recognize two important characteristics of shortwave radio broadcasting: it is "unstoppable," i.e., capable of crossing national boundaries without government interference;[1] and it possesses the ability to achieve almost "limitless" operational goals.[2] Much has been written about the use of international shortwave radio broadcasting as a powerful propaganda weapon.[3] While in some instances claims regarding the effects of propagandistic transnational broadcasts are difficult to quantify and are subject to exaggeration, no one doubts the indispensable role that radio plays in disseminating information to an international audience. Radio broadcasting easily transcends national boundaries, and there is very little any perturbed target country can do about it. Technically, jamming may prevent a shortwave radio broadcast program from entering a country, but it is exceptionally expensive. The former Soviet Union, zealous in protecting its borders from foreign broadcasts beamed into its territory, stopped jamming American shortwave broadcasts in January 1989.[4]

Shortwave radio broadcasting, then, is a special utilitarian communications medium that offers the worldwide radio audience "something beyond the scope of any domestic newspaper, radio or television station— an instant window on the world."[5] The question remains: who provides such window openings?

Key players in this specialized form of broadcasting often are national governments attempting to supplement other international communication forms with a sovereign "radio voice" which is capable, on occasion, of substituting for diplomacy.[6] World powers often attempt to reinforce their positions and their status in the community of nations via shortwave radio broadcasting. Other agencies and groups are involved in this important communications medium as well: church groups, military forces, even clandestine operators.[7] All function with specific goals, with an underlying assumption of effectiveness. Dominant among the participants are international shortwave radio broadcasters that represent governments across a world power continuum ranging from Great Powers to Middle Powers to Lesser Powers.

Traditional descriptions of the world hierarchy may be lacking in the context of today's fluid, transient economy; nonetheless, they offer a starting point for assessment. The three degrees of power—great, middle, and lesser—signify placement points along the illustrative continuum with the understanding that any categorization of power structure connotes characteristics of a nation's foreign relations status. Typically, the Middle Powers are known to be diffident, perfectly peaceful nations that are content with the status quo, do not benefit greatly from the hierarchy of world power, and ally themselves with the more dominant nations.[8] The Great Powers are more assertive in international relations than the middle powers and often supplement forms of diplomatic persuasion with international shortwave radio broadcasting to further project their influence. The Voice of America, the World Service of the British Broadcasting Corporation, Radio Moscow, and Radio Beijing all maintain elaborate broadcasting schedules in dozens of different languages and dialects. These extensive operations, however, represent only a portion of the total hours broadcast by international broadcasting services.

Middle Powers such as Canada, the Netherlands, Switzerland, Sweden, Brazil, Italy, and Portugal engage in international shortwave radio broadcasting to supplement their diplomacy. Even Lesser Powers such as Ghana, Zambia, Ethiopia, and Malaysia broadcast to a world radio audience. The question remains: why do the Lesser Powers or, for that matter, the Middle Powers, engage in international shortwave radio broadcasting?

As the title of this book suggests, Radio Canada International (RCI) is the Voice of a Middle Power. In this book, the descriptive designation "voice" is used because it embodies a programming goal that is extremely difficult to define—that of projecting national identity. Throughout RCI's history there have been numerous references to international shortwave radio broadcasting as a means to communicate national identity to the world.

WHAT IS THE CANADIAN IDENTITY?

Among Canadians, from the grass roots to the intelligentsia, the question of identity continues to generate much discussion and debate. Divided by language, ethnicity, and vast regions, Canada has struggled to discover a self-assured identity. Since Confederation, Canadians have expressed concern about their ability to remain a cohesive, culturally integrated, sovereign state. Despite a fearful undercurrent, Canadians have maintained a passion for identity. Influenced partly by economic and political pressures exerted by its southern neighbor, the United States, the Canadian identity issue has been evident in institutions and allegiances.[9]

This book focuses on one institution, the Canadian Broadcasting Corporation's International Service (CBC-IS, later Radio Canada International) which, from the beginning, pledged to represent all of Canada. The RCI programming goal, "to project the Canadian identity," is elusive unless placed within the context of these two assumptions: 1) to represent all of Canada is an impossible task; and 2) to project Canada under the umbrella of social responsibility, with the inherent need for audience targeting, topical selection, and editing, is a worthy goal. Simply put, to project the Canadian identity means the selection of broadcast topics that reflect elements of Canadian life in the form of news, features, and entertainment. The broadcast phrase "This is Canada" emphasizes the point. It was RCI's task to interpret Canada to the world radio audience.

What does Canada, a Middle Power in North America, hope to gain from projecting its "voice" to the world radio audience? This book probes the policies of the Canadian Broadcasting Corporation's international shortwave radio broadcasting (CBC-IS and RCI) from 1945 to 1985 to determine why and how this representative of a Middle Power broadcast to a world radio audience.

The purposes of this study are as follows:

1. To record a history of the founding of the International Service (IS).
2. To trace the development of the operational policies and to determine the degree of government involvement in formulating policies.
3. To describe the development of the organizational structure and management of the International Service and RCI for the term, 1945-85.
4. To illustrate the ways in which operational policies are implemented by describing program planning for each of the language sections beamed to the following target areas: the United States and Caribbean, South America, Western Europe, Eastern Europe, Africa, and Asia/Australia.

Central to this study is the question: Why did Canada, a Middle Power, choose to participate in the field of international shortwave broadcasting? Operational policy and a treatment of policy development provide insights into the question. The organizational structure and management positions are discussed within the framework of the parent organization, the Canadian Broadcasting Corporation, and both the International Service and Radio Canada International. A description of the ways in which the operational policies are implemented through program planning and programming formats offers information about *how* the Canadian Broadcasting Corporation broadcast to the world audience during this period of investigation.

The scope of this monograph has certain imposed limitations. This study traces the development of operational policy for the Canadian Broadcasting Corporation's International Service and Radio Canada

International. The research attempts to probe *why* the service operates in the manner described. It does not, however, compare CBC-IS and RCI with another service, nor does it determine whether or not the operation is typical of other international broadcasting services or whether or not the policies or methods used in the daily operation can be applied to other services which broadcast transnationally.

Moreover, this history does not attempt to list *each* change that has taken place in organization and programming since the inauguration of the International Service in 1945, through the Cold War era of the 1950s, the corporate consolidations of the 1960s to the change of name, to Radio Canada International, in 1972 and concluding in 1985. Only those changes which motivated a specific policy action are introduced.

Research for this study was conducted at McGill University's McLennon Library, Montreal, the National Library and Public Archives of Canada in Ottawa, and the McPherson Library, University of Victoria, Victoria, British Columbia. Interviews were conducted at the main head-quarters of the CBC, at the branch office of the International Service and the Department of External Affairs in Ottawa, and at the broadcasting facility in Montreal. Files and station records at the main broadcasting facility and the extensive holdings at the CBC Central Registry, Montreal, were examined. Nearly twelve hours of taped interviews with IS and RCI personnel were conducted.

For the initial research, conducted for my doctoral dissertation in 1970-71, I remain grateful to the late Charles R. Delafield, then director of CBC-IS, for offering me the opportunity to study and learn about Canadian international shortwave radio broadcasting. In 1987 I received a Faculty Research grant from the Canadian Embassy, giving me the financial start to update my earlier research. For that, I am most grateful.

A special word of thanks should go to RCI management staff members Betty Zimmerman, Alan Familiant, and Keith Randall for their generous help and support during my research visits in 1987-88.

Colleagues at the University of Southern Mississippi were helpful with the project. Terry Harper, dean, College of Liberal Arts, Karen Yarbrough, vice president, Research and Sponsored Programs, and Tim Hudson, dean, College of International and Continuing Education, all provided financial assistance for travel. Brenda Harper Mattson, director, International Programs, read an early draft of the manuscript and made invaluable comments and suggestions. Drew McDaniel, Ohio University, and Walter Soderlund, University of Windsor, reviewed the manuscript and made helpful comments. I am indebted to Victor Howard, editor, Canadian Series, Michigan State University Press, for his encouragement and editorial counsel. Finally, my wife Ellen deserves special thanks for her understanding, extraordinary patience, and expert word processing skills.

NOTES

1. The last official attempts at preventing radio audiences from listening to foreign services ceased when the Soviets stopped jamming American and British short-wave broadcasts in January 1989. For additional insights into the use of jamming techniques, see Julian Hale, *Radio Power: Propaganda and International Broadcasting* (Philadelphia: Temple University Press, 1975), ix.
2. Don R. Browne, *International Shortwave Radio Broadcasting: The Limits of a Limitless Medium* (New York: Praeger Publishers, Inc., 1982).
3. See Hale, *Radio Power.*
4. The Chinese jammed the Voice of America during the student demonstrations at Beijing in May 1989.
5. Andrew Simon, Executive Director, Radio Canada International, cited in *Program Schedule,* 26 March-30 September 1989 (Montreal: Radio Canada International, 1989), 1.
6. Hale, *Radio Power,* Part One, "The Nazi Model."
7. See *World Radio TV Handbook,* published annually by Billboard Publications, New York.
8. A. F. K. Organiski, *World Politics* (New York: Alfred A. Knopf, 1968), 367-68; see also F. H. Soward, *Canada in World Affairs* (Toronto: Oxford University Press, 1950), 126; and J. J. Granatstein, ed., *Canadian Foreign Policy Since 1945: Middle Power or Satellite* (Toronto: The Copp Clark Publishing Co., 1969), 50. For a more recent discussion of Canada's place in the continuum, see James Eayrs, "From Middle Power to Foremost Power: Defining a New Place For Canada in the Hierarchy of World Power," *International Perspectives* (May/June 1975): 15-24.
9. David Taras, "Introduction," to *A Passion for Identity: an Introduction to Canadian Studies,* Eli Mandel and David Taras, eds. (Toronto:Methuen Publications, 1987), 10.

1

ENTERING THE INTERNATIONAL ARENA

FROM FAR AND WIDE, O CANADA

THE VAST EXPANSE OF Canada has inspired, in part, a unique infrastructure to provide communications for an area encompassing 10 million square kilometers of land and water and a quarter of the world's time zones. Canada is second only to Russia in geographic size since the collapse of the Soviet Union. The United States, almost dwarfed by comparison, shares with Canada an unfortified border stretching across nearly 5,414 kilometers of territory.

Nearly 28 million people presently live in Canada with more than two-thirds of the population residing within 100 miles of the U. S. border. Approximately one-half of the total population is densely clustered in the southeast near the Great Lakes and the St. Lawrence River. The United States casts a long shadow into the most populous regions of Canada, causing concern about "possible threats" to Canadian culture via electronic media spillover and broadcast program procurement from American production companies. Fundamentally, Canada's geographic closeness to the United States has been an important counterbalance in the development of Canadian broadcasting.

An interesting argument can be made that Canadian broadcasting actually has advanced "continental integration" instead of promoting "national unity." The early use of American programming diffused American, not Canadian, cultural elements. The "doctrine of technological nationalism" is, according to the proponents of this argument, a figment of the Canadian imagination. Since 1928, when the first Royal Commission on Broadcasting, the Aird commission, proclaimed that "Canadian listeners want Canadian radio broadcasting," policy makers and legislators have attempted to restrict foreign (mostly American) content. Why? Canadians may have wanted their own programming, but they listened to and enjoyed American radio programs in surprising quantities as well—a trend (carried over into the age of television) that continues to this day.[1]

1

Another important national consideration for the development of Canadian broadcasting is the cultural and linguistic needs of the French and English. These two major groups have been joined by scores of other immigrants, with the overwhelming majority from dominant European cultures. The assorted immigrant groups have been drawn largely to English-speaking Canada, while maintaining their own residual cultural identities. The indigenous peoples, the Indian and the Inuit, provide additional cultural and linguistic variations. With so many Canadians continuing their language and cultural heritage, the notion of a "melting pot" society has given way to more of a "cultural mosaic," with the major heritage pattern originating from the French and English. Much of Canadian history can be viewed "as a continuing search for accommodation and cooperation between the two major cultural communities and the integration of newcomers to the basic patterns."[2] National unity and national sovereignty, then, have been a major overriding concern primarily because of these geographical, linguistic, and cultural factors.

Since Confederation, the development of a spirit of nationalism has been troubling to many Canadians, particularly with the traditionally learned responses to an evocative national symbol such as the flag. Agreement to a Canadian flag did not come easily. The now familiar ensign, red maple leaf centered between two red bars against a field of white, was not adopted until 1965, ninety-eight years *after* Confederation.

The ever-present bicultural accommodation issue, deigned by English-speaking Canadians and supported warily by French-speaking Canadians, remains problematic even among staunch nationalists. The Royal Commission on Bilingualism and Biculturalism (1963-69) recommended that Parliament enact legislation providing that both French and English serve as the official languages of Canada. In effect, this would mean that all federal institutions must provide services in either of these two languages at the customer's request. Parliament obliged the commission with The Official Languages Act (1969), a federal statute that declared French and English the official languages of Canada with an implied reinforcement of bicultural accommodation, while at the same time recognizing intellectual and cultural insularity among the Quebecois. Politically, the act has been sanctioned by all federal parties; among the citizenry, however, there has been concern about the need for two official languages, fostered in part by misunderstanding and intolerant attitudes among both language groups.

Canada's relations with the world's communities have evolved primarily through two major, complex processes. The first process of self-definition through national unity has been the evolution of Canadian nationalism from colony status within the British Empire to independence within the Commonwealth. The second process, more subtle and often more difficult to describe, was the defining and defending of the Canadian identity against economic, cultural, and political pressures from its close neighbor, the United States.[3] A distinctively Canadian communications system offered the hope of remedying these complex issues. From its inception, broadcasting, with its unique property of instantaneous communication, held even greater promise to unite Canadians with a spirit of nationalism.

BROADCASTING THE SEEDS OF NATIONALISM

EARLY POLICY

The scattered, culturally diverse Canadian population has always needed a communications system to help resolve difficult issues associated with the complex internal accommodation and external self-definition processes. In the nineteenth century, the telegraph aided unity, but remained a point-to-point communications system. Newspapers, the first truly mass communications media, were essential to the development of democratic institutions, political parties and, indeed, to the Confederation that united Canada.

In the twentieth century, the emergence of broadcasting in Canada brought new opportunities for information dissemination, generated new communications channels crucial to nation building, and increased awareness of the political processes among the populace. Beginning modestly in 1920, at station XWA (the forerunner of station CFCF), Montreal, radio broadcasting quickly spread across the densely populated areas of Canada to become the dominant carrier of entertainment, news, opinion, and social and cultural values. Unfortunately, the pervasive nature of radio broadcasting offered false hope for Canadian nationalists. Viewed as "the highways of national cultural interaction," the broadcast media proved to have limited success in attaining such a noble goal. In actuality, from the inception of Canadian radio broadcasting, there was the threat of denationalization caused by the pervasiveness of broadcasts from American stations spilling over into the heavily populated areas along the Canada-United States border.

The privately owned, commercial radio stations in Canada were the forebears of a centralized system charged with the responsibility of providing balanced programming for all Canadians. While Parliament groped for solutions to pressing problems associated with this revolutionary communications medium, Sir Henry Thornton, the astute head of Canadian National Railways, envisaged radio broadcasting as an instrument for the clearer delineation of a truly Canadian identity.[4] Thornton's view was premature. It was 1928 before anyone in government paid any attention to the new communications medium, and even then their attention turned to it only because of pressing problems causing public alarm.

One problem which hindered the development of Canadian broadcasting in the 1920s was inadequate frequency management which caused intolerable transmission interference problems with stations in the provinces and in neighboring states. By 1925, there were 555 stations broadcasting in the United States, of which 138 had 500 watts of power or more. One-half of these stations were located in the states bordering the Great Lakes, and their signals penetrated easily into the eastern provinces. Canada, however, had fewer and less powerful stations, only forty-three active stations broadcasting in 1925. Why the disparity of broadcasting stations in the two countries? American stations had simply absorbed all available channels, including frequencies Canada had claimed as its own (19).

There was also the thorny issue of financing the broadcasting. Initially, stations attempted commercialization, but in the main they were established with the expectation they would not be able to pay for themselves. Interestingly, most of the first radio stations were owned by newspapers or by firms engaged in selling radio equipment. While it is easy to understand why businesses involved in the selling of radio equipment would want to enter broadcasting, it is an open question for newspapers. Perhaps the publishers were attempting to promote their newspapers via the new medium, or the publishers may have sensed future competition for advertising revenue. The fact remains that commercialization of radio broadcasting was slow to develop in the 1920s. Certainly the newspaper-station ownerships, as well as newspapers without stations, did not support the notion that the new medium should be solely supported by advertising (27). Furthermore, the proposal of charging a license fee was unpopular among Canadians since the Americans had "free radio." The first Canadian attempt to finance the new medium was termed "indirect advertising," and followed the American model. The advertising dollar generated by radio broadcasting in

Toronto and in Montreal multiplied, and the number of stations increased steadily in the districts surrounding the densely populated metropolitan areas. In sparsely populated regions with smaller cities and towns, the reverse was true. The result was a lack of adequate geographic coverage of Canadian broadcast programming, which caused further consternation among both the populace and the government.

Accordingly, the urban population received Canadian programming, while large segments of nonurban residents heard only American stations. If radio broadcasting was to foster national unity, the large numbers of people living across rural Canada needed access to Canadian radio stations.[5] This access argument presented by government would hold up easily in subsequent debates. The dynamic evolution of radio broadcasting must have been baffling to early framers of Canadian broadcasting policy, since a myriad of problems associated with this new electronic medium seemed to materialize at each development milestone.

For example, broadcasting in Canada was hampered by the inadequate provisions of the 1913 Radiotelegraph Act, a legislative act clearly intended for "wireless" point-to-point communication. The act granted the federal government licensing power, but set forth no provisions for broadcast programming intended for the public. The cautious Canadian government adopted a "wait and see" attitude. It was not long, however, before the government became enmeshed in its first controversy over programming—created by its own inadequate, lackadaisical broadcasting policy. Ironically, it was religion, not politics, that brought the problem to the forefront and caused the resolution of issues which proved to be a turning point in the development of Canadian broadcasting.[6]

By 1928 several broadcasting stations were operated by churches and by other religious organizations across Canada. In Vancouver, for example, the United Church of Canada, the Presbyterian Church, and the International Bible Students Association (an organization of Jehovah's Witnesses) all operated radio stations. The International Bible Students Association owned stations in Edmonton and in Saskatoon. The Christian and Military Alliance had a station in Edmonton.

In Toronto the situation was more complex. CJYC, a commercial station, was owned by Universal Radio of Canada. CKCX shared the CJYC broadcasting facilities and was licensed to the International Bible Students Association. During a reassignment of frequencies in Toronto, which affected the station operated by the International Bible Students, the fact surfaced that the government had received increasing numbers of complaints concerning the content of religious programs as "unpatriotic and abusive of all our churches" (31). The government subsequently revoked the licenses of four stations located in different parts of Canada which were owned by the International Bible Students Association. Lawyers representing the association were sent to Ottawa to appeal the revocation order. Their petition, focusing on the issues of freedom of speech and of censorship, stirred considerable controversy, eventually bringing into question the entire Canadian broadcasting situation. The Canadian government indicated a willingness to at least study broadcasting policy. The broadcast licensees hoped that legislative enactment would follow (34).

THE FIRST LEGISLATION

In June 1928, the House of Commons appropriated $25,000 to finance a commission "to inquire into the radio broadcasting situation throughout Canada, and to advise as to the future administration, management, control and finance thereof."[7] On 6 December 1928, the first Royal Commission on Radio Broadcasting was appointed under the chairmanship of Sir John Aird, then president of the Canadian Bank of Commerce.[8]

The commission's report was submitted to the House of Commons in September 1929, but the Stock Market Crash the next month caused a three-year delay before any action was taken. The Aird commission reported that there was "unanimity on one fundamental issue: Canadian listeners want Canadian broadcasting."[9] According to the commission, private enterprise could not support radio, and the unregulated commercial stations forced too much advertising on the audience. More important, the commission found that the concentration of stations near the metropolitan centers did not provide *national* coverage or opportunities for program exchange between regions. The Aird commission concluded that the Canadian nation could be adequately served only by some form of public ownership, operation, and control, "behind which is the national power and prestige of the whole public of the Dominion of Canada."[10] The commission recommended that Canadian broadcasting should be based upon the public service model and that stations should be owned and operated by a national broadcasting company called the Canadian Radio Broadcasting Company.[11]

In 1931, several provincial governments questioned the jurisdictional authority of the federal government over radio broadcasts and eventually challenged this point of law before the Supreme Court. The British North America Act of 1867, the legal base for divisional powers between the provincial governments and the central government, did not make specific reference to broadcasting. The Supreme Court ruled there were indeed several headings suitable to include radio broadcast communications and therefore assigned jurisdiction to the federal government. With this, the Court declared radio broadcasting a national medium.[12]

In 1932, a special parliamentary committee reexamined the Aird Report and the concept of public ownership of a national broadcasting service.[13] Proponents for public ownership eventually persuaded the committee to submit a recommendation establishing a commission of three members to have the necessary powers to regulate broadcasting in Canada. That same year, Parliament passed the Canadian Radio Broadcasting Act and created the Canadian Radio Broadcasting Commission (CRBC).[14]

The Canadian Radio Broadcasting Act of 1932 established the cornerstone of all subsequent Canadian broadcasting legislation: the broadcasting frequencies were "a scarce public resource," and all broadcast licenses were "a temporary monopoly, to be operated as part of a single national system in the public interest."[15]

Numerous problems plagued this newly created national broadcasting system. Buying and leasing stations, negotiating cable use from private companies and, above all, providing representative Canadian talent in programming proved to be formidable tasks for a three-member commission.[16]

Financing of the CRBC broadcasting operation was inadequate as well. By 1936, therefore, the national network reached less than half the total population. To add fuel to simmering discontent, both French and English Canada believed they were deprived of adequate service. Internal management, bound to limited salary scales imposed by civil service, was severely restricted in the hiring of personnel. All staff appointments required ministerial approval which caused further delays.[17]

Attempts to remedy these problems began in 1933, when legislation was passed to remove senior commission staff from civil service wage restrictions. In 1934, the second parliamentary committee on broadcasting sought to remove some of the workload from the commission members by recommending that a general manager and a broadcasting expert be appointed to direct the operational side of the CRBC. This recommendation, however, did not lead to legislation.[18]

Although the CRBC struggled with operational problems, in four years it did provide the first national network to air programs in both

French and English. During the brief tenure of CRBC, newer facilities were built, including a shortwave receiving station to relay programs from the British Broadcasting Corporation. The CRBC expanded the regular national broadcasting to some six hours a day on a basic network of twenty-six stations, eight of which were owned or leased by the CRBC. Programming from CRBC was optional on an additional thirty-one stations.[19]

This problem-plagued first attempt to establish nationwide radio broadcasting coverage was disappointing to both the commission and the audience, but despite difficulties, the basic mold of nationalized broadcasting to unite all of Canada was set. Canada did not emulate the American and British systems. Instead, Canada experimented on its own and attempted to effect a substantial departure from traditional North American broadcasting policy. Plagued by doubts, confronted with continuing problems, and enduring vehement arguments between opposing factions, Canadians pressed toward achieving their goal—a distinctively Canadian broadcasting system.

A CROWN CORPORATION

In 1936, the third special committee charged with the responsibility of studying the broadcasting situation and of recommending remedial action was established by Parliament. After nearly three months of investigation, the 1936 Special Committee on the Canadian Radio Commission recommended a complete revision of the national broadcasting system. The committee observed that the three-member commission was hard-pressed to formulate and to execute policy successfully. Further, to help alleviate the obvious workload problem, the committee recommended the adoption of the 1934 proposal for the appointment of a general manager. The committee advised the repeal of the Canadian Broadcasting Act and requested its replacement with a new act which would place broadcasting under the jurisdiction of a "public corporation modelled more closely on the lines of a private corporation, but with adequate powers to control, for the purpose of co-ordination, all broadcasting, both public and private. . . ."[20]

Parliament followed closely the committee's proposals and passed the new law on 2 November 1936, establishing the Canadian Broadcasting Corporation (CBC), a Crown corporation, to be owned by the people of Canada.[21] With the creation of the CBC, Canada's basic broadcasting pattern was finally established. The Canadians did not pattern their broadcasting system after the British or the American system, but instead created a distinctive dual broadcasting structure which has endured with some modification: a private commercial broadcasting system and a public corporation with nationalized networks designed to aid the internal bicultural accommodation and external self-definition processes which underscored much of Canada's national development.

BREAKING AWAY

The often emotional issue of national unity prompted strong feelings among some government officials that radio broadcasting could be a boon for "developing a greater National Empire consciousness within the Dominion and the British Commonwealth of Nations."[22] Discussion of the potential importance of international radio broadcasting first took place in the period of Canadian history in which the government engaged more directly in world affairs. Until the mid-1920s, for example, official relations between Canada and other nations were conducted entirely through British channels. In 1867, the British North America Act formed the Dominion of Canada, uniting the provinces of Canada, subdividing the country into Canada West (Ontario) and into Canada East (Quebec), together with Nova Scotia, and New Brunswick.[23] While the British North America Act granted Canada complete internal self-government, the powers to make treaties and to determine obligations between the Empire and foreign countries were reserved for the Parliament in London as part of the British Empire. This doctrine, known officially as the diplomatic unity of the Empire, remained dominated almost exclusively by the British government until the outbreak of the First World War. In fact, the Dominions had no status in international law which would enable them to accept or to receive official diplomatic representations or enable them to sign treaties.[24]

By 1909, however, Canada had reached a status which prompted the government to establish a Department of External Affairs. The title of the department followed the precedent established by the Australian government in 1901, and was intended to demonstrate relations both with the British Empire and with other foreign states. On 4 March 1909, the resolution to establish the Department of External Affairs was introduced in the House of Commons, the act to create it was assented to on 19 May, and went into effect on 1 June.[25]

The assumption of full control over external affairs was a gradual process. In fact, Canada first initiated independent diplomatic status in 1919 when Ottawa obtained separate representation at the postwar Paris Peace Conference, ten years after the creation of the Department of External Affairs. In reality, however, the Canadian government, under the umbrella of the powerful British government, did not actually have diplomatic representatives posted abroad until 1926.[26] Following a series of imperial conferences in 1926, the earl of Balfour, chairman of the Balfour committee, announced that Canada had become a *sovereign* nation. The Balfour Declaration, the precursor of the 1931 Statute of Westminster, noted that Britain had, at long last, relinquished control over the foreign policies of the Dominions. Canada finally had a world voice and negotiated its own treaties with other nations.[27]

THE POLICY OF "NO COMMITMENTS" WEARS THIN

Within the next decade the formal lines of Canadian foreign policy were, for the most part, succinctly postulated. First, Canadian external affairs began seeking the best possible relations with its giant southern neighbor, the United States, and with its Commonwealth patriarch, Great Britain. Second, by population and economic development standards, Canada remained a relatively small country, making it vital to view international affairs within the context of a large overseas trade. A young Canadian foreign policy was destined to be shaped primarily by a desire to remain diffident, to avoid foreign commitments in world affairs.[28]

This policy of "no commitments" was a reflection of the mood of North America. Both Canada and the United States fervently believed isolation was their policy *vis-à-vis* Europe. Both Ottawa and Washington preferred not to get involved in any European troubles. French Canada, always staunchly isolationist, was fearful that English Canada's main aim in foreign policy was to support Britain at all costs, even if it meant the ultimate entanglement, war. Indeed, there was consensus among English-speaking Canadians for endorsement of British foreign policy "more or less automatically."[29]

Both Ottawa and Washington watched cautiously as the democracies of Europe began to rearm. By 1937, Canada had begun to expand national defenses while strengthening relations with the United States. President Franklin D. Roosevelt's Good Neighbor Policy helped to improve relations between the two countries through newer, more aggressive tariff agreements. President Roosevelt and Prime Minister W. L. Mackenzie King, North American compatriots against Nazi Germany, expressed their joint defense efforts in both public statements and in private covert actions.

Upon accepting an honorary degree from Queen's University at Kingston, Ontario, in 1938, FDR proclaimed: "I give to you the assurance that the people of the United States will not stand idly by if domination of Canadian soil is threatened by any other empire."[30] Roosevelt's remarks were reassuring to the Canadian people since most feared that war with Germany was inevitable. Following Britain's lead, on 9 September 1939, Canada declared war on Germany while the United States remained officially neutral toward a war-torn Europe.

Neutrality notwithstanding, there was a secret alliance between the two friendly neighbors long before any American declaration of war. On 18 August 1940, FDR summoned Mackenzie King to a railway dining car at Ogdensburg, New York, and scrawled a memorandum outlining the terms for the acclaimed Permanent Joint Board on Defense agreement.[31] In 1941, before Pearl Harbor, the little-known ABC Alliance, a secret liaison between America, Britain, and Canada, made the common sharing of intelligence information possible.[32]

American neutrality wavered under nearly constant pressure from European allies. Britain was undergoing air attack, its future was clouded by a possible Nazi invasion. Closer to home, Canada agreed to permit American bases in Newfoundland, while in New York City Britain opened its intelligence branch, aptly called the British Security Cooperation, under the direct command of William Stephenson, the astute Canadian-born businessman turned intelligence officer. At the behest of Britain, Canada permitted the training of American espionage agents at Special Training School 103 (popularly called Camp X) located on a farm outside Whitby, Ontario across from Rochester, New York.[33] All this was undertaken before the United States entered the war and was indicative of the close ties, indeed the extraordinary friendship, with Canada.

The Second World War demonstrated to Canadians that no nation could afford to stand aloof from the world community. If a nation did not participate in making world decisions, world decisions could be forced on it; the war had proven that. Ottawa, then, decided that the best course of action was to influence world decisions along predetermined lines with the understanding that as a small nation there would be imposed limitations.[34] As a sovereign power within the Commonwealth, Canada began

to put greater emphasis on projecting a national identity throughout the
world community.

During the 1930s, while Canada was reassessing its external self-definition, government officials began investigating shortwave radio broadcasting as a means for projecting the Canadian identity. In 1932, this
interest was heightened when representatives of the Canadian government
attending an International Telecommunications Conference (ITC) in
Madrid, Spain, were told that Canada had been granted shortwave frequencies for international broadcasting.[35]
Among the Canadian delegates, the general consensus was that such an
allocation was really a national resource that should not be taken lightly.
In fact, this observation surfaced repeatedly in the difficult times of budget austerity when the CBC was called upon to answer the basic query:
why does Canada need shortwave radio broadcasting? The answer, simply put, remained: if the frequencies were not used, another country
would snap them up and Canada would be frozen out of shortwave radio
broadcasting forever.
Shortly after the ITC announcement, a shortwave receiving station was
built at Britannia Heights, near Ottawa, to rebroadcast programs from
the BBC, for propagation studies, and for experimentation. Part of the
facility's function was to keep accurate records of reception conditions on
the various international shortwave bands. Since the early days of the
CRBC network there had been program relays from the BBC but in the
1930s, as the events in Europe began to dominate world news, BBC newscasts were relayed along the CBC network, a practice which continued for
more than thirty-five years.[36]
In October 1937, L. W. Brockington, chairman of the board of governors
of the CBC, wrote Prime Minister King that the board endorsed the establishment of a shortwave radio broadcasting service, since it was "an essential
part of a national scheme."[37] Brockington, an enthusiastic supporter of the
proposed service, outlined internal and external advantages for the stodgy
prime minister's consideration. Externally, such a facility enhanced "national
prestige." He pointed out that Britain possessed considerable numbers of
transmitters and operated on fourteen different wavelengths. In addition, as
if to stress a grave neglect on the part of the Mackenzie King government, he
reported that Brazil and the Netherlands operated transmitters on the short-

wave bands. Brockington reasoned that because smaller nations were involved in international shortwave radio broadcasting, Canada should develop its own shortwave service to enhance its national prestige; to foster international goodwill, and to project Canadian culture by broadcasting "events of national significance and celebration" (400).

Brockington was a visionary. He suggested that since Canada needed population growth, an international shortwave radio broadcasting service could make appeals for immigrants by offering "a home and domestic and political security to a number of distressed and harassed people" (401).

The CBC board of governors, following Brockington's leadership, later that year unanimously agreed to urge the government to take action. A shortwave service, according to the board, could serve to interpret Canada to the world, to advertise the nation abroad, and to facilitate the exchange of shortwave programs with other countries.[38]

In July 1937, Donald Manson, chief executive assistant of the corporation, carefully studied the technical requirements for the proposed service. In an internal memorandum Manson suggested that at least one station "of not less than fifty kilowatts, designed to work on various frequencies" was needed to reach the world radio audience. He outlined objectives the proposed service might pursue in regularly scheduled broadcasts to foreign audiences: exchanging programs with other countries; broadcasting programs in French to the Prairie Provinces (Manitoba, Saskatchewan, and Alberta); providing point-to-point services for governmental agencies during the sessions of the League of Nations. Manson presented the strongest argument to the government with a fateful warning: "It is important that Canada should get on the air with a powerful station at an early date, otherwise there will be no frequencies available, as these are being rapidly preempted by the different countries who realize the advantages of short wave broadcasting."[39]

In 1938, the House of Commons Standing Committee on Radio Broadcasting endorsed the proposal, asserting the project "should be financed as a national project, operated and controlled by the Corporation."[40] A similar committee the next year reiterated the need for the proposed service and expressed concern that if action were not taken, the frequencies would almost certainly be lost to other countries.[41]

The Canadian press rallied additional support. In December 1939, the Ottawa *Citizen* declared Canada was "lagging behind in short wave radio." The influential national newspaper, the *Financial Post*, reported that Canadian trade commissioners posted worldwide were demanding the establishment of a shortwave service for use as a sales weapon. An editorial in the Regina *Star* accused the government of shelving the shortwave project out of fear of offending U. S. isolationist views. The Windsor *Tribune* stressed advantages accruing from the expected tourist trade and the anticipated strengthening of goodwill between Canada and the United States. German broadcasts beamed to North America attacked the Quebec elections, and broadcasts from the Soviet Union offered communist commentary on Canadian workers' views of the war. At least one editorial expressed fear of these "attacks" on Canada by other nations' international broadcasts and urged Parliament to act on the matter.[42]

E. L. Bushnell, general supervisor of programming, CBC, wrote in February 1939, ". . . if we in Canada are to maintain our proper place in the world of today we must be in a position to let other nations know of what is taking place within our boundaries."[43] Moreover, the royal visit of King George VI in late 1939 was used to promote the need for a shortwave broadcasting service. In an internal memorandum directed to members of the corporation, Bushnell advised that the BBC had requested daily transmissions describing events during the royal visit. "As matters now stand," he revealed, "the CBC is without shortwave transmission facilities of sufficient power for the broadcasting of these functions."[44]

Members of the Canadian Parliament expressed concern that Broadcasting House, the headquarters of the external services of the BBC in London, might be destroyed during a Nazi bombing sortie. Interestingly, there was a contingency plan proffered by the BBC to cover just such an emergency—construct a transmitting facility in Canada. The British treasury, however, was reluctant to provide funds, and even the BBC had reservations about the proposed project.[45]

When Rene Morin, chairman of the board of governors, was asked about the financing of the proposed shortwave project, he replied that the board felt it was improper to use CBC funds generated by the license fee system, since the funds were earmarked for domestic broadcasting and not for an international broadcasting service. He stated, matter-of-factly, ". . . if a high-power shortwave station is necessary, it is for the government to build it . . . and provide us with the funds necessary to operate it."[46] Morin's stand on the matter was accepted, since all future references to the financing of the proposed service were made to special government funds, separate from the Canadian Broadcasting Corporation's budget.

WORD WAR

Any planning for a shortwave radio voice beamed to Europe was almost certain to include expressions of concern about possible wartime uses. Canada, already deeply entrenched in the European theatre of operations, considered the importance of shortwave radio broadcasting in psychological warfare. The 1942 House of Commons Standing Committee on Radio Broadcasting observed that the proposed shortwave radio broadcasting service would permit Canada "to play a useful part . . . with respect to counter-propaganda in occupied countries" (114).

There had been attempts at counter-propaganda with broadcasts for the Free French via WRUL, Boston, and the BBC. By any stretch of the imagination, this effort was limited. It was suggested that the Free French build a shortwave radio transmitter in Canada, but there were no available frequencies for such a service. The Canadians, struggling to establish their own shortwave service, would not offer the use of their allocated frequencies to the Free French (114).

Members of the House of Commons spoke in favor of the shortwave service. One honorable member, convinced shortwave radio broadcasting could be an effective weapon against the Axis Powers, emphasized the value Hitler placed on foreign broadcasts. "If we wanted only one proof of the value of the new battlefront of the aether," the member asserted, "we have only to remember that Hitler has decreed the death penalty to listeners to foreign broadcasts (114).

On 27 September 1941, Mackenzie King scribbled in his diary: "I favour the shortwave station & intended to recommend its establishment at last meeting of War Committee had principle members been present."[47] Mackenzie King, not known for his understanding of radio broadcasting as a communications medium, merely seemed to endorse its wartime use instead of taking a leadership role in promoting shortwave radio broadcasting as an instrument of External Affairs.

While politicians viewed an international broadcasting service as an instrument for war-induced counter-propaganda, the CBC personnel referred to the proposed station as an instrument for delineating the Canadian identity. When asked what would be the particular value of such a station, Dr. Augustin Frigon, assistant general manager of the corporation, replied: ". . . to get into the international picture, so to speak, and then give us the opportunity to let people know about us."[48]

The 1942 House of Commons Standing Committee on Radio Broadcasting summarized the need for the proposed shortwave service by noting it would supplement Allied broadcasting services and reach both enemy and occupied territories. Throughout the discussions of the proposed service, concern was expressed about Canadian soldiers and sailors far from home. Such a service, the 1942 committee observed, would bring news from home to the Canadian serviceman. Although recognizing the importance of a wartime shortwave service, the 1942 committee asserted, ". . . it would also be of the greatest possible usefulness in establishing new areas of understanding, goodwill and trade after the war" (854).

The 1942 committee emphasized the vital importance of immediate action and recommended that a shortwave station be established ". . . at the earliest possible moment, to be owned and financed, as to installation, operation and maintenance, by the government and operated by the Canadian Broadcasting Corporation" (854).

On 18 September 1942 a report was submitted to the committee of the privy council from the minister of national war services reiterating reasons for the establishment of a shortwave service and, for the first time, including detailed costs of the proposed operation. It was noted, for example, that the frequencies, viewed by many as a valuable natural resource, could be lost to another country if Canada did not use them in the near future. In addition, the country would benefit not only from the wartime uses of such a service, but also from the fostering of exchange programs with other nations and the supplementary use of French to French Canadians in the Maritimes and the Prairie Provinces. Postwar competition for trade was another concern. The minister of national war services asserted that ". . . Canada would be gravely handicapped if any means are lacking for an effective presentation of the resources, potentialities and products of this country."[49] Shortwave radio broadcasting, according to the report, would meet this important need. To meet these proposed goals, two fifty-kilowatt transmitters with three-directional antennae were to be installed at Sackville, New Brunswick, at a cost of $800,000.[50]

The government agreed to finance the proposed International Service (IS) through direct parliamentary grants. Although the International Service was to be financially supported separately from the CBC, the corporation was to be in charge of the shortwave broadcasting operations because it was better equipped than any other agency and was "the logical one to administer, operate, supervise, and control the shortwave broadcasting stations and associated facilities."[51] Finally, the minister of war services acknowledged that shortwave radio broadcasting beamed to foreign countries could affect Canada's relations with the other countries of the Commonwealth and with foreign countries. Accordingly, "the work of the Canadian Broadcasting Corporation in this field should be carried on in consultation with the Department of External Affairs."[52]

The committee of the privy council, on the recommendation of the minister of national war services, in concurrence with the secretary of state for External Affairs, approved the report and passed the Order in Council. Canada was to have an international radio voice.

INSTALLATION

The CBC began building a transmitter and antenna site at the worst of times. Not only did war priorities claim most of the sorely needed supplies and material, but undoubtedly bureaucratic eyebrows arched at the extraordinary requisitions. First on the list of problems encountered was the geographic location. It was widely known that Canada's close proximity to the North geomagnetic pole caused a severe problem associated with nearly constant emission of electromagnetic energy that created a zone of absorption. Radio frequency (RF) energy, transmitted in wavelengths, are subject to strange phenomena when passed through the so-called zone of absorption. Accordingly, radio signals transmitted across much of northern Canada would not only be weak, but would be plagued by erratic fading if the transmitter was placed within the zone. Preliminary engineering studies conducted in 1934 and 1938 clearly demonstrated that the shortwave transmitting site would have to be located as far as possible from the electromagnetic field generated from the north geomagnetic pole. Studies indicated that the best location for the transmitting site to reach Europe, Africa, and South America was southeastern Canada in the Maritime Provinces (New Brunswick, Nova Scotia, or Prince Edward Island) (12).

The geomagnetic pole emission was but one of the difficult problems affecting location. It was necessary to have a large area of level terrain providing high radio frequency ground conductivity in order for the antenna systems to work efficiently. A search revealed that CBA, a CBC-owned station near Sackville, New Brunswick, met all the necessary prerequisites. Far removed from the geomagnetic pole's zone of absorption, the land, reclaimed salt water marshes (the Tantramar Marshes), offered high ground conductivity for the antenna arrays.[53]

Procuring steel and copper from the Department of Munitions and Supply for the antenna arrays proved to be a formidable task. The war supplies priority system was cumbersome, the bureaucracy a labyrinth of paperwork. And to compound the problem, high-powered shortwave transmitters were in short supply.

The CBC appointed E. C. Stewart, an old hand at engineering services, to serve as liaison officer between the CBC, the Department of Munitions and Supply, and the War Production Board of the United States. Radio Corporation of America (RCA) in Newark, New Jersey, was the primary production company for high-powered shortwave transmitters. The CBC, somewhat bewildered by the bureaucracy in Ottawa, faced similar, if not more, red tape in Washington.

The CBC pressed Ottawa for assistance. Prime Minister Mackenzie King wrote Lester B. Pearson, then Canadian ambassador to the United States, stressing the importance of the shortwave project and urging Pearson to expedite matters. It was January 1943 and Ottawa had pursued the transmitter procurement through channels between the Department of External Affairs and the Office of War Information in Washington, but without success. All production of transmitters was subject to strict, wartime priorities. Ambassador Pearson was instrumental in securing a higher priority for the Canadian requisition of two fifty-kilowatt RCA transmitters, but the procurement process dragged on until 1944, when the transmitters were finally shipped to Sackville and prepared for test transmissions.[54]

While construction of the site was in progress at the Sackville, two floors of an old building at 1236 Crescent Street, Montreal, were renovated for studios and office space housing the programming and administrative staff of the International Service. These production and administrative quarters consisted of three studios and control rooms, a recording room, a master control room, and offices. Montreal was selected not only because of its cosmopolitan value as a major production center, but also because professional writers and production personnel were easily recruited from the urban area. In addition, Montreal was approximately 600 miles from the Sackville transmission site and was accessible via land lines.[55]

Peter Aylen, program liaison officer at the CBC headquarters in Ottawa, was transferred to Montreal to organize the International Service operations in 1944. A CBC employee since 1933, Aylen had held numerous broadcasting positions, including announcer, writer, producer, and station manager in Windsor, Ontario. A graduate of both the University of Toronto and McGill University, Montreal, he served on the staff of the Montreal *Gazette* from 1931 to 1933.[56]

ORGANIZATIONAL STRUCTURE

Under the first organizational chart schematic (fig. 1), policy was administered by the CBC-IS supervisor.[57] The CBC-IS supervisor, Peter Aylen, worked in consultation with the general manager and the director-general of programs for the corporation. Final policy decisions were made by a joint government-CBC committee named, appropriately enough, the Shortwave Joint Committee. In 1944 the following individuals served on the committee:

Dr. Augustin Frigon, acting general manager, CBC (chairman)
Norman Robertson, undersecretary of state for External Affairs
T. A. Stone, External Affairs
Davidson Dunton, general manager, Wartime Information Board
E. L. Bushnell, general programme supervisor, CBC
Peter Aylen, supervisor, CBC-IS.[58]

Figure 1. International Service Organizational Chart, 1945

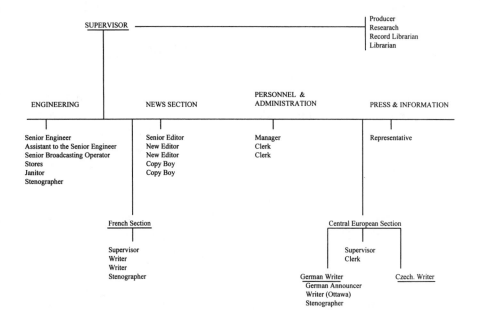

The representative nature of the committee is worthy of analysis. Understandably the CBC shared responsibilities with External Affairs, but it is interesting to note that CBC-IS, budgeted separately, held an oblique organizational relationship with respect to the corporation, yet the corporation held two committee posts—as many as External Affairs. Since it was wartime, the placement of the general manager of the Wartime Information Board was commensurate with the committee's purpose: to advise Aylen about policy matters. Moreover, the Order in Council P.C. 8168, the legal document which authorized the establishment of the International Service, read "the work of the Canadian Broadcasting Corporation in this field [international broadcasting] should be carried on in consultation with the Department of External Affairs."[59] The CBC complied with the Order in Council by establishing the Shortwave Joint Committee and appointing External Affairs members.

During a committee meeting in March 1944, Dr. Frigon suggested it might be advisable to have an External Affairs representative in Montreal review scripts. The undersecretary of state for External Affairs, Norman Robertson, stated frankly that it would not be necessary to have any great amount of reviewing for ". . . the department was interested primarily in a long range projection of Canadian policy, and that . . . a great deal of supervision could be exercised by responsible officials of the shortwave staff."[60]

EARLY POLICY AND PROGRAMMING

Peter Aylen and his associates organized the International Service under the following departments: engineering, news, personnel and administration, press and information. Under the engineering heading, for example, were the staff members associated with the transmitting facilities at the Sackville plant. The news section was headed by the senior editor, while the personnel and administration manager maintained records for the broadcasting services. The press and information representative served as a liaison between CBC-IS and the press.

The programming elements were divided geographically into two primary sections: United Kingdom and Commonwealth, and Central European. Plans were also made for a Latin American section, but during the initial stages of the International Service's operation, only the following programming was implemented: English and French broadcasts directed to the United Kingdom and Commonwealth; German and Czech for the Central European region. The Order in Council P.C. 8168 suggested these divisions and languages.

The apparent effort "to strengthen the resistance within the occupied countries of Europe" was reflected in the programming. Since 1940, Canadian broadcasters had been producing French-language programs carried by both the BBC and WRUL, Boston, and beamed to occupied France. German-language broadcasts had been produced in Ottawa by the radio division of the Wartime Information Board since 1943. Programs in French and in German, written and recorded in Canada, were flown to New York for shortwave transmission by the U. S. Office of War Information.[61]

On 1 December 1944, the last shipment of French and German recordings was sent to the United States. All efforts were then concentrated on the preparation of programs for the International Service. One transmitter (CKNC) broadcast a test transmission to Europe on 16 December. The next day the BBC wired:

REPORT FIRST SHORTWAVE TRANSMISSION 1945 GMT DANCE MUSIC RECORDS AND ANNOUNCEMENT QUALITY VERY GOOD STOP NO INTERFERENCE STOP VERY STRONG CARRIER WITH OCCASIONAL FADES STOP NOISE ONLY EVIDENT DURING TROUGHS OF FADES STOP OVERALL MERIT THREE TO FOUR [good to very good] ON SINGLE RECEIVER AND ON DIVERSITY RECEPTION WOULD MERIT FOUR [very good] STOP (13).

With this encouraging report, the International Service staff began program rehearsals on 20 December, and on Christmas Day, the first Canadian shortwave program went on the air. This Christmas Special, directed to Canadian troops overseas, was broadcast from 6:45 A.M. to 12:00 noon EDST, and consisted of programs from the English and French networks of the CBC, as well as from transcribed features. The BBC sent a congratulatory cable:

PLEASE ACCEPT OUR CONGRATULATIONS ON INAUGURAL TRANS-MISSION CHTA STOP WE ARE DELIGHTED THAT STRONGEST SIGNAL IN NINE-TEEN METRE BAND NOW COMES FROM CANADA STOP (13).

On 26 December, a regular two-and-one-half-hour daily schedule of English, French, and German programs were broadcast on a test transmission basis, and on 6 February 1945, Czechoslovakian programs were added to the test schedule (13). By this time preparations were under way for the inaugural broadcast officially opening the International Service's broadcasting operations. After nearly three years of bureaucratic hurdles and wartime frustrations, Canada was ready to speak to the world.

NOTES

1. Robert E. Babe, *Telecommunications in Canada: Technology, Industry, and Government* (Toronto: University of Toronto Press, 1990), 5-8.
2. Dominion Bureau of Statistics, *Canada 1971: The Annual Handbook of Present Conditions and Recent Progress* (Ottawa: Information Canada, 1971), 31.
3. Ibid.
4. Frank W. Peers, *The Politics of Canadian Broadcasting, 1920-1950* (Toronto: University of Toronto Press, 1969), 440.
5. Royal Commission on Broadcasting, *Report* [Fowler Commission] 1957, Appendix II, "A Brief History of Broadcasting in Canada," 299.
6. Statutes, *The Radio Telegraph Act, 1913*, 3-4 George 5, chap. 43; the first wireless legislation was: Statutes, *The Wireless Telegraphy Act, 20 July 1905*, 4 & 5 Edward 7, chap. 49. See also Peers, *Politics of Canadian Broadcasting*, 29-30.
7. House of Commons, *Debates*, 2 June 1928, 3708.
8. Royal Commission on Radio Broadcasting, *Report* [Aird Commission] (Ottawa, 1929).
9. Peers, *Politics of Canadian Broadcasting*, 44.
10. Ibid.
11. See Aird Commission *Report*, 12-13, for the complete listing of recommendations.
12. Thomas L. McPhail and Brenda McPhail, "Canada," in *International Handbook of Broadcasting Systems*, Philip T. Rosen, ed. (New York: Greenwood Press, Inc., 1988), 49.
13. House of Commons, 1932 Special Committee on Radio Broadcasting, *Minutes of Proceedings and Evidence*, 1932.
14. Statutes, *Canadian Radio Broadcasting Act, 1932*, 22-23 George 5, chap. 51.
15. McPhail and McPhail, "Canada," 49.
16. Walter B. Emery, *National and International Systems of Broadcasting: Their History, Operation and Control* (East Lansing: Michigan State University Press, 1969), 53.
17. Canadian Broadcasting Corporation, *CBC - A Brief History and Background* (Ottawa: Information Services, Canadian Broadcasting Corporation, 1968), 7-8.
18. House of Commons, 1934 Special Committee on the Operations of the Commission Under the Radio Broadcasting Act 1932 (as amended), *Minutes of Proceedings and Evidence*, Ottawa, 1936.
19. Ibid.

20. House of Commons, 1936 Special Committee on the Canadian Radio Commission, *Minutes of Proceedings and Evidence,* Ottawa, 1936. For an overview of the recommendations, see *CBC - A Brief History,* 305.

21. Statutes, *Canadian Broadcasting Act, 1936,* 1 Edward 8, chap. 24. For a detailed legislative history of the CBC, see Alexander F. Toogood, "The Canadian Broadcasting Corporation: A Question of Control" (Ph.D. diss., Ohio State University, 1969).

22. Peers, *Politics of Canadian Broadcasting,* 441.

23. Great Britain, Statutes, *The British North America Act, 1867,* 30 Victoria, chap. 3. The bill became law on 29 March 1867, with Confederation officially accomplished on July 1. See Desmond Morton, *A Short History of Canada* (Edmonton: Hurtig Publishers Limited, 1983), 71-79. *A Consolidation of the Constitution Acts 1867 to 1982* can be found in the Appendix, Robert J. Jackson, Doreen Jackson, and Nicolas Baxter-Moore, *Politics in Canada: Culture, Institutions, Behavior and Public Policy* (Scarborough, Ontario: Prentice-Hall Canada, Inc., 1986), 682-758.

24. *The British North America Act,* 1867, sec. 132 reads, "The Parliament and Government of Canada shall have all powers necessary or proper for performing Obligations of Canada or of any Province thereof, as Part of the British Empire, towards Foreign Countries, arising under Treaties between the Empire and such Foreign Countries." For a thorough discussion of the development of Canadian external affairs, see R. Barry Farrell, *The Making of Canadian Foreign Policy* (Scarborough, Ontario: Prentice-Hall of Canada, Ltd., 1969), 55-63.

25. Statutes, *An Act to Create a Department of External Affairs,* 8-9 Edward 7, 1909, chap. 13. For a brief discussion of the act, see James J. Talman, *Basic Documents in Canadian History* (Princeton, N. J.: D. Van Nostrand Company, Inc., 1959), 136.

26. Farrell, *Canadian Foreign Policy,* 57-58.

27. Jackson, Jackson, and Moore, *Politics in Canada,* 639.

28. J.M.S. Careless, *Canada: A Story of Challenge* (Toronto: Macmillan of Canada, 1963), 370.

29. Ibid.

30. Morton, *History of Canada,* 191.

31. Ibid., 194.

32. William Stevenson, *Intrepid's Last Case* (New York: Villard Books, Inc., 1984), 6. In a footnote Stevenson reports the ABC Alliance was renamed ARCADIA after Pearl Harbor.

33. David Stafford, *Camp X* (New York: Pocket Books, a division of Simon & Schuster, Inc., 1988), xvii.

34. Careless, *A Story of Challenge,* 390.

35. Canadian Broadcasting Corporation, "The International Service of the Canadian Broadcasting Corporation: 1945-1950" (International Service, Montreal, 1950, mimeographed), 8.

36. Ibid. A daily early evening BBC World Service newscast was relayed until September 1971.

37. L. W. Brockington to Prime Minister Mackenzie King, 26 October 1937; cited in, House of Commons, Special Committee on Radio Broadcasting, *Minutes of Proceedings and Evidence*, no. 16, 2 July 1942, 400-401.

38. Fifth Meeting of the CBC Board of Governors, August 5-7, 1937. Similar recommendations were made at the Seventh Meeting of the Board held 22-25 March 1938, and the Ninth Meeting of the Board, held 19-20 December 1938, as cited in, Special Committee on Radio Broadcasting, *Minutes of Proceedings and Evidence*, 14 May 1942, 412-13. See also "References of Board of Governors and of Parliamentary Committees," in, Canadian Broadcasting Corporation, "International Broadcasting Service: Information Prepared on the Desirability of Its Establishment, 1938-1942" (Historical Section, Canadian Broadcasting Corporation, Ottawa, n.d., n.p., mimeographed).

39. Ibid.

40. House of Commons, Standing Committee on Radio Broadcasting, *Minutes of Proceedings and Final Report*, no. 8, 20 May 1938, 195.

41. House of Commons, Standing Committee on Radio Broadcasting, *Minutes of Proceedings and Final Report*, March 1939, 363.

42. *Citizen* (Ottawa, Ontario), 21 December 1939; *Financial Post* (Toronto), 9 December 1939; *Star* (Regina, Saskatchewan), 12 December 1939; *Tribune* (Windsor, Nova Scotia), 24 November 1939; *Tribune* (Winnipeg, Manitoba), 27 December 1939, in "Digest of Editorial Opinion," Special Committee on Radio Broadcasting, *Minutes*, 2 July 1942, 415-16.

43. Ibid., 401.

44. Ibid. Since there was no shortwave facility, news about the royal visit was sent via cable to the BBC for broadcast. This was the CBC's biggest broadcasting job to that date. See *CBC - A History*, 12.

45. See Asa Briggs, *The History of Broadcasting in the United Kingdom*, vol. 2: *The War of Words* (New York: Oxford University Press, 1965), 348-49.

46. Special Committee on Radio Broadcasting, *Minutes*, 2 July 1942, 115.

47. James Eayrs, *The Art of the Possible: Government and Foreign Policy in Canada* (Toronto: University of Toronto Press, 1961), 194.

48. Special Committee on Radio Broadcasting, *Minutes*, 854.

49. Memorandum from the Minister of National War Services to the Committee of the Privy Council, 9 September 1942; included in the Minutes of a Meeting of the Committee of the Privy Council, approved by his Excellency the Governor General, in Order in Council P.C. 8168, 18 September 1942, in Public Archives of Canada, Orders-in-Council (16 September-18 September 1942), Reference Group 2, 1, vol. 2154.

50. Ibid.

51. Ibid. Order in Council P.C. 156/8855, 17 November 1943, officially provided that the Government of Canada would finance the operations of the International Service.

52. Minister of War Services Memorandum, 1.

53. The shortwave transmitting plant was to merge with the CBA facility. It was necessary to construct a new, larger building around the CBA station without interfering with its normal operation.

54. E. C. Stewart, interviewed by the author, audiocassette, Montreal, 14 July 1971.

55. "International Service: 1945-1950," 14.

56. D. R. Proteau, assistant supervisor, publicity, Canadian Broadcasting Corporation, International Service, Montreal, letter to author, 2 May 1972.

57. This chart, reported to be the first organizational structure, was supplied by William McDonald, Historical Section, Canadian Broadcasting Corporation, Ottawa, in 1971.

58. Minutes of the Shortwave Joint Committee Meeting, Canadian Broadcasting Corporation, 21 March 1944; in Canadian Broadcasting Corporation, Montreal, Central Registry File no. IS54-5-1.

59. See Order in Council P.C. 8168. Typically, in legal terminology, the word *should* denotes mandatory action.

60. Shortwave Joint Committee, Minutes, 1944.

61. "International Service: 1945-1950," 13.

2 THIS IS CANADA CALLING

ON 25 FEBRUARY 1945 at 3:00 P.M., as Allied troops were nearing victory in Europe, a confident Mackenzie King officially inaugurated the International Service. The prime minister's first message broadcast to Europe and to Canadians listening in across the Trans-Canada Network were words of greeting "to Canada's armed forces serving on and beyond the seas."[1] Beset by increasing opposition after ten years in power, including six years at war, the Liberals welcomed an opportunity for international exposure. Faltering after the departure of National Resources Mobilization Act "conscripts" to the European theatre in early 1945 that had caused mass discontent, even riots in Montreal, the Liberals were worried about the summer elections.[2]

"Tonight," the aging prime minister intoned, "Canada enters the world radio arena. As we undertake this new service, let us resolve that in peace as in war, we will be true to the values you are so valiantly upholding—ideals which have made our country a nation. The unity of Canada belongs not only to Canada, it belongs to mankind."[3]

Recognizing the war could end soon, King was speaking to thousands of potential voters both at home and abroad. Unity was a key word for the Liberal Party. "If we are true to ourselves," King remarked, "Canadian unity may well serve as a model for the wider unity of humanity. In the unity of mankind lies the one sure foundation of enduring peace."[4]

After King's brief remarks, the program announcer stressed what was to become the primary operational policy of the International Service: "It is our intention that this service now being inaugurated will bring you the best of Canada's radio, news and sports, music, grave and gay, entertainment, amusement, and our point of view."[5]

E. L. Bushnell, the CBC director of programmes who had seen the project evolve from a shaky start nearly ten years before this inaugural program, commented: "In the shortwave band Canada has nothing to sell but friendship, no motives but a desire to understand and to be understood, no aims but peace and the brotherhood of men."[6]

With remotes from Toronto, Winnipeg, Vancouver, Montreal, and Sackville, the variety program marked the formal beginning of the International Service. The radio speeches, although sketchy, reveal the basic operational goals for the CBC-IS. First, and foremost, to boost morale, the International Service was directed to the Canadian armed forces stationed in Europe. Second, Prime Minister Mackenzie King expressed hope that the conveyance of the Canadian identity would serve as a model to the world and would promote friendship and better understanding among nations. Third, the war created a conscious need for a deviation from the "projection of Canada" concept. Parliament wanted involvement in the "psychological war of broadcasting."[7]

PSYCHOLOGICAL WARFARE

The CBC-IS staff of forty professionals quickly settled into regularly scheduled broadcasts with both fifty-kilowatt transmitters beamed toward Europe. Guided by the Order in Council, the CBC-IS undertook an important role in the war effort. Peter Aylen and his staff scheduled fifty-eight hours of broadcasting weekly directed to the Canadian troops in Europe.[8]

The program fare in March and April consisted of CBC domestic network shows already familiar to Canadian servicemen and servicewomen, including well-known dance orchestras, sports reviews, symphony concerts, and dramatic presentations. News reports were broadcast five times daily. While most of the programs were in English, popular programs from the CBC French Network were broadcast as well, offering some semblance of balance.[9]

The remaining twenty-eight hours of the weekly broadcast schedule were in German, Czech, and French, and followed the spirit of the Order in Council directives: "to strengthen the resistance within the occupied countries of Europe," and "to counter-attack German propaganda that had been directed against Canada."[10] The way in which these directives were actually implemented is a lesson in Canadian conceptualization of international broadcasting potential.

The German broadcasts, for example, were characterized as "news bulletins and special programmes throwing new light on Nazi leaders and their aims . . . designed to weaken the German will to resist."[11] Thousands of German prisoners of war were incarcerated in Canada, and producers at CBC-IS were quick to utilize some of them for interviews or short talks directed to their homeland. Helmut Blume of the German-language section, CBC-IS, encouraged prisoners to write about camp life, war experiences, even politics. "Faced with the collapse of their philosophy," Blume wrote, "the ruin of their homeland, the prisoners . . . were beginning to analyze the errors of the German past, to understand our way of life and to learn something about democracy."[12] Blume solicited the prisoners to form "radio groups" in the camps and actually permitted some of them to speak on the German-language service.

It is difficult to evaluate this type of "psychological warfare" without a rhetorical criticism of selected scripts. While rhetorical criticism is not a methodological element of this study, the following excerpt illustrates a typical commentary of a German prisoner broadcast by CBC-IS:

> Due to the . . . isolation of our life in the so-called Third Reich, and due to the strongly propagandistic publications in Germany about foreign countries, I had always imagined Canada to be the dead end of the world. How surprised I was when I saw modern limousines rushing over smooth roads, instead of the trapper cutting his way through the virgin forest with a bush knife! And how thoughtful I became when I realized that I, a German worker, allegedly the best paid worker in the world had barely been able to afford a bicycle, while here in Canada lots of workers own cars and think nothing about it (9).
>
> Similar broadcasts were beamed to Austria but this service later developed into a quarter-hour commentary on international and Canadian news.[13]

Since Czechoslovakia remained under German occupation, Czech-language broadcasts attempted to project Canada by informing the listeners about Canadian industries, agriculture, music, and other art forms.[14] Special attention was given to descriptions of life in Canadian Czechoslovakian communities. To aid Canadian Czechoslovakians in locating missing relatives in Europe, the International Service cooperated with the Canadian Red Cross by providing a personal message service in the broadcasts.[15]

"La Voix du Canada," the primary feature program directed to the French-speaking countries of Europe, included news bulletins of Canadian and international news together with a wide variety of reviews and comments on Canadian events. The French section of CBC-IS continued to

supply the BBC and the U.S. Office of War Information with regular transcribed weekly programs until the end of the war (20).

The three foreign-language services of German, Czech, and French
were used "to aid the war effort,"[16] and continued only for the duration
of the European conflict. Meager by BBC External Broadcasting Service
and Voice of America standards, the Canadian radio presence nonetheless
reinforced Free World views. Canada, a Middle Power with no axe to
grind, offered war-torn Europe yet another example of a free democracy
in action. This middle position in the court of world opinion served
Canadians well in the ensuing months of peace before the beginning of the
Cold War with the Soviet Union.

TRANSITIONS

After VE-Day, 7 May 1945, the operational policies of CBC-IS went in
new directions. The transition, from wartime broadcasting to a total
peacetime operation directed toward general audiences, took approximately one year. What were the new operational goals and how did the
International Service attempt to achieve these goals with its programming? How did the International Service broadcast to a world audience
during the postwar period, 1946-50?

MANAGEMENT

Shortly after the initial transition in 1946 from wartime to peacetime
broadcasting, Peter Aylen resigned his post as supervisor to take a position with the United Nations. His replacement, Arthur Phelps, had served
as the assistant supervisor, CBC-IS. Phelps, a former English professor at
United College, Winnipeg, was well-known to Canadian listeners for his
philosophical radio talks on various aspects of Canadian life broadcast on
CBC domestic networks. The Phelps appointment was short-lived, however, since he retired from the CBC in 1947.[17]

In October 1947, Ira Dilworth, the CBC regional representative in
Vancouver, was appointed supervisor, International Service. Dilworth, a
Harvard graduate with a master of arts degree in English literature, was
active in higher education in western Canada, and had served on the faculty at the University of British Columbia. He was a recognized authority
on Emily Carr and had published several anthologies of English verse (9).

It is interesting to note that all International Service supervisors from 1944-50 held advanced degrees in the liberal arts from major universities, and all were in CBC managerial positions, prior to the Montreal posting. The similarity of their credentials suggests that the CBC selection committee sought to employ educated, professional broadcasters with an understanding and appreciation of the arts, literature, music, and culture of Canada.

ORGANIZATIONAL STRUCTURE

The organizational chart of CBC-IS at this time was expanded to include new language sections and new world areas. The primary target areas were the United Kingdom, Western Europe, Central Europe, Latin America-Caribbean, and the South Pacific (Australia and New Zealand). These world areas were subdivided according to the languages broadcast. Organizationally, the supervisor served as "manager" of the entire broadcasting operation.

During these formative years of the International Service's operation, eleven new language services were initiated with seven employing new languages: Dutch, Swedish, Norwegian, Danish, Spanish, Portuguese, and Italian (see table 1).

Table 1. New Language Services and Target Areas, 1945-50

Language	Target Area	Inaugural Date
Dutch	Western Europe	1 May 1945
Slovak	Central Europe	1 July 1945
English	Caribbean	1 July 1945
Swedish	Scandinavia	23 April 1946
Norwegian	Scandinavia	23 April 1946
Danish	Scandinavia	23 April 1946
Spanish	Latin America	1 June 1946
English	South Pacific	1 March 1948
Portuguese	South America	1 April 1948
French	Caribbean	31 October 1948
Italian	Southern Europe	3 December 1948

POLICY

It is reasonable to ask: Why did the International Service choose to broadcast in the selected languages and to the designated world areas? First, it should be remembered that long-range policy, particularly relating to target areas, was formulated through close consultation with the Department of External Affairs. To accomplish this a committee was appointed with representatives from the CBC, the Department of External Affairs, the cabinet, and the Department of Trade and Commerce. The following individuals served on this committee in 1946:

Dr. Augustin Frigon, general manager, CBC
Norman Robertson, undersecretary of state for External Affairs
A. D. Dunton, chairman of the board, CBC
Donald Manson, assistant general manager, CBC
A. D. P. Heeney, clerk of the privy council
B. C. Butler, Department of Trade and Commerce
E. L. Bushnell, director-general of programmes, CBC
Peter Aylen, supervisor, International Service
G. Glazebrook, External Affairs
F. H. Soward, External Affairs[18]

Interestingly, Dr. Frigon chaired the committee, and Aylen served as secretary. Thus, the CBC held the key positions on the committee and External Affairs served in an advisory capacity.[19]

The new language choices reflected Canadian international interests in those areas determined by the committee. Canada, a key Middle Power, undoubtedly wanted to project its world presence to other Middle Powers: the Netherlands, Denmark, Norway, Sweden, Brazil, and other Latin American countries. There are other possible reasons why Canada wanted to broadcast to these new countries. After liberation, large numbers of Canadian troops had remained in the Netherlands and helped foster interest in Canada. The arrival of Dutch war brides to Canada strengthened ties between Canadians and the Dutch people. The Spanish and Portuguese languages were used "to develop interest in Canada and to further relations between North and South America."[20] Again, this new Latin American service followed the spirit of the Order in Council P.C. 8168, which noted the importance of having a shortwave service to foster relations with South America. The addition of French and English services to the Caribbean reflected Canada's trade interests in this area. Canada directed broadcasts to the South Pacific countries, Australia, and New Zealand, thus maintaining Commonwealth ties with this important area of the world.

The inauguration of a new Italian-language service did not follow the evolutionary patterns of the other European language services. Events in international politics in 1948 provided the main impetus for inaugurating this service.

In early 1948, the Western powers, inherently suspicious of their former ally, the Soviet Union, became alarmed by the general elections in Prague. The Communist Party, clearly in the political minority, waged an effective behind-the-scenes campaign and seized control of the government. The unfortunate *coup d' etat* in Prague was a key turning point in international politics after the Second World War. Western Europe and the New World both realized that they would have to unite if they were to ebb the flow of Soviet expansion.[21]

The Italian general elections, the first since the war, threatened to permit another Communist takeover. The Communists, gaining in popularity among the labor force, battled the Catholic Church in a critical struggle for the control of government. With the Communist victory in Prague fresh in the minds of Western leaders, there was fear that another European country might be absorbed into the Soviet bloc. Thus, the Italian elections of 1948 became a political battle between Western and Eastern ideologies with worldwide implications. The Communists, however, failed to gain control and Italy took its position among the Western nations.[22]

The events of 1948—the Czechoslovakian crisis, the Berlin blockade, the Italian elections—served as catalysts for the creation of the North Atlantic Treaty Organization (NATO) for defense purposes to deter further Soviet aggression.[23] The twelve members of NATO, bonded together by a simple declaration asserting that an armed attack against any one of them would be regarded as an attack against them all, brought the Red Army and the Bolshevist system in Europe to a standstill.[24] The West was determined to make a stand based on the general consensus that a Cold War was better than a Hot War, especially in the thermonuclear age.

Canada became increasingly active in international affairs during the postwar years. In 1948, S. F. Rae, assigned to the information division of the Department of External Affairs, stated: ". . . all responsible governments which are committed to international co-operation believe that the provisions of authentic public information to other countries is an essential aspect of the conduct of foreign affairs."[25] Certainly CBC-IS played an important role in communicating Canadian foreign policies. As a charter member of NATO, Canada held a position of prominence in the general defense of the Atlantic nations. The events of 1948, coupled with the formation of NATO in 1949, had much to do with the establishment of an Italian language service in the broadcasting operations of CBC-IS. It was a reflection of the times; Canada wanted to make its position and its identity known to the European nations, particularly to Middle Powers involved in the East-West confrontation known as the Cold War.

A NEW PROGRAMMING SLANT

The Cold War caused both the West and the Soviet bloc to engage in an endless exchange of words—charges and counter charges—popularly known as "the word war." Like the United States, Canada avoided the term *propaganda* since it carries a pejorative connotation. During the Second World War, both the Americans and the Canadians preferred the term *psychological warfare*, and brought it into official use. Unfortunately, the terms *propaganda* and *psychological warfare* have caused considerable misunderstanding, particularly among the lay public.[26]

Most American *propaganda* programs are based "on the assumption that people tend to act rationally and that *truth always prevails*," while Communist *propaganda* is Pavlovian-based, relying on the conditioned reflex. Nazi *propaganda*, however, followed the obverse of the American propositions: "People tend to act irrationally, and truth—in addition to being indeterminate—prevails far less frequently than skillful lies."[27]

What, then, is *propaganda*? It is difficult to pinpoint a precise meaning for the term because of varied connotations associated with the contexts of its use, particularly in the field of international shortwave radio broadcasting. To further compound the problem of precise definition, the other related terms—word war, war of ideas, and psychological warfare—offer hints at a definition, but add to the confusion. Within the context of international shortwave radio broadcasting, the use of the term propaganda is associated with political broadcasting activities in general. Kris and Leites define the use of propaganda, in agreement with Lasswell, "as attempts to influence attitudes of large numbers of people on controversial issues of relevance to a group."[28] Propaganda is distinguished from education which concerns non-controversial issues. But not all discussions of controversial issues of relevance to a group fall under this definition; they are not propaganda if the *intent* is the clarification of issues, rather than the changing of attitudes. *Propaganda* was the proper term for the political commentaries broadcast to Eastern Europe by CBC-IS.

NEW POLICIES

The events at Prague were disconcerting to Parliament Hill. Convinced shortwave radio broadcasting could provide some assistance to the unfortunate Czechs, caught up in the Russian takeover, new and strategically different operational policies for CBC-IS were encouraged by the government. CBC-IS, content to follow the general policy focusing on projecting "a picture of Canadian life with special reference to social, cultural, and economic development," noted that prior to 1948, the Czech and Slovak audiences in Czechoslovakia were loyal listeners to the "Voice of Canada." In fact, the Czechoslovakian audience was later described as "one of our largest and more responsive European audiences."[29] Thousands of new Canadian citizens from Czechoslovakia had personal interest in their native country and supported lobbyist groups on Parliament Hill. External Affairs, sensitive to the Czech situation, advised CBC-IS to continue Czech- and Slovak-language services, but to focus on two entirely different goals: "(1) to expound and develop the aims and policies of the Western democratic powers and particularly of Canada; (2) to combat communist ideology and Soviet imperialism" (142).

This was quite a departure from the standard peacetime broadcasting policies of the International Service. By 1946, for example, the function of the International Service was as follows: "To project Canada for listeners in the area of international world communication in order that Canada may take her place and be understood among other people . . . to develop a broad and intelligent appreciation of Canadian resources, activities, thought and general culture."[30] Ira Dilworth, general supervisor, International Service, wrote in 1949:

> The basic philosophy behind the "Voice of Canada," as this service has come to be called, is that in this complicated age, nation must speak to nation, and people to people. The words of John Donne, uttered centuries ago, seem peculiarly true today: "I am involved in mankinde."
>
> This speaking must be simple and straight forward, honest and frank, free from bias and negative propaganda. We feel that the service should be, as far as possible, friendly rather than impersonal, reflecting abroad the true character, the institutions, the habits and the aspiration of the Canadian people . . . .[31]

The Czech situation, however, presented new difficulties for the International Service. How could the "Voice of Canada" expound the aims and policies of the Western democratic powers (including Canada) and "combat communist ideology and Soviet imperialism" without engaging in biased propaganda? Dilworth, doubtless sensitive to this concern, explained CBC-IS policy as being:

> . . .to present in a positive fashion, the various aspects of life in Canada as a democratic country, and do this in a compelling and interesting fashion as possible, rather than to attack political points-of-view which may be held in the countries to which the broadcasts are directed. This approach is calculated to win the confidence of listeners and at the same time to spread abroad authoritative, honest opinion and information about Canada. For example, a great deal of time was given last summer reporting the three political conventions in an attempt to show listeners abroad how Canadians elect their political leaders and to reveal the democratic process at work in Canada.[32]

The basic operational policy, then, was the "projection of Canada" concept. Only one segment of the broadcast programming, directed to Czechoslovakia, deviated substantially from this basic policy. And according to Dilworth, the general supervisor, the broadcasts directed to this area were not "attacks" on other political systems, but were designed to "win the confidence of listeners." An analysis of the programming patterns during this period reflects these policies in the International Service broadcasts.

PROGRAMMING PATTERNS

Scheduling

Programming for an international shortwave audience involves considerable planning at both the production and the engineering levels. After determining the target areas and the language sections for each, the engineering section of the International Service had to establish means for transmitting programs to the world audience. Frequency management and antenna facilities largely determine the broadcast schedule.

The HF bands used by shortwave radio broadcasting services are allocated and assigned to meet international agreements made under the auspices of the International Telecommunications Union (ITU), Geneva, Switzerland. The ITU, an agency of the United Nations, has a regulatory function for all forms of telecommunications. The written agreements of the ITU have treaty status among the signatories (presently 160 member-nations) of the union. While the number of assigned frequencies have been increased over the years, the principle of frequency management has remained unchanged.[33] The subject of international frequency management needs clarification to illustrate the complex problems associated with establishing a broadcast schedule at an international shortwave radio broadcasting service.

The International Frequency Registration Board (IFRB) at the ITU is responsible for all uses of available frequencies in the radio spectrum. The HF portion of the radio spectrum is shared by all international shortwave radio broadcasters. There are periodic World Allocation Radio Conferences (WARC) during which the needs of international broadcasting participants are discussed and decisions are made concerning the release of more frequencies. In international shortwave radio broadcasting history there are two landmark WARC decisions, in 1927 and in 1947, that served to establish policy for this communications medium. The underlying theme of both conferences was based on the realization that increasing competition for use of limited electromagnetic radio frequency space demands full and complete cooperation from all participants sharing a common resource. The notion of a common property resource may, at first consideration, appear strange. Yet upon examining the role of the IFRB, it becomes apparent. The IFRB serves as a clearinghouse for "recorded rights and assignments," making it possible for a service to apply for frequencies and broadcasting hours before initiating any transmissions.[34]

In 1947 at the International Radio Conference held in Atlantic City, New Jersey, under the auspices of the International Telecommunications Union, a plan for a coordinated allocation of frequency hours for the shortwave services of the ITU members was established. The engineering section of CBC-IS selected several frequencies on different meter bands and submitted the list to the IFRB for action. The final selection depended upon availability (through international agreement) and reliability for optimum signal strength to the target areas. The reliability factor was largely determined by propagation studies and by reception reports. If, for example, signal reports were consistently poor from a target area, the engineering section would select other frequencies for future transmissions, provided the changes were approved by the IFRB.[35]

Programming:

The 1946 Example. The December broadcasting schedule for 1946 was arbitrarily selected to illustrate how the CBC-IS broadcast to the world audience. The program schedule was a small pamphlet (fourteen pages) containing program notes for each language service and a lead article, with pictures, concerning aspects of Canadian life. It was available to anyone, free of charge, either by mail or through the Canadian embassies.[36]

In 1946, the International Service beamed its broadcasts to two world areas: to Great Britain and Europe (see Appendix A); and to the Caribbean and Latin America. To implement the program schedule, the service used five different frequencies for its transmissions to Great Britain and Europe, and two frequencies for the Caribbean and Latin American services. The transmissions to the European areas were broadcast from 1600 Greenwich mean time (GMT) to 2300 G M T daily (seven hours) in the following languages: English, French, German, Dutch, and Czech (see table 2).

Nearly half of the total European broadcasting time was in English, with the remaining hours divided among the other four languages. An analysis of the English-language broadcast program schedules reveals six primary program types: news and commentary, music, drama and stories, magazine, talk, and other, for those programs which did not fit any of these categories.

News was presented only once per day, six days a week, in a fifteen-minute format. The commentary format, however, was used extensively throughout the weekly schedule, occupying fourteen positions. The primary purpose of the commentaries was to add background material to topical news. These programs could devote all of the time to Canadian events or to international news. Two basic programs used this format: "Canadian Chronicle" and "Canadian Commentary." The program "Canadian Chronicle" was: "A daily survey of people and happenings in Canada as reported by some forty regular correspondents from coast to coast. These form a cross section of stories behind today's headlines."[37] "Canadian Commentary" limited its focus to: "Reports on Canadian housing, trade relations, domestic, and international affairs affecting Canadian people."[38]

Musical programs were popular, and both folk and classical varieties were offered. One program "Concert from Canada," was a half-hour recital featuring Canadian instrumentalists and vocalists. Understandably, these programs were devoted primarily to Canadian artists.

Another segment of programming was radio drama and the productions that wereaired featured scripts with roles for several actors. Short stories read by one person were also in the schedule. Both types of drama were used to project the various elements of Canadian life to radio audiences and were often concerned with an historical event.

Table 2. Weekly Transmission Hours to Europe, December 1946

Language	Time
English	26:45
French	8:45
German	7:00
Dutch	4:00
Czech	6:30
Total	53:00

The talk category matched drama and stories in broadcast time (3:15). The magazine format programming treated a variety of subjects in one program. One show, for example, was "Woman in the New World," a weekly magazine program incorporating news and views of British and Canadian women living and working in Canada.

Programming that did not fit neatly into these formats was designated "Other." "Radio-1946," for example, was described as a program for listeners who were interested in a serious examination of the achievements and shortcomings of radio broadcasting. These fifteen-minute presentations were given by "men of distinction." The following are representative of the radio talks broadcast in this series:

A. Davidson Dunton, chairman, CBC board of governors, on "Our National Radio"
Keith Tyler, director, Institute for Education by Radio at Ohio State University, on "Broadcasting in the U.S.A."
Jack Gould," radio editor, the *New York Times*, on "Radio as Entertainment"
Deems Taylor, music critic and commentator on "Music on the Air"[39]

Two additional programs, "Farm Forum" and "Farm Review," featured Hugh Boyd, agricultural editor of the Winnipeg *Free Press*, as a

commentator. "Farm Forum" was a copy of the experimental radio discussion program originated by CBC domestic radio services which
included listener participation.[40]

CBC-IS broadcast eighty-eight programs in English to Great Britain
and Europe for a total of 26:45 (26 hours and 45 minutes; see table 3).
The majority of the programs seventy-five had a fifteen-minute format,
and only three shows were one hour in length (music and variety).

News and commentary programs were dispersed throughout the schedule for a weekly total of seven hours. Doubtless, the first year of operation after the war can be characterized as a continuing search for program
types to fit the "projection of Canada" theme. Perhaps this explains why
such a large number of programs (26) were categorized as "Other." The
fact that only four hours per week were devoted to music reinforces the
notion that the primary goal of the International Service was to project
news and information about Canada.

Table 3. Total Hours Broadcast Weekly in English to Europe by
Format, December 1946

Program Format	No. of Programs by Program Length			Total Time
	60	30	15	
News and Commentary	0	0	28	7:00
Other	2	2	22	8:30
Music	0	1	14	4:00
Drama and Stories	1	3	3	3:15
Talk	0	4	5	3:15
Magazine	0	0	3	:45
Totals	3	10	75	26:45

The programming for the other language sections—French, German,
Dutch, and Czech—evolved into specific patterns during this formative
period. Since the basic format was fifteen minutes for the majority of the
foreign-language programs, there were topical headings presented by the
weekday. For example, Monday was reserved for economic news;

Tuesday, trade relations; Wednesday, science news; Thursday, sports news, and so on. A specific example from "Hier Spricht Kanada," the German service, had the following daily formats in December 1946:

Monday: Sports News
Wednesday: "For the Wife"
Thursday: Canadian Portraits
Friday: Book Reviews
Saturday: News, Past week in Canada
Sunday: Record Show (music)[41]

All language services beamed to Europe followed similar program format patterns.

The daily broadcasts to the Caribbean and Latin American areas were in English (1:10), Portuguese (:30), and Spanish (1:00). The Spanish and Portuguese services followed the format described in "Hier Spricht Kanada." The English programs directed to the Caribbean also followed a daily pattern and stressed music, drama, and information of interest to that region, e.g., calypso, "discussions bringing West Indians in Canada to the microphone."

Latin America and the Caribbean received a weekly average of 18:40 broadcast time during this period. The following is a weekly breakdown of the languages used: English, 8:10; Spanish, 7:30; and Portuguese, 3:30. The International Service also broadcast to Australia 1:15 every Sunday. These, then, were the minor programming services. The major emphasis in programming was on European target areas.

The main elements of the program schedule for December 1946 are illustrative of the European emphasis. Following the patterns set by other international shortwave radio broadcasting services, a typical CBC-IS program began with news and commentary, then branched into a preset programming format for the allotted time. The service broadcast 71:40 weekly to the world radio audience.

PROGRAMMING PATTERNS: 1947-50

The December program schedule (or nearest available month) for the years 1947-50 revealed total weekly broadcasting times for each language service. The average broadcast times from this period illustrate that the key language directed to Europe was English with a weekly average of 25:11 (see table 4). Further analyses of the English language was the most widely used program type in the schedules with an average weekly total of 7:56 (see table 5). The weekly increases from 6:30 in November 1947, to 8:15 a year later, probably reflected a change of events in Europe. Canada wanted to make its position known to Europeans.

The special programs of United Nations Commentaries, which averaged seven hours weekly, reflected a continuing interest and support for that international body. This programming element is not surprising since Canadians had supported the United Nations from the very beginning. The Dumbarton Oaks Conference proposals for the establishment of the United Nations was approved overwhelmingly by a majority vote of 200 to 5 in the Canadian House of Commons.[42] When the Canadian delegation traveled to San Francisco to participate in the drafting of the U.N. Charter, the International Service sent correspondents to cover the event. The correspondents broadcast fifty-four new *items* in French, English, and German and offered Czech-translation broadcasts to Europe from 25 April until the conference ended on 26 June. The United Nations proceedings at Lake Success and at Flushing Meadows, near New York City, were also covered by the International Service which sent a news staff to prepare reports that were translated in the foreign-language sections.[43]

The primary increases among foreign-language services were in the Czech-language section. The additional 2:15 weekly broadcasts beamed to Czechoslovakia attempted to counter the international turmoil associated with the Communist coup of 1948.

Certain program types say reductions in broadcast time allocations. Music, for example, originally scheduled for four hours per week in 1947, was down to one hour in 1950. Both the dramatic productions and the magazine format were significantly reduced. The main reason for these decreases was the creation of a transcription service and the wider use of relays and program exchanges which proved to be the better, more cost-efficient media for these program types.

PROJECTING CANADA VIA OTHER AVAILABLE MEANS

During the first year of operation, the International Service established a music library containing 1,000 commercial records to be used by producers in broadcasting record shows to troops stationed overseas. But, as the programming emphasis evolved to discussions, commentary, and informative talks, the library was expanded to hold recorded transcriptions of these programs (21).

Table 4. Total Hours Broadcast Weekly to Europe, 1947-1950*

Language	1947	1948	1949	1950	Average Weekly Totals
English	32:45	26:00	19:00	23:00	25:11
French	9:15	9:15	9:15	7:00	8:41
Czech	4:00	6:15	9:45	11:00	7:45
German	4:00	5:00	5:00	6:30	5:08
Dutch	2:20	5:00	5:00	5:00	4:45
Danish	2:20	2:20	2:20	2:20	2:20
Norwegian	2:20	2:20	2:20	2:20	2:20
Swedish	2:20	2:20	2:20	2:20	2:20
Italian	- -	- -	3:30	3:30	1:45
Totals	61:00	58:30	58:30	63:00	60:15

*These times were taken from the December program schedules or the nearest available month.

    The process of making recorded transcriptions was extremely crude. The recording was etched into the surface of a thin aluminum sheeting, which had been cut into a circle, the size of the turntable at a radio station, and coated with plastic. The width of the groove was wider than that found on pressed recordings, thus the quality of the recorded material was acceptable but certainly far from excellent fidelity. Transcriptions were cheaply made, durable, and of such a wide circumference that, they could hold an impressive amount of recorded material.

Table 5. Total Hours Broadcast Weekly in English to Europe by Format, 1947-1950*

Program Format	1947	1948	1949	1950	Average Weekly Totals
News and Commentary	6:30	8:15	8:15	8:45	7:56
Magazine	1:45	1:00	1:00	:15	1:00
Talk	2:00	1:45	2:15	2:00	2:00
Music	4:00	2:15	2:15	1:00	2:23
Drama and Stories	1:30	1:00	1:00	:15	:56
Sports	1:00	:45	:45	--	:38
Other	7:00	11:00	3:30	4:30	6:30
Special (U.N.)	9:00	--	--	6:30	3:52
Totals	32:45	26:00	19:00	23:15	25:15

*These times were taken from the December program schedules or the nearest available month.

Music programming broadcast via shortwave radio presents special problems. With propagation changes comes erratic fading. The poor fidelity of the recorded musiccoupled with fading conditions brought into question the wisdom of programming music on a shortwave radio service. Music was thought to be part of the total "projection of Canada" theme, but with broadcast quality interfering with the audience's appreciation for the music, CBC-IS decided to ship transcribed special music programs overseas. One of the earliest recordings, an album by Canadian composers, was prepared in March 1945 by the International Service. Designed to foster an appreciation of Canadian music abroad, the first music program featured *Suite Canadienne* by Claude Champagne, and Dr. Healy Willan's *Concerto in C Minor*, performed by the CBC orchestra under the direction of Jean Beaudet. The International Service distributed copies of the recordings to Canadian embassies and legations overseas, as well as to foreign radio stations and conservatories (21).

This recorded music shipment was the beginning of the transcription service that was officially inaugurated in 1947. The transcription service had the responsibility of selecting appropriate Canadian music, talk programs, and dramatic presentations for distribution among foreign domestic radio stations. These recorded programs were available free of charge to foreign stations, provided the stations submitted evidence of actual use. The activities of the transcription service from 1947 to 1950 undoubtedly caused the deletion of program types in the regular shortwave schedule, particularly those that were better suited for package mailing, i.e., drama, music, and discussions.

To supplement the live transmissions and the transcription service, CBC-IS developed the technique of relays and the use of special program exchanges. Programs using a relay were broadcast by CBC-IS to a foreign broadcasting service and were then rebroadcast on the domestic service, either simultaneously or at a later time. Special program exchanges, i.e., the production of a special feature recorded in Montreal, then sent by mail to another domestic or shortwave service, were also arranged. Typically, the foreign service sent a special program to Canada for broadcast over CBC domestic networks. This arrangement was not used as frequently as transcription service shipments (21).

All three broadcast types—live transmissions, transcriptions, and special program exchanges—were used to reach target areas. Theoretically, shortwave transmissions, although important, could not reach as many listeners as a domestic service. By placing transcriptions on foreign domestic services, the audience size would be increased since the number of AM radio listeners far exceeded the number of HF shortwave radio listeners. The use of relays and special program exchanges helped purvey the Canadian identity to larger audiences as well. These supplemental broadcasting activities, although introduced on a modest scale in 1947, set a precedent and established a pattern for the future. Exploring non-shortwave means to reach international audiences continued to be a pursuit of the International Service.

PROBLEMS: THE QUESTIONS BEGIN

During the 1947-50 formative period, the major quandary confronting CBC-IS operations was what came to be known as the effectiveness issue. At some point, every international shortwave radio broadcasting service is confronted with the following queries: How effective is the broadcasting service? What is the broadcasting service attempting to accomplish? And, inevitably, how many people do you reach? These questions pose an attack on operational goals. For the Canadian Broadcasting Corporation, the effectiveness issue surfaced after a brief, one-year period of operations.

In 1946, Peter Aylen, addressing a group of Montreal businessmen, asserted:

> It is, of course, difficult to assess in concrete terms the results of such an intangible thing as international broadcasting, particularly in a Europe desperately striving to keep alive, to keep warm and to get organized again. We cannot very well, at least at the present time, have a radio poll as we have here with people going around ringing door bells and telephones and asking, "What foreign station are you listening to?" There remains, therefore, only three major ways to measure success. The volume of fan mail, the quality of the mail and the willingness of stations in foreign countries to relay programs on local networks.[44]

These three criteria—mail quantity, mail content, and placement of programs in foreign stations' programming—were then, as they are now, difficult to defend. First, letters indicate only how many listeners took the time to write and do not show how many actually listened. As Aylen observed, however, radio surveys were difficult to conduct in postwar Europe and, more important, they were costly. Therefore, the CBC-IS was hard-pressed to justify the cost of the service to nonbelievers of shortwave radio broadcasting effectiveness. On 19 July 1948, for example, the Toronto *Telegram* doubted the value of the International Service in an editorial:

> Some doubt of the value of this expenditure must assail the minds of Canadians whose own receiving sets have shortwave bands which are seldom used. On this band are listed such stations as Moscow, Berlin, Rome, London, Paris, Hong Kong, Buenos Aires, Madrid and Australia. It is the show window of the world in a radio sense, yet how often does the average Canadian make use of it and, traveling hopefully from whistle to squeal, attempt to get a glimpse of the great world outside? Is it to be believed that in other countries the people are more enthusiastic shortwavers than we in Canada?[45]

This weak generalization (shortwave listening is not popular in Canada, therefore it is not popular in other countries) indicated a lack of understanding of international broadcasting. The Second World War had increased the popularity of shortwave broadcasting in Europe because often it was the only medium available for objective news. Obviously, the

Toronto *Telegram* was unconcerned about potential radio audiences and was convinced there were better ways to project Canada. The editorial writer noted comments made by the *Financial Post* correspondent stationed in London: "It is a great pity, that Canada does not send Sir Ernest MacMillan and his Toronto Symphony over here for a tour. They would have had a grand reception, and it would remind the British that there are other things in Canada besides making holes in the ice to catch fish."[46]

Both the Toronto *Telegram* and the Brantford *Expositor* endorsed a symphony tour. The Brantford *Expositor* observed:

> The gentle irony of the foregoing should not escape the Canadian powers that be. If the latter could possibly take a little of the money they intend to spend on beaming Canadian radio propaganda to the Russians (who don't listen to it anyway) and divert it to the purpose here suggested, the second investment would pay the greater dividends.[47]

In 1949 the Winnipeg *Citizen* published a letter to the editor which questioned the achievements of the "Voice of Canada," after it was made public that the International Service had received a total of 90,000 letters from listeners abroad since 1945. The writer claimed that a single soap program "has been known to bring in a better response than that."[48] The CBC-IS, sensitive to any criticism, answered the anonymous writer in a letter from Press and Information Representative Ralph Marven who noted that letters were widespread responses from individuals who favor the International Service programming. He offered two examples from letters written from behind the Iron Curtain:

> You have the best newscast and commentaries of all the stations broadcasting in Czech and that is probably why your transmissions are frequently jammed.
> What do we want from you? We know you can't help us. Just as the tree starts blooming in the spring and gives fruit only in the autumn, everything takes time but we believe that no trees are allowed to grow indefinitely. Hitler has not conquered us nor will the Communists. But please keep on encouraging us in your transmissions just as our Jan Masaryk used to do during the war. That gives us new strength which we need now more than ever.[49]

These two letters received from behind the Iron Curtain were exhibited in an attempt to justify the expenditures by promoting the importance of *what* the listeners had to say about the programming rather than *how many* were listening. The effectiveness issue, although just introduced during this period, resurfaced later.

Since government funds were involved, Parliament scrutinized CBC-IS expenditures. In 1948, the Ford Hotel on Dorchester Street was purchased for use as the broadcasting studios and offices for the International Service. It also housed the French networks for the Quebec Region. The Honourable J. J. McCann, minister of finance, proposed a budget of $1,786,500 for the CBC-IS expansions and operating costs. When questioned in the House of Commons, he explained that the shortwave operation was not financed in the same way as the CBC. Moreover, he pointed out that the "shortwave [service] is the property of all . . . the taxpayers, and out of the appropriation we are asking parliament to vote this year that this service be continued."[50] When asked what purpose the service performed, McCann replied, "The most powerful weapon against misunderstanding is the frank exchange of information among nations. This is a time when curtains of any kind, iron or otherwise, are tragic in the extreme when they exist between large groups of mankind."[51] McCann tried to alleviate any bad feelings toward the service by emphasizing Canada's role in world affairs. "She could not if she wished, pursue a policy of isolation," McCann stated before the House of Commons. "Increasingly, Canada has been playing her full role in international affairs. It is, therefore, logical that she should have an international voice and that is exactly what the international service of the CBC is."[52]

McCann's statement and request for support were well-received in the House. One member observed:

> I do not think anybody in Canada begrudges the money to our international shortwave system. It can be one of the greatest things for good we have ever had in Canada in connection with trade if it is properly carried on, and if the broadcasts are properly done. We are a fine democratic country. We must let the people of the rest of the world know what a fine place Canada is in which to live. . . .[53]

Another major problem encountered during this period concerned the transition from the projection of Canada to a controversial participation in the "war of ideas." Broadcasts to Czechoslovakia began in 1945. Lester B. Pearson, secretary of state for External Affairs, later explained that the Czechoslovakian service was not initiated because of an assumption that

Czech was more important than, say, Ukrainian or Polish, but "because Czechoslovakia was the first, and regrettably the only Eastern European country to be re-established after the war with what then appeared to be a stable democratic government."[54] Furthermore, Pearson noted, after the *coup d'etat* in 1948, "it seemed wise to continue that broadcasting because of the audience we had already built up."[55]

The broadcasts to Czechoslovakia, however, prompted some members of the House of Commons to question participation in the so-called "war of ideas." Communism was the primary ideological enemy, and after the fall of Czechoslovakia there was fear of Communist infiltration in government, in industry, and even in CBC-IS. The concern was not only over the content of the scripts, but about the men who wrote them. It was well-known that Eastern European broadcasting staff members at the International Service were born, reared, and educated in that target area. In the minds of the suspicious, it seemed logical that the Communists would plant members of the party in strategic positions abroad as part of a grand conspiracy. The CBC-IS seemed a likely place for infiltrators. Indeed, McCann was asked about this possibility in an exchange in the House of Commons:

Q. [Mr. Drew]: Are the staff or the performers of the international service shortwave broadcasting station being screened by the R.C.M.P. [Royal Canadian Mounted Police]?

A. [Mr. McCann]: Yes they are.

Q. [Mr. Drew]: Is it not correct that the screening which is taking place is being conducted in connection with a suggestion that there has been certain broadcasting conveyed to European countries which was not in accordance with the purpose of setting up this station?

A. [Mr. McCann]: I am informed that the answer is no . . . the topic and the script are screened most carefully. In some instances, the person who is delivering the talk is screened also; but there would be no reason to screen a musician in the employment of the international shortwave station.[56]

The subject of screening undoubtedly flashed an alarm on the Hill. The International Service of the Canadian Broadcasting Corporation was a broadcasting agent for the Government, carefully following policy guidelines dictated by the Department of External Affairs—an arrangement open to question among the suspicious. As the Cold War became more intense, the role of External Affairs in CBC-IS operations directed to

Eastern Europe would become a controversial issue and would become the subject of searching parliamentary inquiry during the next decade.

NOTES

1. Canadian Broadcasting Corporation, "This is Canada Calling: A Variety Program to Mark the Inauguration of the CBC's International Service" (Montreal, 25 February 1945, mimeographed). It was broadcast simultaneously on the Trans-Canada domestic network.
2. Morton, *History of Canada*, 202-3; 207.
3. CBC-IS, "Inaugural Broadcast." The script provides the reader only cues for the control board operator. The complete text can be found in "International Service: 1945-50," 16-17. The *New York Times*, 26 February 1945, reported the occasion with excerpts of King's speech on p.1.
4. "Inaugural Broadcast."
5. Ibid.
6. Ibid.
7. Order in Council P.C. 8168 discussed the need for this type of broadcasting.
8. Canadian Broadcasting Corporation, "Report on International Service" (Montreal: CBC, 1956, mimeographed), app. 13, 5.
9. "International Service: 1945-50," 19.
10. Order in Council P.C. 8168.
11. Canadian Broadcasting Corporation, "A Report on the International Service of the Canadian Broadcasting Corporation" (International Service, Montreal, 1948, mimeographed), 5.
12. Helmut Blume, "Barbed Wire Broadcasts," *Radio*, staff magazine, Canadian Broadcasting Corporation 1 (April 1946): 9.
13. "International Service: 1945-50," 20.
14. Walter Schmolka, head, Czechoslovakian section, interviewed by the author, audiocassette, 14 July 1971.
15. "International Service: 1945-50," 20.
16. See Order in Council P.C. 8168.
17. Canadian Broadcasting Corporation, *Canada Calling: A Schedule of Short-wave Broadcasts from Canada* (Montreal: International Service, December 1949), 1.
18. CBC *Desk Reference Manual* (Ottawa: Canadian Broadcasting Corporation, 1946), 1.
19. Ibid.
20. See Paul-Henri Spaak, "The Atlantic Community and NATO," *Orbis*, 1 (Winter 1958): 411; cited in Alvin Cottrell and James E. Dougherty, *The Politics of the Atlantic Alliance* (New York: Frederick A. Praeger, Publishers, 1964), 13.
21. Muriel Grindrod, *The Rebuilding of Italy* (London: Oxford University Press for the Royal Institute of International Affairs, 1955), 55. For a concise treatment of

this subject, see Guiseppe Mammarella, *Italy After Fascism: A Political History* (Montreal: Mario Casalini, Ltd., 1964), especially chap. 8, "A Turning Point in Italian Postwar Politics: The Political Elections of April 1948," 188-97.

22. Cottrell and Dougherty, *Politics of the Atlantic Alliance*, 19.
23. Prince Hubertine zu Lowenstein and Volkmer von Zuhlsdorff, *NATO and the Defense of the West*, trans. Edward Fitzgerald (Westport, Conn.: Greenwood Press Publishers, 1975), 60.
24. Ibid.
25. House of Commons, Standing Committee on External Affairs, *Minutes of Proceedings and Evidence*, no. 6, 9 June 1948, 146.
26. See, Ferreus, "The Menace of Communist Psychological Warfare," *Orbis* 1 (April 1957): 97.
27. Ibid.
28. See, Wilber Schramm, "Special Problems of Achieving an Effect with International Communication," 429-62; Wilbur Schramm, ed., *The Process and Effects of Communication* (Urbana: The University of Illinois Press, 1970); and, Ernst Kris and Nathan Leites, "Trends in Twentieth Century Propaganda," in Schramm, *Process and Effects*; see also H. D. Lasswell, *Propaganda Techniques in the World War* (New York: Alfred A. Knopf, 1927); and B. L. Smith, H. D. Lasswell, and R. D. Casey, *Propaganda, Communication, and Public Opinion* (Princeton, N. J.: Princeton University Press, 1946).
29. House of Commons, Standing Committee on External Affairs, *Minutes and Proceedings and Evidence*, no. 6, 12 March 1953, 142.
30. *CBC Desk Reference Manual*, 1. For a brief discussion of this development, see Eayrs, *The Art of the Possible*, 194-95.
31. Ira Dilworth, "The Voice of Canada: The International Service of the Canadian Broadcasting Corporation," *External Affairs* 1 (July 1949): 17-22.
32. Ibid.
33. See J. M. Frost, editor in chief, *World Radio TV Handbook,* vol. 41 (New York: Billboard Publications, Inc., 1987), 46, for a tabular listing of the most suitable megaHertz broadcasting bands by world area.
34. Harvey J. Levin, *The Invisible Resource: Use and Regulation of the Radio Spectrum* (Baltimore: Johns Hopkins University Press, 1971), 33-34.
35. Canadian Broadcasting Corporation, "Frequency Management System" (Department of Engineering Services, International Service, Montreal, 1971, mimeographed), app. 1, 2.
36. Canadian Broadcasting Corporation, *Canada Calling: A Schedule of Shortwave Broadcasts from Canada* (Montreal: Canadian Broadcasting Corporation International Service, December 1946).
37. Ibid.
38. Ibid.
39. Ibid.

40. Ibid. For unexplained reasons, Tuesdays were omitted in this schedule.

41. Ibid.

42. See F. H. Soward and Edgar McInnis with the assistance of Walter O'Hearn, *Canada and the United Nations*, National Studies on International Organization (New York: Manhattan Publishing Company for the Canadian Institute of International Affairs and the Carnegie Endowment for International Peace, 1956), 19-32.

43. "International Service: 1945-50," 21.

44. Peter Aylen, speech to the St. Lawrence Kiwanis Club, Montreal, 8 May 1946; in Files, Radio Canada International, Montreal.

45. Editorial, *Telegram* (Toronto), 19 July 1948.

46. Ibid.

47. Ibid.

48. Letter, Ralph Marven to the *Citizen* (Winnipeg), n.d., in Canadian Broadcasting Corporation, Montreal, Central Registry File no. IS4-2-6, vol. 1.

49. Ibid.

50. House of Commons, *Debates*, 6, 1948, 6046-47; see also House of Commons, *Debates*, 1, 1949, 820-21.

51. House of Commons, *Debates*, 2d. sess., 3, 1948, 2821-27.

52. Ibid.

53. Ibid.

54. House of Commons, Standing Committee on External Affairs, *Minutes of Proceedings and Evidence*, no. 4, 30 May 1951, 87.

55. Ibid.

56. House of Commons, *Debates*, 2d. sess., 3, 1948, 2825. Note: There were several different style formats for dialogue employed by the government transcribers for recording the Minutes and Proceedings of Evidence. For consistency, this format is used.

3 THE COLD WAR INTENSIFIES

TENSION MOUNTS

IN THE EARLY MORNING hours of 25 June 1950, North Korean troops stormed across the Thirty-eighth parallel into the Republic of South Korea, placing the Free World on alert. Fighting spread rapidly, and soon the Communist invaders threatened Seoul, the seat of a struggling democratic government which was supported heavily by the United States and the United Nations (UN).

The United States responded quickly to the Communist aggression in Korea. American troops stationed there tried to hold the line but were forced to retreat with heavy losses. The United Nations rallied with military support for South Korea. Nevertheless, the world soon faced another armed conflict with a clear demarcation line: West against East; Free World against the Soviet-China bloc. Although recognized officially as a "Police Action" sanctioned by the UN, the Korean Conflict was a testing ground for Communist aggression. UN participants, including Canada, waged war for three bloody years at a cost of 99,000 killed in action, and 250,000 wounded, while those missing or captured numbered more than 83,000.[1] The end result was a shaky peace and a demilitarized zone separating North from South.

A divided Europe and an ugly war in Korea helped create a strong sense of unity among the Western powers. Canada, a leader among the Middle Powers and active supporter of the United Nations and NATO, became increasingly aware of its responsibilities in a world complicated by international turmoil and open conflict. The CBC-IS, the agent charged with voicing Canadian foreign policy abroad, reaffirmed its mission in the 1951 Canadian Broadcasting Corporation's *Annual Report*:

> In order to keep step with the growing tension in the world today and the increasingly important role being played by Canada in international

53

affairs, considerable changes have taken place during the past two years at
the Voice of Canada. There has been a change in emphasis in programming
. . . and the service has been expanded.[2]

The announcement underscored additional CBC-IS efforts to combat
the Soviets' so-called "battle for men's minds." The International Service
inaugurated a Finnish service on 3 December 1950, and more important,
a Russian service beamed to the Soviet Union began on 4 February 1951.
The Honourable Dana Wilgress, former Canadian ambassador to the
Soviet Union, addressed the Soviet shortwave radio audience in Russian:

> In these days of international tension, ignorance and misunderstanding
> of other countries and peoples are exploited by the propaganda of the rul-
> ing circles of the USSR to create fear and suspicion. We believe that one of
> the surest ways to mutual understanding and peace is through the free
> exchange of information. The Canadian people earnestly desire this
> exchange. . . .[3]

With the inauguration of a Russian-language service, CBC-IS began a
full-scale broadcasting operation directed to Eastern Europe, adding a
Ukrainian service (also meant for the Soviet Union) in July 1952; a Polish
service in 1953; and a Hungarian service following that country's revolu-
tion in 1956.

With this new emphasis on Eastern European broadcasts, the
International Service embarked on a controversial course. As a result, policy guidance for CBC-IS underwent intense scrutiny. Concern that Canada's
international "Voice" might be involved in the "word war" caused some
members of Parliament to take a fresh look not only at *what* was being
broadcast, but also at *who* was responsible for the preparation of these
broadcasts. For example, how was policy guidance decided upon, particularly for Eastern European broadcasts, and how was this advice passed
along to CBC-IS?

ON THE MATTER OF POLICY . . .

Achieving consensus on policy is difficult because the term is largely
ambiguous, and has been overworked, misused, even misapplied by politicians, government officials, and the lay public. Policy has been defined as:
"A purposive course of action followed by an actor or set of actors in

dealing with a problem or matter of concern."[4] For this discussion, the "problem or matter of concern" is Canadian participation in international shortwave radio broadcasting. "A purposive course of action" is guidance provided to the International Service by the Department of External Affairs concerning matters of target areas and languages used which, in turn, are based upon foreign policy commitments. The implementation of this *guidance* is reserved for the "actors or set of actors," namely, CBC-IS personnel.

Within the context of this definitional outline, the policy concerning broadcasts beamed to Eastern Europe came under close scrutiny. From its inception, CBC-IS was never to be the direct radio voice of the federal government. The Canadian Broadcasting Corporation was chosen to be the agent-in-charge of the external broadcasting operations in consultation with the Department of External Affairs. The controversy surrounding broadcasts beamed to Eastern Europe focused on the *degree of consultation*, and the liaison between CBC-IS and the Department of External Affairs. Simply stated, Parliament wanted to know: how and to what degree was the government involved in the broadcasting operations of CBC-IS? In other words, what were the mechanics of governmental policy formulation and implementation that could influence international shortwave radio broadcasting?

The Department of External of Affairs is represented on the cabinet by the secretary of state for External Affairs.[5] In the Canadian parliamentary system, no official from the Department of External Affairs can make foreign policy because only the secretary of state for External Affairs, the prime minister and the cabinet hold that responsibility. More important for an analysis of communication channels, "the Canadian cabinet must take the responsibility for all Canadian foreign policies and the way these policies are implemented."[6]

Information dissemination could be traced via the secretary of state for External Affairs, which in turn had the responsibility for implementation of policy guidelines in the international broadcasts. The CBC, the figurative organizational head of CBC-IS, was represented in the cabinet by the minister of national revenue.

The total funding for CBC-IS came from government grants and not from license fees which funded the CBC, creating a puzzling situation among political observers. For example, it was known that CBC-IS was an appendage to the CBC and that all CBC-IS personnel were CBC employees. Yet the government funded CBC-IS, not CBC, which was sup-

ported by a license fee. The Cold War had prodded Canada into participation in the "word war" with the Soviet bloc, prompting questions:
Which agency was responsible for International Service actions? Was it
the CBC or External Affairs? Or both?

THE KEYSERLINGK AFFAIR

In 1949, refugee groups in Canada began to criticize the Czech- and
Slovak-language services claiming that certain members of the CBC-IS
staff "were at the very least uninterested in this kind of broadcasting, or
were actively disloyal."[7] Robert Keyserlingk, self-appointed firebrand
and editor of the Catholic weekly, *The Ensign*, emerged as an adamant
critic of the International Service. His inflammatory editorials urged the
following: A purging of the CBC-IS staff, of the kind that had swept the
National Film Board after the 1948 Communist coup in Czechoslovakia,
for tighter security screening; and replacing the head of the International
Service with a government appointee rather than a CBC member.[8] In
January 1951, Keyserlingk attacked the CBC-IS in a broadcast over
CJAD-AM, Montreal, charging that "the chief of the Central European
Section . . . was apparently particularly anxious not to make bad friends,
even amongst the Communists."[9] He told the radio audience that the
head of the Communist Bohemian Radio, Mr. Hronek, visited the
International Service studios and offices and "was not only courteously
received" but, Keyserlingk noted, was shown the entire operation (1).
Keyserlingk continued his assault on the integrity of CBC-IS personnel
and operations: ". . . in the battle of ideas as bitter, as dangerous and as
fatal as our present struggle against Communism is, studied neutrality at
taxpayer's expense can be misleading to the people on the other side. . .
" (1). Keyserlingk demanded a more polemic stance in the broadcasts
beamed to Eastern Europe. The listeners in Communist-held countries
needed "moral encouragement," Keyserlingk asserted, "not pleasant feature stories, how eskimos live. . . " (1). Such bland programming, he reasoned, was an "anti-anti-communist slant" (1).

The Keyserlingk attacks, although filled with innuendo and little concrete evidence, undermined the integrity of CBC-IS. The liaison between
the Department of External Affairs and CBC-IS became the focus of attention. Parliament Hill wanted to know who was responsible for policy matters concerning the broadcasts beamed behind the Iron Curtain, and for
the policy guidance at the International Service.

In May 1951, George Drew, leader of the opposition in the House of Commons remarked, "I have no doubt whatever that this service (CBC-IS) has a useful place in the struggle for men's minds which is taking place in the world today. . . . What I am . . . concerned about is the measure of supervision that is being exercised by the Department of External Affairs. . . ."[10] Drew pointed to the Keyserlingk broadcast as a prime example of criticism leveled against CBC-IS programming directed to Eastern Europe. Lester B. Pearson, secretary of state, replied:

> It is, of course, easy to give currency to criticisms of this kind which give a general impression of pro-communist sympathies to the organization of the CBC international service. That service, is, I think, doing valuable work for Canada, and playing a useful part in the psychological war against communism—which, as the hon. gentleman mentioned this afternoon, is an important part of the total war battle for men's minds.
>
> These general criticisms would be more convincing if they were more precisely substantiated; and that may be attempted when the committee [Standing Committee on External Affairs] meets (3003).

On May 30, Pearson appeared before the Standing Committee on External Affairs to explain his department's liaison with CBC-IS. He explained the relationship as "continuous consultation through visits of officers of the department [External Affairs] and CBC-IS and vice versa, and by means of letters, the telephone and the teletype."[11] Pearson continued:

> The Department of External Affairs now assumes the responsibility for the general line of policy but, of course, the International Service, as an agency operating in a highly technical field, is responsible for adapting policy to the medium of shortwave broadcasting. Therefore, the CBC is responsible for the writing of scripts or the commissioning of scripts by experts in various fields. We do not censor these scripts, but we are, of course, concerned in seeing that the general line of policy is followed. . . (85).

The committee's major concern was the European broadcasts. Pearson noted that broadcasts to other world areas—Latin America, for example—were perceived as "a projection of Canada." In the broadcasts beamed to Europe, Pearson stressed the most important component was "participation in the war of ideas" (85). This revelation increased parliamentary concern over *how* this policy was implemented.

In March 1951 a new section, policy coordination, was established at CBC-IS and supervised by a policy coordinator. Pearson testified before the Standing Committee on External Affairs:

> The policy coordinator holds daily policy meetings with the head and some members of the various language sections, and he transmits and interprets to them our guidance. The language sections then produce their materials along the lines we have suggested and before the broadcasts, the material is checked by the policy section to make sure that the general line is being followed (85).

There were now two links to the Department of External Affairs within the CBC-IS. Understandably, the supervisor maintained contacts within the department but, in addition, the policy coordinator assisted in the liaison. It was the policy coordinator's responsibility to check the scripts for policy implementation, particularly with political commentaries.

Pearson's explanation concerning the relationship between the Department of External Affairs and CBC-IS was reasonable. Liaison was a critical issue among certain key members of Parliament and Pearson's submission to the committee meticulously described the way in which the Department of External Affairs insured strict adherence to official policy. Keyserlingk, however, unleashed yet another editorial attack on the International Service. The October 1951 edition of *The Ensign* contained a scathing editorial entitled, "We Rest Our Case." Keyserlingk reiterated the old charges condemning the Eastern European broadcasts, including the redundant "anti-anti-Communist slant," and extended his discontent by attacking the Latin American section:

> Now, complaints are reaching us that the Spanish-language broadcasts of the CBC shortwaved to Latin America are replete with anti-religious bias and astute secularist propaganda. This is causing annoyance amongst many Latin Americans who feel Canada has no right to offend traditional religious attitudes.[12]

The editorial did not specify dates or specific programs, nor did it identify the origin of the complaints. H. W. Morrison, head of the Latin American Section, countered:

> Among . . . 11,930 letters received in Spanish [during the last three years] there was one which criticized us on religious grounds . . . this letter accuses

of us broadcasting *Catholic* propaganda. No one else has expressed even
annoyance with any of our broadcasts.[13]

Morrison submitted a three-page report outlining broadcast themes
and noted: "It is difficult to refute an undocumented generalization such
as this."[14] On 18 October, Ira Dilworth, the CBC-IS supervisor, wrote a
letter to A. D. Dunton, chairman, board of governors, CBC, complaining
about the lack of explicitness in the Keyserlingk editorial. Doubtless frus-
trated over answering such vague charges, Dilworth asserted:

> Mr. Keyserlingk is concerned with who is responsible for policy in rela-
> tion to our programming in the International Service. I have to accept that
> responsibility. If Mr. Keyserlingk would only come out and say plainly and
> not depend upon innuendo that I am a less good Christian or a less loyal
> Canadian or a less intelligent opponent of communism than he is, I should
> be glad to deal with him directly. . . .[15]

Dilworth attached Morrison's explanation to his letter. On 22 October,
Dunton replied in a letter: "If Keyserlingk's methods of attack on the CBC
are Christian, then many of us have long misread the Bible. Perhaps some
day Providence will provide an answer."[16]

The Keyserlingk attacks, coupled with concern expressed by members of
Parliament over policy, in general, and the liaison issue, in particular, com-
pounded the CBC's dilemma. These charges, although weak, had given the
CBC-IS adverse publicity. Policy concerning Eastern European broadcasts
became a controversial issue with Dilworth and the corporation was caught
in the middle. The result was to forge a "closer liaison" with External
Affairs. Keyserlingk believed that a CBC appointee, a professional broadcaster, was not qualified to make judgments concerning programming content which would reflect Canada's foreign policies. Thus, Keyserlingk
argued in his editorials that a government appointee, preferably someone
from External Affairs, be named as head of the International Service.[17]

THEN CAME DÉSY . . .

In November the announcement came, not from the CBC, but from the
prime minister in the House of Commons, that the Canadian ambassador
in Rome, Jean Désy, had been seconded to the post of director-general of
the International Service, effective 1 January 1952.[18] The selection of a

senior diplomat, an officer in the Department of External Affairs who was temporarily assigned to the post "to bring the benefits of his long and close familiarity with Canadian foreign policy to bear on the technical problems of broadcasting," was made to offset the liaison and policy criticisms.[19]

The Désy appointment, however, caused instant confusion. The Order in Council P.C. 8168, which authorized the International Service, clearly specified that the CBC would be the agent-in-charge of the shortwave broadcasting operation in consultation with External Affairs. The question of whether the corporation or the Department of External Affairs was responsible for the CBC-IS became an issue, since Désy was not a professional broadcaster. The Standing Committee on External Affairs questioned L. D. Wilgress, assistant undersecretary of state, about this unparalleled relationship:

> Q. [Mr. Graydon]: I just wanted to know this. Mr. Désy is called the Director-General, if I understand it correctly, of the Canadian Broadcasting Corporation International Service . . . supposing a Director-General is not giving satisfaction, what minister of the cabinet can remove him? The Department of External Affairs Minister or the Minister of National Revenue? In other words, who is his boss?
>
> A. [Mr. Wilgress]: The CBC would be the boss in that case. The CBC as you know, reports to parliament through Dr. McCann [Minister of National Revenue].
>
> Q. [Mr. Graydon]: So really, the report to parliament would not come through External Affairs at all, it would come through the Minister of National Revenue?
>
> A. [Mr. Wilgress]: On a matter of administration through the Minister of National Revenue.
>
> Q. [Mr. Coldwell]: I suppose advice on such a step as that would be given by the Department of External Affairs to the Canadian Broadcasting Corporation?
>
> A. [Mr. Wilgress]: Naturally (53).

A few weeks later, the committee asked Désy about his administrative relationships with the CBC and with government:

> . . . may I repeat once again that I and the CBC-IS staff are responsible, in turn, to the management of the CBC and to the Board of Governors [of the CBC] who report to Parliament through the Minister of National Revenue.

I am not serving two masters. Whereas the Minister of National Revenue may be compared to my Father Superior, as they say in clerical circles, the Secretary of State for External Affairs is more like a 'directeur de conscience,' a spiritual director. I am at liberty to follow the advice of my spiritual director but should I commit any sin I have to turn to my Father Superior, either for absolution or reprimand.[20]

Later, during the same session, Désy was asked to further clarify his relationship with government:

Q. [Hon. Member]: I ask you specifically, Mr. Désy, whether, since your appointment in charge of the service, you had made periodical reports to the Prime Minister personally and received directions from him?

A. [Mr. Désy]: My reply is no (150).

The Standing Committee on External Affairs, satisfied with Désy's official status, then turned its attention more directly to the center of the controversy: the mechanics of liaison.

In 1951, Lester Pearson had described the liaison between External Affairs and the International Service as being "continuous consultation" by visits of officers from both agencies, by means of letters, telephone, and teletype. This was not satisfactory by standing committee standards. When Désy was appointed director-general, he was called upon to explain how he had "strengthened" the liaison. Asked by a committee member how the mechanics of liaison operated in 1952, Désy replied:

. . . the Department of External Affairs was supplying my service with the information that they had available and this was done when I came to Ottawa, consulting the various officials of the department and finding out if they had anything of importance to communicate to me. I am entitled to read all the secret memoranda, secret telegrams, secret documents coming from all over the world from our missions, and those documents enable me to form an opinion as to what is good and what is bad—what is, in other terms, the psychology or the temperature of the various countries concerned with regard to this or that subject (150).

In March 1953, however, part of that responsibility was relinquished by the creation of a political coordinating section in the Department of

External Affairs and by another temporary transfer of an External Affairs officer to Montreal to assist in the exchange of information from Ottawa. A standing committee member asked Désy:

Q.[Committee Member]: Is he the man that commutes between Ottawa and Montreal?

A. [Mr. Désy]: Yes.

Q. [Committee Member]: How often does he go back and forth between Ottawa and Montreal?

A. [Mr. Désy]: Once or twice a week, as a rule once a week, and the telephone is always at our disposal, as well as the teletype. May I point out that the important documents arrive only once a week, and the documents are sent to me after the diplomatic bags arrive (150).

This brief exchange identified another problem associated with the liaison issue—geography. Montreal is 125 miles from Ottawa. One member of the committee, concerned about the day-to-day operations carried on at such a distance from the national capital, demanded to know:

. . . why in the world should we operate the CBC International Service by putting Jean Désy in Montreal and then having a commuter service where a man commutes back and forth once or twice a week to tell him what the Department of External Affairs wants beamed to other countries is beyond me. I think what we should have is a CBC International Service right here in Ottawa and Jean Désy or whoever is responsible for the material that goes out should be right here in the spot where consultations can continually go on instead of having some kind of remote control policy such as this where somebody takes a bag of stuff from Ottawa down by train or plane and then brings it back and that I think would be a great nuisance with respect to the whole set-up . . . .[21]

This objection was unanimously overruled when it was made known that the CBC-IS was located in Montreal for "technical reasons," and that to move the service would be costly (46). The primary concern regarding distance was timeliness. The standing committee preferred daily contact and a daily delivery of notes and information which was not always possible because of the geographic separation.[22]

Beginning in 1952, the liaison between CBC-IS and External Affairs was close, and during the Désy tenure, was strengthened by both the new political coordination section at External Affairs and the temporary transfer of a second department official to Montreal. Désy continued to be the primary link between CBC-IS and External Affairs.

Although credit can be given to Jean Désy for maintaining strict control over policy, particularly with regard to Eastern European broadcasts, his flamboyant managerial style became an issue in the House of Commons hearings. Désy made extravagant changes in his new office space and purchased new furnishings, arousing doubt about his managerial competency. Appearing before the Standing Committee on External Affairs, Désy was asked about his appropriations for office furniture:

Q. [Mr. Kirk]: . . . Now, may I ask if there are furnishings other than the usual chairs, desks, and so on?

A. [Mr. Désy]: Well, the furniture and furnishings in my office according to the list which was given, I think, by the Minister of National Revenue, includes . . . chairs, desks, bookcases, wastepaper baskets, telephone tables, trays, and so on. A good many of these things were in the office in 1947, 1948, and 1949. But a few pieces of furniture were bought when I arrived, to replace those pieces which had been transferred to Toronto or to some other office in Montreal. . . .

Q. [Mr. Coté]: . . . Did you not bring home with you paintings of your own?

A. [Mr. Désy]: I am going to answer that. The paintings, the draperies, the sculptures and the china—yes, even the rugs, belong to me. . . . This is an old practice in my case. In the various missions I have headed, in Belgium, Holland, Italy, and in Rio de Janeiro, practically all of the works of art came from my private collection.[23]

Désy's flair for the extravagant carried over into the broadcasting operations as well. In Montreal the CBC-IS presented a special concert conducted by the Brazilian composer, Hector Villa-Lobos. The concert, presented to a live audience on 17 December 1952, was recorded simultaneously for a transcription service shipment to Brazil. The cost for this one production was $24,278.50, and members of the House, the press, and the Standing Committee on External Affairs questioned the need for such an exorbitant expenditure for one program.

Already under fire for his office furnishings, Désy responded that the program was a cultural exchange. He commented on the adverse criticism that had been leveled against the program:

Music editors (in the press) stressed four main objections: (1) The concert showed that Canadian composers are better and more advanced than their South American confreres; (2) The experiment was too costly; (3) The presentation was ill-timed coming just before the Christmas holidays; (4) Instead of spending huge sums of money on bringing a Brazilian composer to Canada, CBC-IS should use the money to help Canadian composers and musicians (154).

Désy argued that up until this program production, the CBC had "greatly favoured Canadian artists and composers by recording their works and performances and making the transcriptions available to foreign radio stations," but he believed strongly that to maintain goodwill, the CBC-IS "must occasionally show . . . willingness to do for foreign artists what we expect foreign countries to do for ours" (154). Désy's explanation fell on deaf ears. This type of "cultural exchange" was not repeated on such a grand scale. Désy's questioning before the Standing Committee on External Affairs concerning his flair for the extravagant, specifically with regard to office furnishings and the specially recorded Brazilian concert, reinforced his reputation for fiscal liberality.

In April 1953, a member of Parliament commented in the House of Commons that Désy was "our prime salesman" of Canada. "Yet," the member charged, "when speaking to the Richelieu Club in Quebec, . . . Mr. Désy [remarked]: 'The two principal ethnic groups in Canada have natural, historical and constitutional rights to which new Canadians of other origins have no claim.' " This statement, the member asserted, was "strange" coming from the director of a broadcasting service that is supposed to promote immigration. The member called for the government to "instruct Désy not to make statements calculated to antagonize new Canadians."[24]

Although his flamboyant managerial style overshadowed his tenure, Désy did make substantial changes in the operations at CBC-IS. The Eastern European broadcasts became more polemic during his term of office, but his management of the budget did not coincide with established fiscal practices. Désy's administrative actions caused one writer to observe: "He carried out his changes with a notable lack of tact, and [as a result] the International Service remained demoralized for several years."[25]

LIAISON: THE QUESTIONS CONTINUE

In 1954, Jean Désy became Canadian ambassador to France. Charles R. Delafield, who had served as assistant director-general under Ira Dilworth and Jean Désy, was then promoted to Director of CBC-IS.[26] Doubtless, the CBC-IS staff was relieved with the appointment of Delafield, a CBC employee since before the war; he was not only a seasoned professional broadcaster but had also served in the CBC-IS administration. His appointment could only foster internal stability at the International Service. Externally, the Cold War created a wave of propaganda-phobia among some members of Parliament. International shortwave radio programming, among the world services, had been branded as propaganda machines. The World Service of the BBC, although a stalwart of objectivity, had joined forces with the Voice of America to broadcast "counter-propaganda" to the Soviet bloc via 100 transmitters. By the time Delafield took over at CBC-IS, this concerted cooperation by key NATO members had been under way for five years and had received considerable press attention.[27] Parliament reasoned that if Canada was participating in international shortwave radio broadcasting beamed to the Soviet bloc, how would the CBC-IS staff know *what* to broadcast?

Later in 1954, Delafield was called to answer questions before the Standing Committee on External Affairs. Inevitably the nagging questions about the relationship between CBC-IS and External Affairs surfaced. When asked about the liaison issue, Delafield answered that the political coordination section at External Affairs had proven to be an effective alliance:

> We have benefitted tremendously from the assistance of this special section. We feel that this section should be fully maintained since the need of day-to-day continuing link in our broadcasting generally, and of course particularly to Eastern Europe. This operation is completely two-way and is supplemented by regular personal contact and telephone communication with and from members of the International Service staff.[28]

Delafield explained that all CBC-IS scripts treating international affairs were sent to this special section in the Department of External Affairs. The political coordination section, in turn, made these copies available to the diplomatic missions overseas. The guidance received from the Department of External Affairs was reviewed by "senior members of the Service at the regular morning meetings on policy," and pertinent information was "passed on to the language heads through the policy coordination department." [29]

The two-way system at this time appears to have worked in the following manner: The political cocordination section at External Affairs provided policy guidelines to the director-general and to the policy coordination department at CBC-IS. The Policy Coordination staff at the International Service sent all political commentaries to the External Affairs political coordination section for examination to ascertain whether official Canadian foreign policies were being followed in these broadcasts. Usually the scripts were broadcast before they were sent to External Affairs. The Department of External Affairs was a supervisor of policy and not a manager of the CBC-IS daily operation. The Standing Committee on External Affairs questioned Delafield on this very point. If there was disagreement about the content of the political commentaries, who had the final responsibility?

Q. [Mr. Starr]: Does the Department of External Affairs influence the content of the International Service broadcasts?
A. [Mr. Delafield]: We are always guided by their advice.
Q. [Mr. MacNaughton]: Who has the final veto?
A. [Mr. Delafield]: I do not think the question has actually arisen, so I would not know.
Q. [Mr. MacNaughton]: But in a case where it did arise, who would have the final say? . . . Is it the CBC or the Department of External Affairs? . . .
A. [Mr. Delafield]: I think that perhaps External Affairs might make some comment on that point. . . .
[Mr. R. M. Macdonnel, Assistant Under Secretary]: I would certainly endorse what Mr. Delafield has said about there being no disputes of this sort having arisen, and I think it is very unlikely that they would arise. However, we feel quite confident that the CBC would give due weight to suggestions made in the political field. . . .
Q. [Hon. Member]: It would almost be a case of "when in doubt, leave it out."
A. [Mr. Macdonnel]: That might possibly be so.
Q. [Hon. Member]: Where would the final responsibility lie?
A. [Mr. Delafield]: It rests with the CBC.
Q. [Hon. Member]: You say: "It rests with the CBC."
A. [Mr. Delafield]: Yes. The CBC is the agent chosen by the government for the establishment and presentation of the International Service (400-01).

The exchange between Delafield and members of the standing committee demonstrates that the relationship between the CBC-IS and External Affairs was cooperative. Perhaps more important, the exchange demonstrates that the International Service conducted a near autonomous operation: The CBC-IS took advice from External Affairs, but the transfer of guidance on Canadian foreign policy to the broadcasting programs was entirely the responsibility of the International Service.[30]

In addition, an advisory committee offered another coordination point between the Department of External Affairs and other government agencies with regard to the International Service broadcasts. The Shortwave Joint Committee had been active since the first year of the CBC-IS operations and included senior officers of the Department of External Affairs and the Department of Trade and Commerce. The committee was chaired by A. D. Dunton, chairman of the board, CBC, who coordinated information concerning possible program ideas for the "projection of Canada." The Interdepartmental Committee on Canadian Information Abroad, the chairman of which also served as the head of the information division of the Department of External Affairs, was made up of representatives of the following departments: Trade and Commerce, Citizenship and Immigration, National Film Board, the Bank of Canada, the Exhibition Commission, and CBC-IS.[31]

Since the Canadian government had elected to participate in the "war of ideas" campaign along with the BBC and the Voice of America, there was suspicion among members of the Standing Committee on External Affairs that CBC-IS might also be working closely with the other broadcasting services. The standing committee inquired, on occasion, whether or not External Affairs was the sole advisor to the International Service for the broadcasts beamed to Eastern Europe. In 1953, for example, Undersecretary Wilgress was asked about the relationships between the three Western broadcasting services:

Q. [Mr. Coté]: Does the Canadian Broadcasting Corporation International Service operate on the same pattern, for instance, as does the . . . Voice of America?

A. [Mr. Wilgress]: It corresponds to the Voice of America of the United States and to the BBC shortwave service. . .

Q. [Mr. Coldwell]: I think there is a rather different conception between the BBC and the Voice of America on what should be sent to these countries. If that is so, which line do we take, for example, the Voice of America or the BBC?

A. [Mr. Wilgress]: I think we take something of a middle line between the two. The Voice of America [is] on a more direct psychological warfare and concerns itself less with statements of facts, news, and commentaries on the news. We probably are in between the two.

Q. [Mr. Coté]: Is there any coordination?

A. [Mr. Wilgress]: There is consultation.[32]

This same line of questioning was put to Jean Désy when he appeared before the standing committee in 1953. When asked about any possible agreement between CBC-IS, the Voice of America, and the BBC External Services with respect to broadcasts to countries behind the Iron Curtain, Désy replied that "both the BBC and the Voice of America send us their material by teletype or otherwise. We know day after day the position taken by the Voice of America on this subject and by the BBC on another subject. . . . There is a constant flow of information. It is sort of a Niagara of teletypes."[33]

A. D. Dunton, chairman the board of governors, CBC, appeared before the Special Committee on Broadcasting in 1953 and was queried about possible coordination and cooperation with the Voice of America concerning broadcast content: "Do they follow the same line?" Dunton answered: "We follow our own line, and they follow theirs. There is informal cooperation and often visits are exchanged, and we, I believe, have a good idea of what they are doing, and they of what we are doing, but there is no coordination."[34]

Although there was no policy coordination between the CBC-IS and the Voice of America or the BBC, there was scheduling coordination to offset the jamming of all three services. A. D. Dunton acknowledged severe jamming but predicted some of the broadcasts from the three services were getting through largely because of a concerted effort to coordinate frequency use. According to Dunton, the Russians would have had to use large numbers of jamming transmitters to block all of the frequencies utilized by the three shortwave services. This, Dunton explained, occurred through "very careful coordination."[35]

During the period of Cold War intensification, the relationship between CBC-IS and the Department of External Affairs became more clearly defined. Responding to the pressures of criticism, the CBC and the government moved to secure closer liaison between the International Service and External Affairs with the temporary assignment of Jean Désy to the post of director-general, CBC-IS. Désy became the primary link to the political coordination section of the department, which was established in March 1953. To assist in the liaison, a foreign service officer was assigned to Montreal as special courier for documents from Ottawa to Désy's desk. This arrangement proved to be satisfactory. The primary focus of the guidance provided by External Affairs concerned the policy guidelines for the Eastern European broadcasts. The CBC-IS personnel remained the agents-in-charge of the broadcasts and were responsible for the content.

When Charles R. Delafield became director of the International Service, however, the Department of External Affairs withdrew the foreign service officer from Montreal. The communications between the two organizations then flowed directly from the political coordination section at External Affairs to the policy coordinating Section, CBC-IS, which then passed the information to the heads of the language sections. Again, although there was policy guidance for all language services, the principal concerns of this liaison were the political commentaries and news talks directed to Eastern Europe.

The advisory committee, the Shortwave Joint Committee, and the Information Abroad Committee were concerned with the "projection of Canada" *concept* and provided advice to the CBC-IS on what might be included in broadcasts to further this basic purpose.

The CBC-IS continued to include the "projection of Canada" themes in its programming to Western countries to promote goodwill and under-standing toward Canada as a nation, but the active involvement in the "war of ideas" with the Soviet Union and its allies began to receive the greater emphasis. The Désy appointment established closer ties with External Affairs, and with the subsequent administrative changes within the CBC-IS (policy coordination), and the Department of External Affairs (political coordination), the appointment seemed to resolve the coordination problems. The heightened concern over the role External Affairs played in providing guidance to the International Service in its Eastern European broadcasts makes an examination of the operational policies of this period an important consideration.

OPERATIONAL POLICIES FOR EASTERN EUROPE, 1951-59

On 30 May 1951, Lester B. Pearson, secretary of state, appeared before the Standing Committee on External Affairs to explain CBC-IS policy for the Eastern European broadcasts. The Pearson statement, an overview of the development of International Service policy, reiterated past operations.

First, he noted the concerns about reaching Canadian troops stationed overseas. Second, after the war, when "the world was entering an era of peace and international collaboration," Pearson observed that CBC-IS policy adopted an emphasis on "the projection of Canada."[36]

The "threat of Soviet Imperialism" established a need for a third phase of operational policy development: "participation in the war of ideas." Pearson was very careful to delineate differences between broadcasts beamed to Western Europe, especially to NATO countries, and those directed to the Soviet bloc. Programming to Western Europe maintained the overall emphasis of "the projection of Canada" theme because there was "a spirit of community and the appreciation of our common heritage and destiny" (85). Pearson explained that those countries beyond the Iron Curtain must receive programming that will "check the inroads of Soviet imperialism, in an attempt to bring truth about the west and about Soviet imperialism . . . and to strengthen the morale, faith and determination of the many friends of freedom and democracy who still live behind the Iron Curtain but whose voices have been silenced" (85). Interestingly, Pearson added that this policy was directed to the Kremlin leaders and not to the people of the Soviet Union and its allies, "with whom," Pearson noted, "we wish only friendly, cooperative relations based on mutual respect, and whose traditions we still honor" (85).

Called before the Standing Committee on External Affairs in 1953, Undersecretary of State Wilgress testified that Pearson's 1951 statement continued to be CBC-IS basic policy toward European broadcasts and stressed effectiveness focused on news and political comment on international affairs:

> Indeed this is perhaps the most important contribution which shortwave broadcasting can make in the war of ideas. One need only to reflect for a moment the complete absence of reliable news in a country where the press and radio are mere branches of the State propaganda machine to realize the value that attaches to unbiased news. People who live under these conditions have almost no other way of learning what is going on in the world.[37]

This statement prompted Gordon Graydon, a member of the Standing Committee on External Affairs, to ask:

Q. [Mr. Graydon]: . . . What do you say in a general way to these people behind the Iron Curtain? What do we hold out to them? Is it containment, liberation, or what is it?

A. [Hon. Mr. Pearson]: No, we try to give them a picture of our free way of life and to emphasize its superiority over the life of the regime under which they have to live. We also, on occasion, try to show up the absurdity and falsehood of the things that are being told. But we do not normally appeal directly to their desire to free themselves because that would not be doing them a favour at this time . . . .[38]

Wilgress attempted to clarify the Canadian perspective on the "war of ideas," otherwise known as propaganda:

Without slanting the news or distorting it, it is possible to counter much what is said about us behind the Iron Curtain. In this way Soviet charges against the West can be answered and Soviet policies can be put in the proper perspective. It is not considered desirable to imitate the polemic tone of the Soviet and satellite radios. It is *ideas* [italics mine] and not individuals that should be attacked.[39]

Even Désy, the External Affairs selectee for heading the controversial broadcasting operations beamed to Eastern Europe, proffered the following as general aims of the International Service:

(1) To expound and develop the aims and policies of the western democratic powers and particularly of Canada;
(2) To combat communist ideology and Soviet Imperialism;
(3) To project as far as possible a picture of Canadian life with special reference to social, cultural and economic development.[40]

"In broadcasts to the iron curtain," he added, ". . . the first two aims are most heavily stressed and the third is used for specific propaganda advantage"(142). Obviously, Désy believed that the projection-of-Canadian-life theme had persuasive appeal. This remark, however, caused a member of the standing committee to ask if he could explain the objective of the other broadcasts not directed to the Iron Curtain. Désy replied:

The general aim of our service to friendly countries is primarily to make Canada better known; to explain Canadian life in all its aspects, and to keep them abreast of our developments in all fields, economic, financial, agricultural, cultural, literacy, artistic (143).

Désy explained how the "projection of Canada" could have "specific propaganda advantage":

> Of course when the occasion arises, if there is an attack directed against
> Canada at some international gathering, we will avail ourselves the oppor-
> tunity to correct the accusations made against us. But, the basic aim is the
> projection of Canada abroad (143).

Apparently the political commentaries were the persuasive elements used
for "specific propaganda advantage" but, as noted previously, these commentaries were only a small part of the programming.

In 1954, Charles Delafield carefully outlined the purposes and objectives of the International Service before the standing committee:

(a) To secure general political and social goodwill and understanding for
    Canada in European, Latin American and Commonwealth countries;
(b) To project abroad Canada's aims and policies and the life and culture of
    the people;
(c) To provide a reliable source of international and Canadian news for peo-
    ples of Eastern Europe; to counteract communist propaganda about the
    western world, through news, factual information, a vigorous statement
    of our views on current topics to encourage the Soviet people to question
    their governmental policies and to oppose its aggression tactics; and in
    the satellite countries to keep alive their contact with western democra-
    tic life and seek to frustrate the efforts of Soviet domination;
(d) To provide an appropriate climate for diplomatic and trade relations
    with other countries and to promote the general activities of government
    departments in their work abroad.[41]

Reflecting the philosophy of External Affairs, Delafield implied a direct
propagandistic approach to the broadcasting operations: A "vigorous
statement of our views on current topics" smacks of a polemic stance, as
does the statement, "to encourage the Soviet people to question their governmental policies." An attempt to prod the radio audience into under-
mining the Soviet government is certainly a traditional propaganda device.
It should be noted, however, that there were *four* general objectives and
the Eastern European objective represented only a small part of the total
broadcasting operation.

A CHANGE IN PRIORITIES

As the Cold War intensified, Canadian shortwave radio broadcasting operations adapted, as best it could, to meet the challenges imposed by a "word war" with the Soviet bloc. Limited by frequency assignments, the number and power of transmitters, operating funds, the size of its staff, and the number of weekly hours programmed, the CBC-IS management was forced to adopt a priority listing. Although the programming operated under all four basic objectives, there were important priority preferences agreed upon by both External Affairs and the International Service.

On 22 May 1954, the decision was made to adjust the priorities associated with programming output. Effective 1 April 1955, the following recommendations were put into effect:

(1) Increase broadcasting hours to Soviet and satellite areas with programs scheduled at better listening times;
(2) Reduction of the West European and Latin American transmissions and staff;
(3) Development of relays and transcriptions;
(4) Further assessment of overseas reception conditions;
(5) Attendant budgetary reductions related to reductions of transmission hours;
(6) Removal of Canadian Forces Broadcast Service costs from I.S. appropriations.[42]

In the House of Commons, Minister of National Revenue, J. J. McCann, the cabinet minister charged with responsibility for the Canadian Broadcasting Corporation, explained:

. . . in effect, the CBC acts as an agent for the government in carrying on the shortwave broadcasting service to other nations. The policies and scope of expenditures . . . are set by the government, and funds for it are provided in annual estimates submitted by the government to parliament.[43]

Moreover, the revenue, McCann noted, had been reduced "significantly" necessitating a reordering of operational priorities. The services beamed to countries behind the Iron Curtain, McCann observed, "should not be reduced but should be continued with the same effort, as part of the general endeavour by the countries of the west to get some rays of timely information to people under communist domination" (1806).

Broadcasts to Western Europe were decreased, providing additional broadcast times for the Eastern European operations. Lamenting the reductions, McCann remarked:

> I think it is regrettable in many ways that we should have to lose our daily contacts with the apparently quite considerable audiences for Canadian broadcasting in the Scandinavian countries, the Netherlands, and Italy. It is hoped to retain some connection and some of the good will that has been built up through programs broadcast on weekends and if possible sent for direct relay by broadcasting systems in the countries themselves (1806).

The decision to trim appropriations for CBC-IS operations met with some opposition in the House of Commons. The Honourable Ambrose Holowach (Edmonton East), a proponent of the shortwave service, commented on the cuts and the redirected policy guidelines:

> . . . I do not know what the policy is today, but the trimming that has occurred would indicate that the policy has become mellow and has lost much of the punch it once had. . . . The question arises, why? Is it because of co-existence (1841-42)?

Holowach's support for the shortwave service was colored by his apparent lack of understanding concerning operational broadcast policy for Eastern Europe. Speaking before the House, Holowach recounted his meeting with some Europeans who had listened to CBC-IS transmissions:

> I was astonished. They told me of broadcasts to countries behind the iron curtain on such subjects as Eskimos, our northern lands, dog-sled races, the St. Lawrence Seaway and reindeer herds. Imagine someone behind the iron curtain crawling into the loft of a barn or into a haystack where a radio is hidden, tense with anticipation, tense to receive a vibrant message. He turns the radio knob and what does he get? Talks on reindeer and on the St. Lawrence Seaway (1842).

Holowach charged the CBC-IS with "inefficiency in the matter of realistic policy" and noted "a serious crippling of the effectiveness of this vital service" thus creating a need for strengthening, not weakening, Canadian international broadcasting efforts (1842).

Unfortunately, financial matters ruled against Holowach and the CBC-IS; the budgetary reductions remained in force, the extraordinary shift in priorities accomplished. An interesting sidelight concerning the financing of the International Service emerged in the House of Commons debates. It was made known that in 1948 the Ford Hotel in downtown Montreal had been purchased and renovated to house the CBC International Service production studios and offices. The remaining space was for the CBC French Network production facilities. The Ford Hotel was purchased not by the Canadian Broadcasting Corporation, but by the government for the International Service. In fact, the French Network leased facilities from the International Service. The arrangement provided the International Service with revenue, reducing the government expenditures for the short-wave service's operations.

The financial terms between the government, the CBC, and the International Service were a curious departure from established practice. The Order in Council P.C. 8168, which authorized the establishment of the International Service, clearly stated that financial support for the over-seas broadcasts should come from direct government grants. The domes-tic CBC broadcasting services were funded by receiver licensing. The Canadians paid an annual radio and television receiver license fee that was similar to the British collection method. A demarcation line was drawn. Broadcasts beamed to foreign audiences should not be part of the CBC domestic funding. Separate and far from equal, CBC-IS was charged with the responsibility to speak for Canada, but without much financial support. Lean years lay ahead, and management scrambled to meet the changes in operational priorities. The manner in which CBC-IS dealt with an increased emphasis on Eastern Europe, particularly the coordination between External Affairs and the supervisor of sections, is discussed in the following section.

MANAGEMENT

The first major change in the managerial structure was the appoint-ment of Charles R. Delafield as director, CBC-IS in 1954. Delafield, an academic-turned-broadcaster, held a Bachelor of Arts degree in history from the University of Windsor and a Master of Arts degree in Ancient History from the University of Toronto. After a year of university teach-ing, he became secretary to Hart House, the student center at the University of Toronto, for six years. In 1938, he joined the CBC national program office in Toronto and later became national supervisor of religious broadcasts. In 1947, Delafield was transferred to Montreal as the Assistant General Supervisor of the International Service. Delafield took over as Director when Jean Désy resigned to assume ambassadorial duties in Paris.[44]

Four managerial posts were related directly to programming: supervisor of sections, news, supervisor of information services, and program operations (see fig. 2). The supervisor of sections post were established during this period and was a key addition to International Service management. The individual filling this position was responsible for serving as manager of the entire programming operation. He supervised all language sections, program representatives in Ottawa and Toronto and, more important, headed the policy coordination section that had been created in 1953 to effect closer liaison with the Department of External Affairs. In a multilingual broadcasting service, the heads of sections were the professional broadcasters to the target countries. The head of a language section was responsible for the preparation of all material actually broadcast. He was required to know his target area and the kinds of programming needed to project Canada to the audience. Arthur L. Pidgeon, a former supervisor of sections, explained:

Figure 2. International Service Organizational Chart, 1959

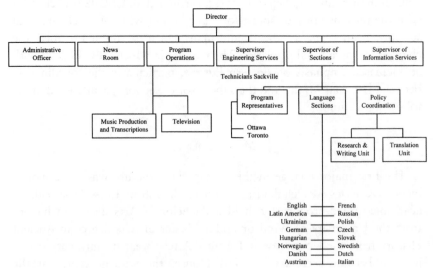

Under our system, we have always made the section head the man responsible for the final product. No one else can be. There are so many elements that go into the final product which no one else can control, even the intonation of the voice. After all, this is a spoken-word service; it's not a written service, and the only man who really knows how this is sounding, what kind of impact it has, and what kind of message it is giving, is the man who can understand the language and is responsible for it.[45]

The policy coordinator had the responsibility of channeling policy guidelines from the political coordination section at External Affairs to the heads of sections at CBC-IS. The policy coordinator's office was the center of the ensuing controversy since the political commentaries were written and translated there for use, either in part or in entirety, by all of the language sections. Pidgeon candidly revealed how the Policy Coordination operated in the 1950s:

. . . a multi-lingual service . . . must try to choose material that is relevant to its target area, that is of interest to its target area, that in a sense, relates to it. It must also, of course, . . . reflect Canadian point-of view. But we did give the section, the individual language section, a fair amount of freedom, in light of the target area that they are serving. In other words, if we commented on NATO to Great Britain, we might not comment on NATO to Czechoslovakia because Great Britain was a member of NATO and Czechoslovakia would have a very different point-of-view. Or, if we did comment on NATO to Czechoslovakia, we wouldn't necessarily be commenting the same way; not that we wanted to say something different but we had to realize that the audience could not accept, for example, particular styles . . . it would have to be a commentary that was needed for that particular area.[46]

Audience analysis, then, was an important task for the commentary writers in the policy coordination section. With a close liaison with political coordination at External Affairs, the CBC-IS policy coordinator provided a sense of direction for the multilingual broadcasting service. Pidgeon described in some detail how he performed the necessary tasks:

Now, the policy coordinator was the man who was consulted by the various sections about the subject matter. He was the man who was responsible for the writers . . . when I first went there [to CBC-IS]. For example, the

German Section would have an idea. We'd have a morning meeting and they would say, "Well, look, we want to talk about this in Germany today. This is the important subject for Germany. They are all keen about it. Now they want some kind of Canadian reaction, obviously, so let's use it." We'd say, "Fine, put so-and-so on it and then come on up and talk it over with me when you get your ideas on paper." And then later we'd talk it over. Maybe in my knowledge of what I'd been reading and so forth, I'd say, "Look, this doesn't represent our point-of-view. The way we feel about the subject is this." In other words, it was a matter of discussion and the purpose of it was to make certain that we were reflecting, in a sense, our own country and not somebody else's point-of-view.[47]

In a multilingual shortwave broadcasting service that targets a number of different countries many of the staff writers, announcers, and even the section heads are natives of the target countries, particularly those in Eastern Europe. In the early 1950s, some of the CBC-IS section heads were staffed by political refugees. They had immigrated to Canada for political reasons, and therefore, had their own emotional approach to many political subjects, which, according to Pidgeon, created a problem for some of the writers. "With the best will in the world," Pidgeon recalled, "when they sat down to write a topic or commentary, they would reflect their point-of-view. Now this we had to watch because we were not setting ourselves as an immigration service. We were a Canadian service."[48]

To assist the International Service staff writers, professional specialists in economics and politics were asked to write commentaries quite frequently for broadcast on the shortwave service. Journalists from across Canada served as guest writers, offering still greater representation of Canadian opinion on issues and topics under discussion.[49]

The work of the newsroom was closely related to the work of the programming units, i.e., the supervisor of sections, section heads, and policy coordination. The news coverage consisted of the following subscribed services: Canadian Press, British United Press, Reuters, and Agence France Presse. News was considered to be the kernel of the whole broadcasting service, and formed a part of every language section's transmissions.[50]

The supervisor of information services post had the responsibility of mailing program schedules, answering the mail, and providing the listeners with additional information about Canada. If, for example, a listener wrote a letter and requested additional information about a particular subject, the supervisor of information services either supplied the information directly or passed the listener's request to another agency. The Information Services also provided the heads of sections with programming feedback from the letters of listeners, thereby aiding the overall production planning procedures.

Program operations received greater prominence after 1955. This post was responsible for the transcription service and also, after 1955, the distribution of television programs abroad. Program operations made the selections for the spoken-word and the music transcriptions, in collaboration with the language sections, and was responsible for the mailings. The program operations section worked with the CBC domestic television services and selected short television features for distribution abroad. It is difficult to state precisely why the International Service was the agent-in-charge of the distribution of television programs or, for that matter, why it had an interest in television. Perhaps it was merely a reflection of the time. Television broadcasting had greatly expanded in Europe by 1955, and the novelty associated with the medium probably caused a decline in shortwave radio audiences. The distribution of Canadian television programs enhanced the overall information dissemination activities of CBC-IS by periodically reaching the television audience. Television program distribution was only a minor part of the program operations section.

Finally there were two additional managerial posts: administrative officer, the person who kept personnel records and attended to budgetary matters; and supervisor of engineering services, who was in charge of frequency management, transmission schedule planning, and the transmission facilities at Sackville, New Brunswick. In 1955, there were 173 persons working at CBC-IS.[51]

PROGRAMMING PATTERNS

The intensification of the Cold War was reflected in the increases in Eastern European broadcast time from 1951 to 1959. Since the CBC-IS operated only two transmitters with a fixed number of frequencies and hours, priority had to be given and broadcast time shifted from one target area to another. The total weekly Eastern European broadcast time in 1951, for example, was 16:45, but by 1959, it had climbed to 34:15 (see table 6). Czech- and Slovak-language services were combined in the program schedules with Czech the primary language. In other words, only a ten- or fifteen-minute segment of the daily program was devoted to Slovak. As noted in the table, the Czech and Slovak languages had nearly ten hours broadcast weekly (9:45), in 1951 and 1952, but this total was reduced in 1953 to 6:15. The primary reason for the reduction was to add a Polish service. In effect, this additional service took 3:30 away from the Czech and Slovak services.[52]

Russian-language broadcast time, on the other hand, was increased from 7:00 in 1951 to 10:30 in 1955, while the Ukrainian service fluctuated between 3:30, 5:15, and 7:00 hours during this period. Thus the combined Russian- and Ukrainian-language broadcasts accounted for 14 hours weekly to the Soviet Union in 1955 and reached 17:30 hours in 1959, or almost half the total broadcast time directed to the East European target areas.

TABLE 6. *Total Weekly Program Hours Broadcast to Eastern Europe*

Language Service	1951	1952	1953	1954	1955	1956	1957	1958	1959
Czech & Slovak	9:45	9:45	6:15	6:15	8:00	8:00	8:00	8:00	8:00
Russian	7:00	7:00	7:00	7:00	10:30	10:30	10:30	10:30	10:30
Ukrainian	--	5:15	5:15	5:15	3:30	3:30	5:15	5:15	7:00
Polish	--	--	3:30	3:30	5:15	6:15	5:15	5:00	7:00
Hungarian	--	--	--	--	--	--	1:45	1:45	1:45
Totals	16:45	22:00	22:00	22:00	27:15	28:15	30:45	30:45	34:15

RUSSIAN-LANGUAGE PROGRAMMING

The Russian service offers a good illustration of the programming patterns for Eastern Europe during the height of the Cold War, 1950-55.[53] Each broadcast began with a detailed newscast on international events— "unbiased information" on the most important events of the day and "a commentary" on significant political events.[54] The political commentaries gave the opinion of Canada and other Western countries on contemporary international events.

Since the broadcasts were predominantly one-half hour in length, the daily program patterns were planned. Sundays, for example, were described as follows:

. . . we bring our listeners a talk on religious and moral subjects from the series "Christianity in Canada," as well as an article on the anniversaries of the preceding week in which we mark more important historic and cultural events in Canada during the past week.[55]

Interestingly, providing religious programming was one of the objectives of these broadcasts directed to the Soviet Union. In 1955 Lester Pearson, appearing before the Standing Committee on External Affairs, suggested that broadcasts containing religious themes would "strengthen the morale, faith, and determination of the many friends of freedom and democracy who still live behind the iron curtain but whose voices have been silenced."[56]

Mondays on the Russian service were devoted to articles in Russian-language newspapers published in Western countries. A common characteristic of the programming content was the use of "testimonials" proffered by former Soviet citizens living in Canada:

What can be said about my present life, when compared with my socialist life of the past? For instance, before the war, I was occupying, in Kiev, a small room in a co-operative tenement, and I was envied by many people. And my wife was feeling lucky to be able to use the hall to heat her coffee on the kerosene lamp. On account of the exiguity of my room, I was not wasting time in tidying up my place of abode and I had very little to spend for furniture and fuel. I was then realizing economies and could buy state bonds. For want of a compulsory National Loan, we have been obliged to buy a home and a new car. My wife, who has her own bank account, has bought a number of bourgeois trifles, as for instance, a chesterfield, a refrigerator, a washing machine, a television set, a toaster and a lot of gadgets, the names of which I don't even know. Our floors are covered with carpets, much like the Sultan's palace. . . .[57]

Testimonials were not limited to males. The following excerpts were taken from a radio address broadcast to Soviet women:

Entering the factory my first thought was that I came to the wrong place. Cars were driving into the wide yard and well-dressed men and women were getting out. All wore expensive fur coats, had beautiful hair-does [sic], and were powdered and rouged. "These are probably all office workers," I thought. I came early, for fear to be late, and now I remained at the entrance waiting for the women workers to appear. But they did not come. The same elegant young ladies continued to enter through a wide glass door. I felt conspicuous in this well-dressed crowd, even if before coming to Canada I thought I looked quite presentable.

Summoning my memory and reaching into my scant supply of English words, I asked: "How many packages are we supposed to do in a day?" Astonished, she looked at me and replied: "As many as you can." "How? There is no norm?" "And what is a norm?" she asked. "Well a norm is a minimum you must do to fulfill a plan." "A norm, a plan?" The girls looked at me as if I was out of my mind. No, everyone was doing as much as she could. For may part I was flabbergasted and must confess now that I did not believe her.

To my surprise I was not fired. With every day I saw that my word was becoming better and faster. During the whole week no one came up to me telling me to hurry. Friday night we were given envelopes with money. There was no queuing up before the cashier's windows and no signing for loans or subscriptions. Than I found out the astonishing fact that we do not work on Saturdays. "But why," I asked, "is there a holiday tomorrow?" "Oh no," I was told, "we never work on Saturdays. We have a five-day week." Here you have a five-day week promised by the communists. But it prevails not where they are in power, not in the countries of People's Democracy, but in capitalist Canada. We have two days of rest every week, which we can use as we like. There is no shock-work, Saturday work or Sunday work. You are free and can do what you please. . . (226).

These were strong appeals to the Soviet listener. Obviously contrasting the Canadian worker with the carefully controlled production lines in the Soviet Union, the overall tone of the broadcast was highly polemic. Words such as "flabbergasted," "astonished," "surprised," described the reactions of this worker to conditions in Canada. While informative, the broadcast took political stabs at the Communists: "Here you have five-day week promised by the communists. But it prevails," the speaker condescends, "not where they are in power . . . but in capitalist Canada" (226).

On Tuesdays, the Russian service broadcast a "Life in Canada" series so that "the listeners can learn about conditions of life in our free country and understand still better our democratic traditions."[58] Wednesdays were devoted to acquainting the listener with problems of the Canadian economy. The program notes explained:

This series of talks is designed to bring about an understanding of the essence of the economic system of the free and democratic countries, in which private initiative plays such an important part. On the same day we transmit talk from the series entitled, "Soviet Propaganda and the Truth" in which the whole falsehood of Soviet propaganda is unmasked (2).

Continuing its own brand of polemic broadcasting, the International Service attempted to answer Soviet propaganda directly by pointing to "falsehoods." A similar theme was broadcast on Thursdays with the program, "Answering the Soviet Press"; a report on the life of Canadian working people supplemented this broadcast (2).

On Saturdays, the CBC-IS openly attacked the Soviet system in a series entitled "Communist Theory and Practice," which was an attempt to "show once more the discrepancies between words and actions of the Bolsheviks, as well as a commentary entitled, 'Canadian Viewpoint on International Events'" (2).

This examination of Russian-language program patterns reveals a definite purpose: open attack on Communist ideology. News and commentaries on the news were the primary ingredients of the broadcasts. The broadcast week was filled with themes of Canadian freedom (religious and political) and economic successes (individual and corporate). Canada was indeed participating in the "war of ideas" along with other Western powers. In fact, the first daily transmission to the Soviet Union coincided with the BBC and the Voice of America "to reinforce the battery of western transmitters broadcasting to the Soviet Union in order to overcome jamming."[59] This triple battery of broadcasts required jamming transmitters to be set on a dozen frequencies, because each service used three or more frequencies for maximum penetration. The theory held that the Soviets could not block all frequencies giving an opportunity for at least one of the Western powers' broadcasts to get through.

The other Eastern European broadcasts in Ukrainian, Czech, Slovak, Polish, and Hungarian followed similar patterns, described as being: ". . . a news service which is comprehensive, true and objective; . . . programs which explain Canadian life in all its variety; and the correcting of misrepresentations in Communist propaganda and the exposing of the hypocrisy of Communist democracy" (52). The primary means for communicating such propaganda was the political commentary (see examples in appendix B).

WESTERN EUROPE

English language broadcasts dominated the program schedule throughout the period under study with the French language second. There was a significant decrease in broadcast time for most Western European languages from 1954 to 1955 (17:05 hours), reflecting the shift in emphasis to Eastern Europe. German was an important language with approximately seven hours weekly or two half-hour programs daily (see table 7).

In 1955 the number of broadcast hours beamed to Europe in Dutch, Italian, Swedish, and Danish were cut to weekend programs, one hour each. The Finnish language service was canceled. It is interesting to note the transitions in broadcasting times during this period. The Western European services broadcast 39:35 hours in 1951, decreased to a low of 18:00 in 1955, but by 1959 had regained to a total of 28:45. Although Eastern European broadcasting was still important in 1959 (34:15), there seemed to be a renewed emphasis on Western European broadcasting. Apparently the 1959-60 period reflected the spirit of "peaceful coexistence" in Canadian foreign policy, with the priority emphasis changing to a less polemic broadcast policy line.[60]

Table 7. Total Weekly Program Hours Broadcast to Westen Europe
1951-1959*

Language Service	1951	1952	1953	1954	1955	1956	1957	1958	1959
English	9:10	8:45	8:45	8:45	3:30	3:30	3:30	3:30	9:15
French	9:30	8:10	7:00	7:00	3:30	3:30	3:30	3:30	9:15
German	6:30	6:30	6:30	6:30	7:00	7:00	7:00	7:00	5:15
Danish	2:20	2:20	2:20	2:20	1:00	1:00	1:00	1:00	1:15
Dutch	5:15	5:15	5:15	5:15	1:00	1:00	1:00	1:00	1:15
Finnish	:45	:45	:45	:45	--	--	--	--	--
Swedish	2:35	2:35	2:35	1:00	1:00	1:00	1:00	1:00	1:15
Italian	3:30	3:30	3:30	3:30	1:00	1:00	1:00	1:00	1:15
Totals	39:35	37:50	36:40	35:05	18:00	18:00	18:00	18:00	28:45

*These times were taken from the December program schedules or nearest available month.

LATIN AMERICA

In the mid-1950s, with the rearrangement of priority commitments in Canadian policy, Latin America was de-emphasized (see table 8). Weekly broadcast hours for all Latin American services reached a high of 26:50 in 1951 and fell to a low of 17:30 in 1955. Again, by 1959, the services had regained nearly two hours of weekly broadcasting time. A weekly total of 17 or 19 weekly hours of broadcast time for all Latin American services was very little for such a large area. Diplomatically, economically, and militarily, Europe was a higher priority for Canada than Latin America. The Department of External Affairs' policy guidance influenced the European orientation of programming, and it was the responsibility of the CBC-IS to reflect Canadian foreign policy commitments and interests.

AUSTRALASIA

The remaining area of the world covered by the International Service broadcasts was Australasia, or the South Pacific area, where English was the only language broadcast. Broadcast time to that area increased from 2:20 hours in 1951 to 5:15 hours by 1959. Certainly the predominant reason for reaching this area was to promote Commonwealth trade.

Table 8. Total Weekly Program Hours Broadcast to Latin America and Carribean, 1951-1959

Language Service	1951	1952	1953	1954	1955	1956	1957	1958	1959
Spanish	14:55	13:45	14:00	14:00	5:15	5:15	5:15	5:15	5:15
Portuguese	6:25	8:10	5:15	5:15	5:15	5:15	5:15	5:15	5:15
French	1:45	3:30	3:30	3:30	3:30	3:30	3:30	3:30	4:05
English	3:30	3:30	3:30	3:30	3:30	3:30	3:30	3:30	5:15
Dutch	:15	:15	--	--	--	--	--	--	--
Totals	26:50	29:10	26:15	26:15	17:30	17:30	17:30	17:30	19:50

*These times were taken from the December program schedules or nearest available month.

PROGRAMMING PATTERNS: A SUMMARY

With the exception of Eastern Europe, the programming patterns for the other world areas were similar to the 1945-50 period—they were primarily news and a "projection of Canada." The main difference between this kind of projection and those directed to Eastern Europe was the political orientation of the Eastern European broadcasts. The other broadcasts merely attempted to reflect the "Canadian identity" as viewed in Parliament, the press, and the arts. The program schedule, *Radio Canada Calling*, contained articles on various themes as part of the total projection concept. Although the broadcasts did not necessarily follow these themes, the topics were included in at least some of the transmissions. The following themes of the monthly program schedules in 1954 are representative of the types of information projected during the period under study:

January	Canada's Food Exports
February	Canada's Fur Enterprises
March	Homes for Canadians
April	Canada's Commercial Fisheries
May	Canada and International Aviation
June	Mail from Listeners
July-August	Canada's Growing Stature
September	Canada at Sao Paulo Exposition
October	Canadian Trade Commissioner Service
November	Canada's Newcomers
December	Season's Greetings[61]

With the reordering of priorities in 1955, there was an increased use of supplementary broadcasting activities. Relays, for example, were defined as ". . . programs prepared on disc or tape . . . and shipped out for domestic playing by another broadcasting operation. Sometimes, as in news features, they are picked up from shortwave transmissions and relayed" (5). The use of relays was increased to offset the reductions in broadcast times. This was particularly the case for those services which were reduced to weekend broadcasting: Dutch, Swedish, Danish, and Italian.

The rationale behind these supplementary broadcasting activities was simple: if the external broadcasting service had to be curtailed, then the relays and transcription services could assume the role of on-the-air programming. This proved to be a difficult arrangement. An example from the Netherlands is typical of the complications that were experienced when arranging relays and transcription shipments to a foreign country.

In 1955, the Dutch Domestic Service had only two large transmitters for broadcasting to the entire country,and they were shared by four major systems representing not only religious groups, but political parties as well. The four organizations were: Nederlands Christljk Radiooverening (NCRV), Protestant; Katholieke Radio Omroep (KRO), Catholic; Vereniging van Arbeiters Radio-Amateurs (VARA), Socialist; and Algemene Vereniging Radio Omroep (AVRO), neutral. These four broadcasting organizations were headquartered at Hilversum, and all were supported by membership fees. The situation was further complicated because a central organization, Radio Unie, owned the studios and transmitters and employed all the technical staff, but did not originate any programs. Radio Unie was responsible for the coordination of the domestic stations and foreign broadcasting organizations. The CBC-IS produced transcribed programs for all four organizations in the Netherlands, but not without difficulty, for there was rivalry among the many stations and several demanded "exclusive rights on the personality voicing the program" (6). Largely because of these problems, the International Service placed only forty-five programs through the radio organizations in the Netherlands in 1955. The Dutch section at the International Service relayed news items to Dutch possessions scattered across the globe (3).

The Norwegian, Swedish, and Danish sections at CBC-IS attempted to place programs on state systems in Scandinavia. Again, this was not an easy task because each of these countries maintained a single national network with a quota established on the number of programs accepted by each national broadcasting organization. Sweden presented almost insurmountable problems since Radiojanst insisted on using its own correspondents or freelance contributors. Canadian news received very little attention through these outlets; consequently, CBC-IS was successful, albeit sporadically, in persuading Radio Sweden to carry special items "of a newsreel character" for local program insertion (4).

Other sections at the CBC-IS were more successful in their efforts. For example, three organizations readily accepted CBC-IS Italian language programs: Radio Italiana (RAI), Rome; Svizzero Italiana Diffusione, Berne; and Radio Vaticana in Rome. Between January and August 1956, twenty-one programs were broadcast by RAI, fourteen to the Swiss Radio, and six to the Vatican Radio (8).

These supplementary broadcasting activities were not directed only to the target areas that had been reduced in the program schedule of the external broadcasts from CBC-IS. For example, the International Service prepared two fifteen-minute programs weekly for broadcast by Radio Athens. One of these programs was a spoken-word transcription while the other was a musical type. The spoken-word program, usually an interview, was described by a CBC-IS staff member as featuring Greek-speaking Canadians who represented various aspects of life in Canada (8). The Austrian section, which began in 1950, did not broadcast directly from the Montreal studios and was concerned only with relays. In 1954, 118 news items were placed on the Austrian radio network, totaling 17:45 for the year (8).

The language sections that were not severely reduced in program time on the shortwave schedule also utilized relays and transcriptions to a greater extent in 1955. The German section, for example, used all of the available German networks for relaying news items. During 1955, CBC-IS placed sixty-three items (14:15 hours program time) over German networks. These news items were of a topical nature and consisted of interviews, reports, and actuality broadcasts (9).

The largest operation for relays, transcriptions, and external broadcasting was the English section. "Canadian Chronicle" continued to be the main program and contained short news reports from across Canada. The BBC domestic program "Radio Newsreel," which reportedly had an estimated nightly audience of three to four million people, occasionally used "Canadian Chronicle" items. Moreover, "Canadian Chronicle" was taped and distributed on a monthly basis to Ceylon, Australia, Hong Kong, Southern Rhodesia, South Africa, Pakistan, Indonesia, India, and to cooperating stations in the United States (9).

The French section, which had broadcast time reduced 66.3 percent during the 1955 priority shifts, did not expand the shortwave relays. Instead, the section developed a wider use of transcriptions (9). The Latin American section (Spanish and Portuguese) shifted its emphasis from shortwave direct broadcasting to a wider use of transcriptions. In February 1955, the Spanish transcription service was created:

> The catalogues of Spanish transcriptions now comprise a list of one hundred and ten programs; eleven half-hour programs on "The Canadian Provinces"; thirty-six half-hour plays in Spanish, many of them by Canadian authors; twenty-four fifte-minute documentaries on Canadian industry,

history and geography; twenty-four fifteen-minute programs of Canadian popular music; and two special programs on Columbus Day. . . (14).

Finally, during this period, the International Service continued to exchange films with foreign television services. Under the auspices of Eurovision, Canada exchanged items of interest for "Children's International Newsreel" with the United Kingdom, France, Belgium, Switzerland, Italy, Austria, Holland, Japan, Sweden, Denmark, West Germany, Finland, Portugal, Australia, and Luxembourg. Twice a month, for each item sent, each country received a minimum of sixteen items focusing on children's activities. In 1959, for example, the International Service sent 52 items and received 617 items from abroad for Canadian viewing. The International Service also cooperated with another Eurovision series, "International Agricultural Newsmagazine."[62]

From 1951 to 1959, the programming patterns of the CBC-IS were divided into two major types: those directed to Eastern Europe and those beamed to the rest of the world. For most areas, the broadcasts reflected a projection of the Canadian identity. As previously discussed, the only deviations from this basic objective were in the political commentaries directed to Eastern Europe. There were problems, however, that confronted the International Service management team during this decade.

In retrospect, three major problems can be associated with CBC-IS during this important, yet controversial decade of international shortwave radio broadcasting: the liaison issue; the question of the broadcasts' effectiveness; and the 1955 budget reductions.

LIAISON: THE DÉSY APPOINTMENT

Jean Désy's appointment as director of the International Service on 1 January 1952 was fraught from the beginning with confusion, disdain, and puzzlement among CBC-IS management personnel. While Désy brought with him considerable experience in the Foreign Service of the Department of External Affairs, his credentials as a professional broadcaster were nonexistent. His primary function was to strengthen the liaison between the Department of External Affairs and the CBC-IS. Under his direction this goal was indeed accomplished.

Désy's managerial style was suspect. Possessing an ostentatious flare, he devoted considerable time to redecorating his office, overseeing a pet project, the Villa-Lobos concert, and answering inquiries before the Standing

Committee on External Affairs. He was, simply put, a flashy shoe on a wrong foot. The Désy tenure was short lived, its mark lasting: the Eastern European broadcasts became more polemic, the liaison with External Affairs more intricate ("a Niagara of teletypes"). Yet despite these accomplishments, his work was overshadowed by the claim that "he carried out his changes with a notable lack of tact, and the International Service remained demoralized for several years."[63]

EFFECTIVENESS

Understandably, whenever government appropriations are involved, there are always questions related to whether or not the incurred costs are needed. Although the CBC-IS was supported only meagerly by government grants, it had to deal with the effectiveness issue. In 1953 Désy was asked about operational justification. Who listened to shortwave radio broadcasts coming from Canada? Désy countered with a vague answer which pointed to two main sources of information: reports from missions and an ongoing analysis of listener mail.[64] The reports from the missions were based upon their own surveys, and Désy shrewdly avoided any description of methodology:

> According to our missions, which, of course, had neither the time nor the trained personnel to carry out an extensive survey, our broadcasts to European countries cannot be said to be highly popular, except in Scandinavian countries where they are extremely well received and deemed the best publicity medium we have (140).

In 1950, the BBC conducted public opinion surveys in Denmark and Sweden and in October 1952 conducted a survey in Germany. The CBC-IS contributed financially to both projects. The Danish sample of 2,125 respondents during the week of 3-8 March 1950, indicated that 2.4 percent were regular listeners to CBC-IS. This figure was projected to an estimated audience size of 72,720. Sweden was projected to include 35,000 listeners, based upon the same methodology and sample size, and Germany 600,000.[65] Since the survey work was not regularly scheduled and did not include all target countries, the CBC-IS was hard-pressed to provide questioning members of Parliament with scientific audience research data.

Charles R. Delafield, immediate successor to Désy as director, CBC-IS, testified before the standing committee that mail surveys, public opinion polls taken in a target country, "size of scheduled mailing lists," and questionnaires mailed to a random sample of listeners provided some information about audiences. Wisely, however, Delafield recognized the limitations imposed by these methods:

> Mail surveys are the simplest ways of gauging audience size but also the least scientific. They tell only how many letters are received from various countries. They are more valuable for what they say about broadcasts than for how many they are. You do get a certain amount of comment on programs, but it is so limited and simple that it is difficult to analyze it. Most of the mail tends to say, "We have a great deal of interest in Canada. We have been listening to the program and would you please give us more of it," or they ask questions which they want answered in future programs. Public opinion polls are the most scientific, depending on the reliability of the organization, but they are also the most costly. We are able to do only one or two countries annually. We also gain much valuable information from the surveys of the BBC and the Voice of America (430).

These methods of gathering audience research data worked only for the target countries that permitted survey work. Countries in Eastern Europe presented special obstacles since foreign research companies were not permitted to gather audience data within their boundaries. The standing committee, concerned more with Eastern Europe than with any other world area, pursued the following line of questions:

> Q. [Mr. Kucherepa]: Have you any way of assessing the audience reaction to your programs behind the iron curtain?
> A. [Mr. Delafield]: It is very difficult. Of course, there are two main sources of negative understanding of the reaction. First of all, our broadcasts behind the iron curtain are jammed unfortunately as heavy as those emanating from the BBC and the Voice of America. This, therefore, signifies that presumably our broadcasts are as straight forward and as positive as those of our two major partners in these shortwave broadcasting operations (430).

Jamming, largely a defensive measure, was looked upon by the International Service as a negative reaction from the Soviet officials, generating the assumption that the Canadian shortwave radio broadcasts must be effective. The CBC led the standing committee to believe that the straightforward and positive nature of the Eastern European broadcasts must have been viewed by Soviet officials as detrimental to the mass audience. Unfortunately, there was little substantive evidence to prove that the mass audience received any of the broadcasts, much less to gauge how they felt about them.

A. D. Dunton, chairman of the board of governors, CBC, was asked by the Standing Committee on External Affairs about jamming:

> Q. [Mr. Reinke]: Is there any way, Mr. Dunton, in which the results of these broadcasts (to Eastern Europe) can be measured? Have you any indication of the extent to which we are getting our information across or is there so much "jamming" that it is difficult to estimate the results?
>
> A. [Mr. Dunton]: You mentioned "jamming." As to countries behind the iron curtain . . . very little information comes through Russia, but some does reach us through confidential channels and it is known that in spite of the "jamming" some broadcasting does get through. We know the overseas service has been heard by at least some people in that country, and the Canadian service has certainly contributed to the general British and American effort to get something through to the Russian people. We know from information in our possession that at least a good part of the very wide audience we had in Czechoslovakia before the coup there has been retained. . . .[66]

In reply to a question concerning mailings from Eastern Europe, Dunton observed that few letters had come from Czechoslovakia and most had been "smuggled out" to avoid detection. "We have had a trickle reaching us since the coup," Dunton testified, "all smuggled letters asking us to 'keep it up' and that sort of thing" (337).

This lack of supportive evidence undoubtedly made it more difficult to defend the expenses necessary for the operations of the CBC-IS. In 1954, for example, a member of the House actually suggested abolishment. After all, the honourable member observed:

> I remind the House that this service was originally inaugurated during the war, and my understanding is, that its main purpose was to keep in contact with our troops overseas. When our troops came home, there was not need for this type of communication. It is quite true that the broadcasts have some propaganda value overseas but I do not think that the costs, which have been increasing year after year, are anywhere in line with the value

received by the Canadian taxpayer. The elimination of the expenditure could save the taxpayer $2,400,000.[67]

Later, Honourable George A. Drew questioned the expenditure and based his objections on a lack of sufficient audience research to justify the costs. He did, however, offer suggestions:

> There is one way, one sure easy way, by which we could have some evidence as to what is being accomplished by the international shortwave broadcasts. We could have placed before us reports from the Canadian embassies in those countries beyond the iron curtain where they have a chance to hear them. Let us have a report from Moscow where we have a Canadian embassy as to how many Russians hear that broadcast. Let us have a report as to how often the members of the Canadian embassy in Moscow listen to the Canadian report. Let us find out how many Russians they have heard of who have heard that report. Let us ask the representative in Czechoslovakia how many Czechs have heard broadcasts; or in Hungary, or in Poland, or in Bulgaria, or in any other country to which we are beaming these broadcasts at this time. Let us have a full and effective statement from those Canadians who have been actually over there as to what they have found. Mr. Chairman, we have had not one word of evidence before us which justifies the expenditure of another cent on that particular type of broadcast (4331).

In 1955, the Standing Committee on External Affairs recommended a shift in priorities and a reduction in funds for the International Service. If the International Service could have demonstrated the value of the broadcasts in more concrete terms, perhaps the budget might have been increased rather than decreased. The effectiveness issue would surface again.

NOTES

1. John D. Hicks and George E. Mowry, *A Short History of American Democracy*, 2d. ed. (Boston: Houghton Mifflin Company, 1956), 859.
2. Canadian Broadcasting Corporation, *Annual Report*, 1950-51 (Ottawa: Canadian Broadcasting Corporation, 1951), 46.
3. Ibid.
4. Jackson, Jackson, and Moore, *Politics in Canada*, 564. See James E. Anderson, *Public Policy Making*, 2d ed. (New York: Holt, Rinehart and Winston, 1979), 3, for an elaboration of this policy definition.

5. In Canada, cabinet ministers alone have the political responsibility for making policy.

6. Farrell, *Making of Canadian Foreign Policy*, 7-9.

7. Peers, *Politics of Canadian Broadcasting*, 422.

8. Ibid.

9. Broadcast Script, 14 January 1951, 1, in Canadian Broadcasting Corporation, Montreal, Central Registry File no. IS4-2-6, vol. 1.

10. House of Commons, *Debates*, 14 May 1951, 2993.

11. House of Commons, Standing Committee on External Affairs, *Minutes of Proceedings and Evidence*, no. 4, 30 May 1951, 85.

12. Editorial, *The Ensign*, 13 October 1951, as cited in memorandum from H. W. Morrison to Ira Dilworth, 16 October 1951 in Canadian Broadcasting Corporation, Montreal, Central Registry File no. C14-12-29.

13. Ibid.

14. Ibid.

15. Ira Dilworth to A. D. Dunton, 18 October 1951, in Canadian Broadcasting Corporation, Montreal, Central Registry File no. C14-12-29.

16. A. D. Dunton to Ira Dilworth, 22 October 1951, in Canadian Broadcasting Corporation, Montreal, Central Registry File no. C14-12-29.

17. Peers, *Politics of Canadian Broadcasting*, 422.

18. House of Commons, *Debates*, vol. 4, 1952, 4247. Seconded is a term which means temporarily assigned. In this case, Désy remained an officer of the foreign service, External Affairs, and was on loan to the CBC for a fixed term. See House of Commons, Special Committee on External Affairs, *Minutes of Proceedings and Evidence*, 26 March 1953, 99.

19. House of Commons, Standing Committee on External Affairs, *Minutes of Proceedings and Evidence*, no. 2, 26 February 1953, 45.

20. House of Commons, Standing Committee on External Affairs, *Minutes of Proceedings and Evidence*, no. 6, 12 March 1953, 138.

21. Standing Committee on External Affairs, *Minutes*, 26 February 1953, 46.

22. Arthur L. Pidgeon, interviewed by the author, audiocassette, 20 July 1971. Mr. Pidgeon served as Policy Coordinator, CBC-IS in 1951.

23. House of Commons, Standing Committee on External Affairs, *Minutes of Proceedings and Evidence*, no. 6, 12 March 1953, 154.

24. House of Commons, *Debates*, 24 April 1953, 4345-46.

25. Peers, *The Politics of Canadian Broadcasting*, 441.

26. House of Commons, Standing Committee on External Affairs, *Minutes of Proceedings and Evidence*, no. 12, 10 June 1954, 385.

27. *New York Times*, 14 May 1950.

28. Standing Committee on External Affairs, *Minutes*, 10 June 1954, 385.

29. Ibid.

30. This was further substantiated by Delafield in 1955. See House of Commons, Standing Committee on External Affairs, *Minutes of Proceedings and Evidence*, no. 6, 10 May 1955, 363.

31. Ibid.

32. House of Commons, Standing Committee on External Affairs, *Minutes of Proceedings and Evidence*, no. 3, 2 March 1953, 67.

33. House of Commons, Standing Committee on External Affairs, *Minutes of Proceedings and Evidence*, no. 6, 12 March 1953, 142.

34. House of Commons, Special Committee on Broadcasting, *Minutes of Proceedings and Evidence*, no. 1, 26 March 1953, 98.

35. Ibid., 96.

36. House of Commons, Standing Committee on External Affairs, *Minutes of Proceedings and Evidence*, no. 4, 30 May 1951, 85. Pearson had testified briefly on policy for Eastern Europe on 17 May. See House of Commons, Standing Committee on External Affairs, *Minutes of Proceedings and Evidence*, no. 1, 17 May 1951, 17.

37. Standing Committee on External Affairs, *Minutes*, 26 February 1953, 44.

38. Standing Committee on External Affairs, *Minutes*, 17 May 1953, 17.

39. Standing Committee on External Affairs, *Minutes*, 26 February 1953, 45.

40. Standing Committee on External Affairs, *Minutes*, 12 March 1953, 142.

41. House of Commons, Standing Committee on External Affairs, *Minutes of Proceedings and Evidence*, no. 12, 10 June 1954, 400-401.

42. Canadian Broadcasting Corporation,"Report on International Service," (Montreal: CBC-IS, October 1956, mimeographed), sec. A, 1.

43. House of Commons, *Debates*, 8 March 1955, 1806.

44. Standing Committee on External Affairs, *Minutes*, 10 June 1954, 400.

45. Arthur L. Pidgeon, interviewed by the author, audiocassette, Ottawa, 30 July 1971.

46. Ibid.

47. Ibid.

48. Ibid.

49. Ibid.

50. "International Service, 1945-50," 18.

51. Canadian Broadcasting Corporation, "Report on International Service" (International Service, Montreal, 1956, mimeographed), app. 14, 2.

52. The CBC-IS operated only two transmitters with a fixed number of frequencies and hours. This limited operations and demanded prioritizing and a shifting of broadcast time from one target area to another.

53. After the Geneva Conference in 1955, the Eastern European broadcasts *limited* "the Cold War approach." Memorandum from E. A. Prince, Assistant Head, Policy Coordination Department, International Service, to C. R. Delafield, 12 September 1958.

54. Canadian Broadcasting Corporation International Service, "Program Notes on Eastern European Language Section," in Publicity and Audience Relation, International Services, Montreal.
55. Ibid.
56. House of Commons, Standing Committee on External Affairs, *Minutes of Proceedings and Evidence*, no. 4, 30 May 1951, 85.
57. House of Commons, Standing Committee on External Affairs, *Minutes of Proceedings and Evidence*, no. 7, 17 March 1953, 226. These scripts were submitted by Jean Désy and were reported to be typical examples from this period.
58. CBC International Service, "Program Notes..." 2.
59. Canadian Broadcasting Corporation, *Annual Report*, 1950-51, 52.
60. Charles R. Delafield interviewed by the author, audiocassette, 7 July 1971. The move toward a less polemic broadcast policy line was initiated in 1955 and became more pronounced in 1959.
61. *International Service*, 1956, Section B, 5.
62. Canadian Broadcasting Corporation, "Report on C.B.C. International Service" (International Service, Montreal, 1959, mimeographed), app. 9.
63. Peers, *Politics of Broadcasting*, 442.
64. Standing Committee on External Affairs, *Minutes*, 12 March 1953, 139.
65. Standing Committee on External Affairs, *Minutes*, 10 June 1954, 394.
66. House of Commons, Standing Committee on External Affairs, *Minutes of Proceedings and Evidence*, no. 5, 5 May 1955, 337.
67. House of Commons, *Debates*, vol. 4, 3 May 1954, 4331.

4

CONSOLIDATION, INTEGRATION, AND STABILITY, 1960-70

A CALL FOR AUSTERITY

IN THE WINTER OF 1956-57, a disturbingly oppressive inflation had begun to erode the Canadian economy. The Bank of Canada and the Finance Department of the government were convinced that inflation was a major threat and argued for a "tight-money" policy to combat it.[1] When Conservative leader John G. Diefenbaker became the thirteenth Canadian prime minister in June 1957, the domestic economy was in a state of near recession. Interest rates soared to their highest levels in forty years. The Diefenbaker government, faced with huge budgetary deficits, had to generate an expansive economy.[2]

The Treasury Board, concerned about the general instability of the Canadian economy, issued a general call for budgetary revisions among all agencies. The appropriations for CBC-IS became a target. In early January 1960 a letter from the board to the CBC and the Department of External Affairs requested a full-scale investigation of the broadcasting priorities, organizational status, financing of the International Service operations and, quite significantly, the feasibility of using the Sackville transmitting facilities for broadcasting to the vast territory above the sixtieth parallel.[3] Priority decisions, efficiency of the organizational structure and the means of financing were all related directly to the CBC-IS appropriations. Yet the use of the Sackville facilities for domestic broadcasting could only mean additional reductions in the number of hours broadcast to foreign audiences. A perplexed International Service staff asked: Why the sudden government interest in the North Country?

During his bid for re-election in 1958, Diefenbaker, who was known for his "pulpit" oratory, spoke with messianic fervor about the land north of the sixtieth parallel:

97

A Canada of the North. This is the Vision . . . Canadians, realize your
opportunities! This is the message I give you, my fellow Canadians. Not one
of defeatism. Jobs! Jobs for hundreds of thousands of Canadians. A new
vision! A new hope! A new soul for Canada![4]

Diefenbaker's dream of developing the North meant constructing new
arteries of communications, new cities, new hydroelectric projects to provide power for the South. According to Diefenbaker the North, a large
remote region covering 40 percent of the Canadian land mass, represented
untapped wealth in natural resources.[5]

Canadians scattered across the North numbered 80,000 and understandably had experienced considerable difficulty relating with the South.
Communications were hard pressed to serve the remote northern regions.
Although radio broadcasting was the best means to reach the diverse populations of a White minority, Native Canadians, Inuit, and Métis, there
were not enough satellite transmitters to cover the vast territory.
Doubtless this lack of communications channels added tension to the
troubling reality that the White minority held most of the jobs positions,
while many of the majority, the Native Canadians, Inuit, and Métis, lived
in poverty.

In late 1958, reflecting Diefenbaker's policy of development for the
northern regions, the Treasury Board authorized appropriations for the
establishment of the Northern Service, a branch of the Canadian
Broadcasting Corporation. The Northern Service, with headquarters in
Ottawa and production facilities in Montreal, began broadcasting operations with several low-power AM stations at Whitehorse and Dawson in
the Yukon Territory, and Yellowknife in the Northwest Territories.
Additional stations were later established in several different locations
across Canada's North.[6]

Even these low-power stations could not cover all of the 1.5 million
square miles above the sixtieth parallel. Since a HF wavelength could
reach into such a vast area, shortwave radio broadcasting was the only
effective means to reach the northern population. The Fowler Committee,
a special committee formed to study different aspects of broadcasting (discussed later in the chapter), was sensitive to the requirements, and recommended construction of two shortwave transmitting facilities in
Vancouver, and Winnipeg or Montreal, to augment the Northern Service.
This recommendation was not approved, however, since more financial
allocations were needed for implementation. Instead, the Engineering

Department of the CBC advocated that the International Service short-wave transmitting facilities in Sackville should be used for the broadcasts beamed north. Beginning in 1958, the Northern Service began sharing transmitter time with the International Service on a trial basis.[7]

The *1960 Joint Report* had to address the feasibility of continuing, and possibly expanding, shared transmitter time between the Northern Service and the International Service.

Such allowances for serving the North affected budgeting and operational priorities.

SHIFTING PRIORITIES

As part of the annual operations review, the corporation and the Department of External Affairs reviewed the relative priorities for Western Europe, Eastern Europe, and Latin America, as well as the broadcasts in both English and French. Canadian foreign policy dictated that the first priority for International Service operations continued to be Eastern European services. The *1960 Joint Report* explained that Canadian international short-wave radio broadcasts were the best means to reach audiences in Eastern Europe. With the exception of Poland, jamming of shortwave broadcasts remained problematic across Eastern Europe. Despite the Soviets' sporadic attempts at blocking Western international broadcasting services, the *1960 Joint Report* urged continuance of Canadian broadcasts since there was considerable interest and curiosity about the West. The recent Canadian-Soviet trade agreement, still in wet ink, promised better economic ties between the two powers. "In order that Canadian views may have their maximum possible influence on the citizens of the Soviet Union and its satellites," the report concluded, "broadcasts to the area should continue."[8]

There was agreement between CBC and External Affairs that the volume of broadcasting to this important area of the world be maintained. The two agencies agreed that the transmissions in Czech, Hungarian, Polish, and Russian should be scheduled at times when a maximum audiences could be reached, and that the projection of the Canadian scene should receive greater prominence in the transmitted programs. It was thought that this change in emphasis from polemic rhetoric embodied in political commentaries to a more bland "projection of Canada" theme would permit use of scripts originally written in English and French. An important by-product of this move would be a reduction in the International Service's central writing and translation staff.[9]

Western Europe received daily transmissions, relays, and transcriptions in English and French; daily transmissions and relays in German; limited transmissions in Danish, Norwegian, Swedish, Dutch, Italian, and Spanish; and relays in Finnish and Greek. Because of possible budget reductions, all of these languages could not be retained. With reluctance, the International Service dropped the Danish, Dutch, Italian, Norwegian, and Swedish services and retained the English, French, and German transmissions beamed to Western Europe. Relay services in Finnish and in Greek were canceled as well. The primary explanation for these cutbacks focused on the fact that Canadian attitudes and general information about Canada was available and was circulated in Western Europe. Music transcriptions and television program exchanges augmented shortwave transmissions and these activities would be continued.[10]

Latin American areas did not fare as well. The increased requirements of the Northern Service mandated a shift in priorities for Latin American services. Transmissions to Latin America were to be reduced and transcription services were to be developed "as extensively as possible."[11]

In 1960, there was a general realignment of operational policies. The Eastern European services would continue untouched by the budgetary reduction and the rescheduling of broadcast times to accommodate the CBC Northern Service. Services beamed to Western Europe and Latin America were significantly reduced, and English and French broadcast times to other areas were reduced to satisfy the Treasury Board's demand for greater economy.

ORGANIZATIONAL STATUS AND FINANCING

The Treasury Board inquired about the organizational status and the financing of the CBC-IS operations. A review of the *1960 Joint Report* revealed that the International Service was a separate entity of the CBC, "developing its own programme policies under general political guidance from the Department [of External Affairs]" (8). This unique arrangement was described as "a special one" which really meant that information on foreign policy was given only to CBC-IS personnel:

> Since the Corporation operates as an independent government agency, it might be difficult . . . for the Department of External Affairs to continue to offer adequate political guidance for international broadcasting purposes if the International Service were to be integrated with the Corporation. The

Department would in such circumstances be able to make freely available to the International Service only such material as could be made available to the press and public information media: a patently unsatisfactory arrangement (8).

The concern over the relationship of CBC-IS with External Affairs, however, dealt not only with the classification of documents but also with the matter of financing. At that time, the *1960 Joint Report* observed, there were three possible procedures regarding International Service appropriations: as part of the Department of External Affairs; as an integral part of the CBC; as separate from the CBC. External Affairs did not want the appropriations for the International Service. "The assumption of budgetary control over the CBC-IS would make the Department directly responsible for broadcasting activities," and that, External Affairs argued, "would require it [the Department] to assume functions for which it has neither the experience nor the staff. . . . "(9)

The second financing procedure, making the International Service appropriation an integral part of the CBC vote, was not satisfactory because there might be difficulties associated with the passing of classified information to the CBC-IS staff. Therefore the third procedure, designating the International Service as a separate part of the corporation's appropriations, was preferred and the *1960 Joint Report* recommended that it be retained (10).

The realignment of priorities called for eight hours of transmission time dedicated to the Northern Service during the evening hours. In addition the Northern Service, a division of CBC, could rent the facilities in the Radio-Canada Building in Montreal, as well as those at the Sackville transmitter site, which, would provide additional revenue for CBC-IS (10).

In the House of Commons C. B. Chevrier (Laurier), who was assigned to a parliamentary committee on government spending, was questioned about the expenditure reductions at CBC-IS that caused cutbacks for Western Europe. He told the House there were two "economic reasons" for the curtailment: the development of the North Country required short-wave radio for adequate coverage and the ideological division between Eastern and Western Europe. Eastern Europe needed Canadian broadcasting since there was no other means to reach the Communist held countries behind the Iron Curtain while Western European countries "fostered a free exchange of information with Canada." Besides, Chevrier concluded, the Voice of America did not broadcast via shortwave in its national language to Denmark, Sweden, Norway, the Netherlands, and Italy.[12]

Despite the cutbacks, there was a major development in using "other means" to reach international audiences. The emphasis on relays, transcription services, and program exchanges was given higher priority than ever before. It made sense. Supplementary programs could be mailed or relayed to foreign agencies for broadcast on medium-wave stations and, theoretically, would reach large audiences. Since the CBC-IS possessed only three transmitters and a limited number of frequencies, the adjustments in priorities demanded a wider use of these "other means." These changes in operational priorities were the result of economic pressures exerted on the International Service by the Treasury Board. National economics would continue to play a key role in changing CBC-IS policy priorities.

AN ABOLISHMENT RUMOR: A NEAR CRISIS

In late 1963, word circulated in Ottawa that the government, for unexplained reasons, was considering a drastic curtailment, if not outright abolishment, of the International Service. The origin of the rumor was difficult to trace. It was, perhaps, "an informed Ottawa source" that leaked the story to the press, which in turn questioned the CBC. The fact that the Treasury Board reduced CBC-IS appropriations in 1955 and in 1961 undoubtedly added greater credence to the rumor. The CBC responded quickly by waging a campaign of information. One key management officer of the International Service later remarked, "We were fighting for our lives."[13]

The information campaign worked. On 24 January 1964 Paul Martin, secretary of state for External Affairs, announced:

> . . . the Government has decided that no reduction should be made in the estimates of the Canadian Broadcasting Corporation International Service for the fiscal year 1964-65, and, at the same time view . . . the desirability of an eventual integration of its activities with the Canadian Broadcasting Corporation.[14]

The organizational positioning of CBC-IS within the corporation, while quasi-connected to External Affairs in a non-supervisory, but advisory capacity, was never fully understood by even the most informed observer in Ottawa. Since the early days of the Cold War, questions had been raised in the House of Commons about the mechanics of liaison between these three organizations. Answers seemed to satisfy all concerned until the next series of questions. The Martin announcement of "the desirability of an eventual integration" of the International Service with the CBC prompted the government to grant a one-year reprieve. This safety net for the service was granted so that a detailed analysis of International Service operations could be made by a special committee.[15]

The Canadian press published both support and disfavor for the CBC-IS. The Ottawa *Journal* commented: "If Canada has built a reputation for telling the truth objectively and impartially in North American accents, then the International Service serves democracy well and is worth being presented with facilities to do its work efficiently."[16] In Victoria, British Columbia, the *Daily Times* observed there was "a matter of national prestige." All major countries, the editorial asserted, "including Commonwealth nations, and most of the minor ones, maintain shortwave stations—many of them more powerful than Canada's. . . ."[17]

The *Examiner* in Peterborough, Ontario, attacked the International Service, for the following reason:

> . . . listening to shortwave broadcasting has declined in popularity since the introduction of television and even the British Broadcasting Corporation is said to be considering large reductions in its overseas broadcasts. Shortwave broadcasts of other countries indulge in shameless propaganda; so much so that they require alert listeners and informed opinion of their value is to be accurately gauged. If the CBC must make economies, the shortwave service would be a good place to start.[18]

Blair Fraser wrote in *Maclean's*: "If the International Service fails to prove its case, to the satisfaction of a very unsentimental committee of civil servants from various departments, it probably won't survive beyond the one-year reprieve. . . . But if it does manage to justify its existence, it may win not mere survival but a new lease on life."[19]

Blair Fraser's prediction was accurate. The CBC-IS not only survived a major crisis, but received an appropriations increase:

> As expected, the Government did not reduce the funds earmarked for the shortwave radio International Service, operated by the CBC for the Government. The amount for this purpose went up to $2,100,000 from the current year's estimated $1,865,000.[20]

Eighteen months later, the Canadian press reported that the International Service had overcome the abolishment threat and had actually experienced a resurgence with an announcement of a major modernization program "in the near future."[21]

In 1965, the CBC recommended in its annual report "not only a continuance but a development of Canada's participation in international broadcasting through the International Service." Specifically, the annual report cited recommendations for the purchase and installation of three new 100,000-watt transmitters at Sackville; modifications of the antenna systems; and further development of cooperation with foreign broadcasting systems in the relaying of Canadian programs. The final recommendation called for "maximum integration of the CBC domestic and international services."[22]

The International Service had gained considerable strength since the near abolishment episode. Canada was planning an elaborate centennial celebration for 1967, including a world's fair in Montreal, to commemorate the 100th anniversary of Confederation. International Service personnel asserted that Expo '67 in Montreal could offer a wealth of program material which could promote international goodwill and understanding. International shortwave radio broadcasting from Canada could reach large overseas audiences. There was an apparent recognition in Ottawa that the International Service could provide a needed function in projecting the centennial celebration to the world radio audience.

Yet there was another reason why the International Service was on a popularity upswing. There had been a 69 percent increase in audience mail in 1964, an indication of greater acceptance and recognition among international audiences. The jamming of Canadian broadcasts had all but disappeared in Eastern Europe and mail from that region had increased.[23]

With an increased budget and a recommendation for more modern transmitting facilities, the International Service's future looked promising. But the formation of a special committee to study the status of broadcasting in Canada generally, and the activities of the CBC specifically, meant that still another review of the International Service's operations was forthcoming.

GOVERNMENT SUPPORT: THE FOWLER REPORT

The Broadcasting Act, 1958[24] had established a Board of Broadcast Governors (BBG) to regulate Canadian broadcasting. The CBC, with its numerous affiliates and services, was an agent of the Crown and not licensed by the BBG. This situation generated questions concerning the lines of authority between CBC and the Board of Broadcast Governors. The status of Canadian broadcasting was unsettled and led to the formation of a committee to answer the questions associated with broadcast legislation and to make recommendations for change. On 25 May 1964, Maurice Lamontagne, secretary of state and registrar general of Canada, announced the appointment of the 1965 Committee on Broadcasting and the naming of Robert M. Fowler as Chairman. The committee's report was submitted on 1 September 1965.[25]

The Fowler Committee appraised broadcast legislation, inquired into the structural organization, the financing, and the relationship between government and the CBC, the proposed television services, and the operations of the International Service. Concerning CBC-IS, the Fowler Committee reviewed the broadcasting operations and facilities, the constitutional status, public relations, and the official title of the International Service (vii, 179-89).

CBC-IS OPERATIONS AND FACILITIES

The Fowler Committee recognized the importance of international broadcasting and called it "an indirect aid for foreign policy." Reiterating past statements concerning the role of the International Service, the Fowler Committee endorsed the idea of "the projection abroad of a Canadian image that reflects the nature of the country and its people, their policies, beliefs, and tastes. . . " (179).

As with others who had studied this issue in the past, the Fowler Committee recognized that the international shortwave broadcasting service had the potential to attract immigrants, even tourists, by broadcasting that "Canada . . . is a good place to live or visit." The Fowler Committee observed that Canada ranked fifth in the world for exports; consequently, a promotion of Canadian international trade would be beneficial. Shortwave radio broadcasting, the committee asserted, provided an important "link between Canadians and their relatives and countrymen living overseas" (179).

The Fowler Committee noted that radio in Canada had taken second place behind television but that television was "still an exotic luxury to most of the peoples of the earth" (180). Radio, the committee reported, was widely used in other parts of the world:

In the densely populated and rapidly developing parts of Asia and Africa,
listening to broadcasts from abroad is an everyday experience for those with
radio sets, particularly the young men of better education who are the present opinion-makers and future leaders of their communities. Sales of radio
sets are increasing at a spectacular rate. . . (180).

The Fowler Committee held the view that radio had a valid place in world
communications and it was very much in favor of the International
Service operations.

Although generally impressed with CBC-IS operations, the committee
expressed concern about the effectiveness of the shortwave broadcasts. The
International Service had been subjected to budgetary reductions in 1955,
1960, and again in 1963. Inability to demonstrate the effectiveness of the
shortwave broadcasts probably was a key element in the decision to cut
services and budget. The Fowler Committee weighed the evidence and
stated, rather pointedly, that "it is difficult, if not impossible, to measure
the effectiveness of external broadcasting" (180). The committee quoted
sources from Great Britain and the United States regarding CBC-IS audience size projections in Western Europe. The number of West Berlin and
West German Republic listeners to the International Service was estimated
to be about 170,000 while France boasted an estimated audience of
between 300,000 and 450,000 listeners. In Latin America the estimated
audience was reportedly about the same as for Radio Moscow but less than
that for Radio Havana or the British Broadcasting Corporation (180).
These audience surveys were undertaken sporadically from 1960 to 1963.
Such sparse data sets could not possibly show any trends of audience loy-
alty and were, at best, indirect estimates of audience size at a given point
in time. The statistical confidence level was undoubtedly low, making the
results almost meaningless. Despite problems with research methodology,
the audience survey data sets were contained in the report.

Another indirect measurement of effectiveness, audience mail, was
included in the Fowler Committee report. Total letters received from 1962
to 1964 increased by 20,446. The committee was encouraged by the
increase in number of listener responses, But there was no attempt to
explain the use of letters as indicators of listener response. Letters indicated how many listeners took the time to write to the International
Service, and were not a suitable means for measuring anything more.

A BBC study found that Canada ranked nineteeth out of twenty-two
countries in total weekly broadcast hours. Among all twenty-two coun-

tries, during the period 1950-63, the average weekly total was 88.1 hours. At the time of the Fowler Committee investigation, Canada broadcast in eleven languages for nearly ninety hours per week. The committee reported that other countries broadcast considerably more hours per week: the USSR, 1,500 hours in forty-eight languages; the Voice of America, more than 800 hours in thirty-five languages; China, more than 800 hours in thirty-five languages. The committee argued that even if Canada could not afford anything close to the level of activity and scale of expenditure of the Great Powers, the International Service "should be heard abroad more widely and more clearly than it is at present" (186).

The Fowler Committee agreed with the CBC about the essential importance of installing more powerful and modern transmitters. The committee recognized that the CBC-IS was still using the two original fifty-kilowatt transmitters which, by this time, were obsolete. Spare parts were difficult to obtain and in 1962, a third transmitter of the same type was purchased from Venezuela with the intention of stripping it for replacement components. The transmitter was in reasonable working order and was pressed into service. The committee warned that failure to modernize the Sackville equipment would cause unused frequencies allocated to Canada for external broadcasting to be lost to other nations. The committee also stressed that the three out-dated 50-kilowatt transmitters presented "a sorry contrast" to the two 250-kilowatt and four 100-kilowatt transmitters operated by Ghana. Furthermore, the committee noted that Canada's transmitters were not being used exclusively for international broadcasting. They were also the only outlet for the Northern Service and for the Canadian Armed Forces. "It is high time," the committee emphasized, "for these antique relics from the dawn of the electronic age to be scrapped, for they are costly to maintain and have long since been inadequate for their purpose" (186).

The committee recommended immediate action to install more powerful transmitters and modernize the antenna arrays at a cost, estimated by the CBC, of $3.7 million. With this modernization effort, the committee believed ". . . it would not be unduly extravagant to plan for perhaps 150 hours a week of external broadcasting, at an estimated cost of around $5 million a year" (186). All this was, by Blair Fraser's prediction a year earlier, a "new lease on life" for the International Service.

QUESTIONS OF CONSTITUTIONALITY, PUBLIC RELATION, AND TITLE

The Fowler Committee studied the CBC, International Service, and External Affairs organizational arrangement and found it "ill defined." Since its inception, none of the broadcasting acts had made specific reference to an international broadcasting service either as a part of the corporation or as a separate organization. Although the Order in Council P.C. 8168, dated 12 September 1942, authorized the establishment of CBC-IS, there was no direct reference to it in any subsequent broadcast legislation. Calling the CBC-IS "a semi-autonomous body," the committee noted that the International Service was "loosely attached to the CBC organization" and it possessed a strange administrative status:

> Although CBC-IS is integrated with CBC for purely administrative purposes, funds for its expenditures are separately voted by Parliament and are not subject to corporate control. One odd result is that CBC-IS is the owner and CBC the lessee of the Radio-Canada Building in Montreal, which is the headquarters of the French Network and Quebec Region. But the most serious aspect of the present arrangements is that CBC-IS is suspended in constitutional space between the CBC and the Department of External Affairs, with each ascribing responsibility to the other (187).

The Fowler Committee proposed a more formal organizational and budgetary integration of the International Service with the CBC and noted four possible benefits from this new arrangement. First, the well-established and publicized fact thatCBC was independent from political control offered assurance that the CBC-IS would not become an instrument of government propaganda. Second, the merger would provide better opportunity for representation abroad for program exchanges and distribution without budget duplication. Third, the committee believed that integration would afford the opportunity for "a much needed rotation of staff" to prevent inbreeding. The Fowler Committee charged that International Service personnel were in "cloistered seclusion" from the main CBC organization. Fourth, "the outlook of Canadian external broadcasting could be more readily broadened to cover the whole wide sweep of Canadian interests abroad" (188).

The Fowler Committee discovered that the Department of External Affairs gave "desultory attention" to program policy for international broadcasting and maintained only informal contacts. The committee did not fault this arrangement but stressed that the CBC-IS should maintain closer relationships with other departments and agencies that held a special interest in Canadian external relations, such as the departments of Trade and Commerce and Citizenship and Immigration, the National Research Council, and the National Film Board. The committee charged that the CBC-IS had neglected these departments and, in fact, had "infrequent contacts, if indeed it has had any at all." For these reasons, the committee concluded:

> . . . we believe that the International Service should be formally recognized as a principal division of the CBC; that its physical assets should be vested into the Corporation; and that the CBC should assume full responsibility for operating the shortwave broadcasting equipment at Sackville, N.B. (188).

This proposal for integration of the CBC-IS with the corporation was made primarily for budgetary reasons. The International Service had always been a part of the corporation, albeit "loosely" as described by the committee, and had depended upon the corporation for personnel support. All of the directors, with the exception of Désy, had been CBC employees in the domestic services before they were transferred to Montreal to work with the International Service. In addition, all employees of the International Service were receiving the same benefits, (retirement, vacation time, sick leave, etc.) as employees of the CBC. The primary difference was the allocation of financial support.

The Order in Council P.C. 8168 stressed that it was unfair to charge the external broadcasting services to the corporation because that money was collected for domestic broadcasting services. Therefore, the only fair procedure was to support the International Service through special parliamentary grants, separate from corporation appropriations. "Financial provision for external broadcasting," the committee wrote, "should be kept in flexible relationship to changing external policy, and should therefore be authorized annually by Parliament" (189). According to the Fowler Committee, then, the important point was this: the appropriations for the International Service should remain flexible (the amount determined by changing external policy) and be voted on separately from CBC appropriations but allocated to the corporation instead of directly to the International Service. Thus, the appropriation for the International Service would be received and administered by the corporation. This proposed procedure, according to the committee, would insure that the taxes paid by Canadians for supporting the CBC domestic services would not be used for external broadcasting and would place the International Service more directly under the administrative control of the corporation. The Fowler Committee recommended that the financial requirements of the CBC, both capital and operating, should be provided by a statutory annual grant of $25 for each television household in Canada as reported by the Dominion Bureau of Statistics. The operating formula was designed to cover both amortization of capital interest on capital borrowing but it did *not* include operating provision for the International Service (312-13).[26]

The committee cautioned the International Service about the importance of public relations: "CBC-IS has been doing excellent work for more than twenty years," the committee stated, "yet most Canadians are probably unaware of its very existence." What the public needed was "reassurance that its money is being well spent on this activity. . . " (187).

The final recommendation for the International Service concerned the title of the organization. The committee thought the International Broadcasting Service of the Canadian Broadcasting Corporation was unimaginative and cumbersome in English and when translated into French. The Fowler Committee asserted: "A simpler and more appealing title should be found. The one that commends itself to us is Radio Canada International" (189).

The overall tone of the Fowler Report was favorable and undoubtedly relieved any remaining apprehensions the CBC-IS might have had since the 1964 crisis. If all of the recommendations were implemented, the International Service would have a more clearly defined constitutional status and would have new transmitting facilities as well. Indeed, the future looked very promising.

1966: THE *WHITE PAPER* ENDORSEMENT

In 1966, the *White Paper on Broadcasting*, prepared by Judy LaMarsh, secretary of state, endorsed the recommendations of the Fowler Committee and proclaimed: "The Government is convinced of the importance and value of the International Service, and is generally prepared to accept the recommendations of the Advisory Committee [Fowler Committee] with regard to the necessary renewal of the physical plant and the extension and improvement of programming."[27] Integration, the *White Paper* affirmed, should be undertaken "forthwith." This endorsement and recognition of the importance of external broadcasting by a white paper undoubtedly underscored a general feeling of confidence among CBC-IS management. Improvements would be made in transmitting facilities, and integration, a concept discussed quite frequently since the 1964 crisis, would be implemented, insuring greater stability.

Such confidence was short-lived, however, because as Canada and the International Service prepared for the centennial celebrations and Expo '67, the Treasury Board began reexamining all government expenditures. Another economy campaign was under way.

CRISIS AND CONSOLIDATION

Canada was in a festive mood in 1967. One hundred years had passed since Confederation and the Canadians commemorated the centennial all across Canada and at Montreal with Expo '67, aptly titled, "Man and His World." With all the geographic space in Canada, even around Montreal, it is curious that the Expo planners decided to build the theme park on islands in the St. Lawrence River. The islands were made from earth moved from the excavations underneath Montreal as the city constructed its first subway system. "Man and His World" was, in the words of historian Desmond Morton, "an extravagance beyond excuse."[28]

Robert Shaw, deputy director of Expo, explained that a world's fair was a "commercial market place" while an international exhibition, such as Expo '67, dealt with "ideas and values."[29] The theme, "Man and His World," sought to stress international goodwill with seventy nations providing sixty-two national pavilions which assumed "ambassadorial" rather than "commercial huckster" roles.[30]

As part of this 1,000-acre international exhibition, the CBC built a $10 million International Broadcasting Center to house facilities for visiting broadcasting personnel.[31] The CBC-IS periodically broadcast from the center. All International Service programming concentrated on aspects of the centennial celebrations and Expo '67. The CBC 1967-68 *Annual Report* described the year as "one of the most exciting years in the history of the Service."[32]

One by-product of this broadcasting activity was increased audience mail response to CBC-IS programming. More than 74,000 letters, cards, and reception reports were received during the Centennial Celebration year (compared to more than 68,000 in 1966). Additionally, 46,523 program hours of recorded Canadian music were shipped to radio organizations all over the world, a fourfold increase from the previous year.[33]

There was a general feeling of accomplishment among International Service personnel. International goodwill was the theme of Expo '67 and the CBC-IS had been helpful in sending that basic message to the world radio audience. Ironically, the Canadian Treasury Board was not impressed. By November, a new report was circulating around Ottawa that the International Service was again in jeopardy; a member of the Treasury Board had recommended discontinuance in the name of austerity. To make matters worse, it was reported that the board was in agreement on the issue, as were certain members of the cabinet.[34]

Incredibly, on 30 November, the government announced that it intended to abolish the International Service. Charles R. Delafield, director if the International Service, called in all heads of language sections and told them to alert their staffs that they could expect a government announcement on Monday that the service would be abolished. One employee later described the announcement as "a bolt of lightning."[35]

The shock over the upcoming announcement soon changed to frustration and apprehension among CBC-IS personnel. There were 207 employees at the International Service. Some might be transferred to other assignments within the corporation, but many in the various language sections possessed talents and qualifications that were unique to international broadcasting. Their prospects for future employment were not good.[36]

In the shadows of the recent endorsements and recommendations from both the *White Paper* and the Fowler Committee, none of this made much sense. The Treasury Board undoubtedly made the recommendation to abolish on little knowledge of the International Service's operations.[37]

Ottawa warned the International Service management to expect the official announcement on Monday, 2 December, which gave the service four days to lobby support in the capital. Delafield and his staff prepared a Position Paper, then rushed to Ottawa to distribute it to members of Parliament, the press, and pertinent organizations.

The Fowler Committee had warned the International Service of the importance of public relations. Now faced with possible abolishment, Delafield and his staff moved quickly to make amends. Their Position Paper outlined the CBC-IS operations and reviewed Canada's position in the world radio arena. The Position Paper asserted that a daily output of news and views from Canada beamed to a world radio audience cost each Canadian 16 cents per year.[38]

The cost of broadcasting meant little if the allocated frequencies for Canada's use on HF were no longer used. The Position Paper called the frequencies "a precious national asset" and asserted that to abandon them would be "to lose them forever" (1).

The use of the Sackville facilities was outlined. Since the CBC Northern Service and the Armed Forces Service depended on the International Service transmitters, how could the Treasury Board ignore these sanctioned operations? If the transmitting plant at Sackville was closed, the Position Paper argued, the Northern Service and the Armed Forces Service would have to cease operations as well. In fact, only 54 percent of transmitter time was allocated for the International Service. The remaining 46 percent was for the other two services. If the Treasury Board were to cancel out the International Service and keep the Northern Service and the Canadian Armed Forces Service, only 12 percent of the total cost would be saved since fixed operational costs would be necessary to continue the two services. Then there was the matter of contracts for leasing BBC transmitting facilities in the European areas and the contracts with CBC bargaining units for employees. The Treasury Board had not investigated the ramifications of these important elements. A unilateral cancellation of the contracts was not likely without severe penalty. What about the financial implications of staff dismissals? By contract, proper notice of employment termination (three months) with separation pay and settlement of pensions and retirement rights would, according to the Position Paper, cost "in the neighborhood of one million dollars." The paper concluded: "Surely it is unthinkable that now the government of Canada should be the first and only one in the world ever to have withdrawn from the international broadcasting field" (1).

Reactions to the proposed abolishment were overwhelmingly on the side of the CBC-IS. The British Broadcasting Corporation reacted to the proposed abolishment with a terse statement that asserted in part: "Such a weakening of the Western voice from one quarter is damaging to all" (2). The Canadian Union of Public Employees wrote Prime Minister Lester Pearson: "At a time when the radio voice of the free world is weakened by increased efforts by totalitarian countries, it would be in our view, a disaster to cut this service at this time (2). Yvon Cherrier, national president, Association of Radio and Television Employees of Canada, and George Frajkor, national councillor, Canadian Wire Service Guild, jointly wired Prime Minister Pearson and members of the cabinet requesting a clarification of the "abolishment rumour" and urging the Government "to reaffirm its intention as expressed in the White Paper on Broadcasting to extend and improve the International Service."[39]

In the House of Commons Andrew Brewin (Greenwood) asked Paul Martin, secretary of state for External Affairs: "Is the government of

Canada giving consideration to cutting out the international services of
the CBC? If so, in light of the fact that this service constitutes the voice of
Canada to the outside world, will the government think again before taking this step?"[40] Martin replied simply: "Mr. Speaker, I will take notice of
this question."[41]

Martin and other cabinet members were under fire from the press
about the proposed abolishment; on 2 December, there were reports that
the cabinet was split over the issue.[42] The Montreal *Star* reported that
"Attempts to cancel the service, which for more than two decades has
been regarded abroad as the 'Voice of Canada' have not been admitted by
official government spokesmen."[43]

Globe and Mail columnist Dennis Braithwaite charged: "The corporation's
[CBC] budget is $150 million; scrapping IS [International Service] would
reportedly save about $3.8 million, a mere trifle." Braithwaite suggested there
might be other ulterior motives behind the proposed abolishment of CBC-IS.
"Have the communist countries objected to these transmissions?" And, "Has
President Charles de Gaulle, or some of his Quebec followers, perhaps,
objected to the IS broadcasts in French?" He continued: "For a nation that
this year spent hundreds of millions on an almost hysterical effort to catch the
world's attention, haven't we become strangely reticent and isolationist all of
a sudden?" Who was behind the abolishment movement? Braithwaite named
Deputy Finance Minister Robert Bryce as "the man putting the Indian sign on
the International Service."[44]

Although Braithwaite implied there may have been other reasons for
abrogating the International Service, Delafield attributed the abolishment
proposal to a lack of knowledge and understanding about the
International Service operations.[45]

In the House of Commons on 4 December, T. C. Douglas (Burnaby-
Coquitlam) asked Prime Minister Pearson, ". . . is it the intention of the government to silence the voice of Canada at the end of this month?" Pearson
replied, ". . . we are looking into the operations of all government agencies
with a view to cutting down expenses wherever that is possible. I can assure
my hon. friend that no decision has been taken to abolish the service."[46]

Douglas countered with another question:

> Q. [Douglas]: Will the government be making a statement in the house far
> enough in advance of the actual discontinuance of this program to give
> members an opportunity to express their opinion in respect of this very
> important decision?

A. [Right Hon. L. B. Pearson]: Yes, Mr. Speaker; especially in view of the newspaper comment I think it is important to make an announcement of this kind as quickly as possible. It is my hope that this can be done this week during the debate on the budget (4982).

Michael Starr (Ontario) asked Pearson if he had received any representations from interested groups in Canada favoring retention of the CBC-IS. Pearson answered:

A. [Mr. Pearson]: Yes, Mr. Speaker, I have received a great many representations. Indeed, every time it is rumoured that we are going to reduce or cut back a service or look at it on any ground of expenditure, I receive a great many representations (4982).

Andrew Brewin (Greenwood) asked Pearson if he would ". . . look at the 1966 white paper on broadcasting, issued by his own government, which stressed its conviction of the importance and value of the international service?" Pearson stated, "I am also aware of that, Mr. Speaker" (4982).

Pearson's announcement in the House of Commons that the cabinet had postponed any action on the proposal for abolishment gave hope to CBC-IS management and staff. They had survived the four-day campaign.

The Montreal *Gazette* reported that the termination of CBC-IS would not amount to much savings since the Sackville facilities would have to continue operating for the Northern and Armed Services broadcasting operations.[47] This was, perhaps, the strongest point the CBC-IS had presented in its defense. In his sweeping expenditure reforms, Deputy Finance Minister Robert Bryce probably was not aware of other agencies that were using the Sackville plant. It was a poorly justified action for the Treasury Board.

Editorials in the Canadian press were overwhelmingly in favor of retaining the International Service. The *Globe and Mail*, for example, asserted that the CBC-IS was "a service worth keeping" and asked:

What image do Mr. Sharp's [Minister of Finance] men want Canada to have abroad? Should we hibernate from the world, let Voltaire have the last word as an image-maker with his "few acres of snow"? Or do the money-men in Ottawa hope we will be known by that vigorous new slogan invented for our military aircraft, "Detect and Destroy"? Better by far to pull an air force squadron back from Germany and keep the International Service.[48]

The Montreal *Star* paid special tribute to the International Service's programming of music by Canadian composers. Such use of Canadian music, the *Star* affirmed, presented "a broad and representative cross-section of the musical developments in this country."[49] The International Service was instrumental in producing a seventeen-album series featuring Canadian composers and performers. Recorded by RCA Victor, the sales for the series numbered more than 42,000.[50]

On 4 December, the Toronto *Star* charged that ". . . the proposal to end the CBC International Service—at a saving of $3.8 million—is the sort of clumsy hacking that gets rid of good meat when there's still plenty of budgetary fat to be removed."[51] Two days later, the *Star* editorialized again on the abolishment issue recognizing the importance of shortwave radio broadcasting in purveying the Canadian identity. "At a time when Canada is struggling to establish itself as an independent nation with a secure identity, it is foolish to silence completely our modest attempt to tell the world something of our affairs, our culture and our attraction."[52]

Favorable editorial comments for the International Service came not only from major daily newspapers but from small-town weeklies as well. For example, the Wallaceburg *News* focused on the liaison issue as probable cause for misunderstanding and lack of appreciation for the International Service broadcasts: "Perhaps it was because of its mixed sponsorship. It was run by the CBC but its budget was not part of the CBC budget. External Affairs was instructed to keep an eye on it. In the result the baby belongs to nobody."[53]

Letters to newspaper editors, an indirect measure of public opinion, discussed the proposed abolishment of CBC-IS. A German immigrant wrote a letter to the Montreal *Gazette* claiming that CBC-IS broadcasts influenced him to emigrate from Saarbruecken: "I came to Canada rather well informed and upon my arrival in Montreal, found that I.S. transmissions were true and helpful. Through personal contact with the German Section of I.S., they helped me in searching for a position here as an electrical engineer."[54] An American listener wrote to the Halifax, Nova Scotia *Chronicle Herald*: "The International Service introduces Canada to foreigners who may have forgotten that the United States shares the North American continent with other cultures. Do you want the Voice of America to speak for you? If you do not, I urge you to protest the reduction of this service immediately in a letter to Prime Minister Pearson."[55]

Helmut Blume, dean of the Faculty of Music at McGill University in Montreal and former head of the German section at CBC-IS, telegrammed

Pearson and his cabinet protesting the abolishment notion. Blume wrote, in part:

> . . . musicians are acutely aware that the CBC International Service, throughout the last twenty years, has been the chief promoter of Canadian music through its many recordings and transcriptions of Canadian works and their distribution abroad. . . . We strongly urge you to prevent any attempt to silence the Voice of Canada and its musical culture in international broadcasting.[56]

Overall, the editorial consensus was for retention of the International Service. Were there reasons other than economy for the abolishment? Did the Department of External Affairs have a distrust for mass media, especially an international broadcasting service? Could a broadcast beamed overseas make critical diplomacy more difficult, prompting a cancellation of CBC-IS? These questions represented unfounded suspicions. Repeatedly, since the inception of the International Service in 1938, the Department of External Affairs recognized the importance of international broadcasting in foreign affairs.

The 1967 crisis reinforced the need for total integration of the International Service with the CBC. The relationship between the Department of External Affairs and the International Service was, perhaps, confusing to most who questioned the constitutional status of the international broadcasting operations. The Fowler Committee and the *White Paper on Broadcasting* had recognized this administrative oddity and had recommended that the International Service integrate more formally with the CBC. In 1960, the Department of External Affairs cautioned that CBC-IS integration with the Corporation would make the transfer of classified foreign policy documents difficult, if not impossible. But the separation, although favored by External Affairs, presented numerous problems in budgeting and, above all, in the constitutional status of the International Service.

INTEGRATION

On 8 December, the crisis officially ended when External Affairs sent a telex message to Charles Delafield at the International Service: ". . . the activities of the CBC-IS are being placed under the direct budgetary control of the CBC. . . . We hope that the closer integration between the overseas programmes and the CBC will result in greater economy and efficiency in their operations, and that they will continue and, when circumstances permit, expand their unique role in projecting CDA [Canada] overseas."[57]

Order in Council P.C. 1968-525, authorizing integration, became effective upon the adoption of the 1968 Broadcasting Act, assented to on 7 March 1968. Both the Order in Council P.C. 1968-525 and the Broadcasting Act granted the International Service a more clearly defined constitutional status:

> His Excellency the Governor General in Council, on the recommendation of the Secretary of State, pursuant to subsection (2) of section 39 of the Broadcasting Act, within the conditions of licenses issued to the Canadian Broadcasting Corporation by the Canadian Radio-Television Commission and subject to any applicable regulation of the Commission, is pleased to direct the Canadian Broadcasting Corporation to provide, in consultation with the Department of External Affairs, an International Service by means of shortwave broadcasting supplemented by relays, transcriptions and sound and visual recordings, providing thereby a continuing expression abroad of Canadian identity, and to consolidate accounts of the Corporation and merge any capital assets which may be held in the name of Her Majesty for the purposes of the International Service with the assets of the Corporation; Orders in Council P.C. 8168 of 18th September 1942, P.C. 167/8855 of 17th November, 1943, P.C. 128/4848 of 27th November 1947, P.C. 1955-6/488 of 6th April, 1955, P.C. 97/1983 of 21st March, 1944, P.C. 140/2247 of 4th April, 1945, P.C. 13/2400 of 28 May, 1948, and amendments thereto, are hereby revoked; the foregoing to come into effect upon proclamation of the Broadcasting Act.[58]

The specific reference to the International Service in the 1968 Broadcasting Act was in subsection (2) of section 39:

> The Corporation may within the conditions of any license or licenses issued to it by the Commission and subject to any applicable regulation of the Commission, act as agent for or on behalf of any Minister of the Crown or as an agent of Her Majesty in right of Canada or of any province, in respect of any broadcasting operations that it may be directed by the Governor in Council to carry out, including the provision of an International Service.[59]

For the first time specific reference to the International Service was included in a broadcasting act. The financing of the International Service was changed with the total corporate merger. Funds allocated by the government for international broadcasting operations would be given to the corporation for distribution to the International Service.

The 1967 crisis, although a major threat to the very existence of the International Service, brought about governmental action that was intended to rectify the puzzling organizational structure. It was, after all, the organizational liaison between the Crown corporation and External Affairs and a lack of communication between all parties, especially between the Treasury Board and the CBC, that caused the furor over the proposed abolishment of the International Service. Implementation of the new integration policy that offered stability, and hopefully longevity, was an arduous challenge for the International Service administration.

NOTES

1. Blair Fraser, *The Search for Identity: Canada, 1945-1967* (Toronto: Doubleday Canada Limited, 1967), 164.

2. Peter C. Newman, *Renegade in Power: The Diefenbaker Years* (Toronto: McClelland and Stewart Limited, 1963), 208.

3. Canadian Broadcasting Corporation, "CBC International Service: A Joint Submission of the Department of External Affairs and the Canadian Broadcasting Corporation," (hereafter cited as "1960 Joint Report") (Montreal: CBC, 1960, mimeographed), 1.

4. Gerald Clark, *Canada: The Uneasy Neighbor* (New York: David McKay Company, Inc., 1965), 337.

5. Ibid.

6. Canadian Broadcasting Corporation, "General Information" (Canadian Broadcasting Corporation Northern Service, Ottawa, 1971, mimeographed). See also Royal Commission on Broadcasting, *Report* [Fowler Commission], (Ottawa, 1957), 212-14.

7. CBC, "General Information."

8. "1960 Joint Report," 4.

9. Ibid., 5.

10. Ibid. See also Canadian Broadcasting Corporation, *Annual Report 1960-61* (Ottawa: Canadian Broadcasting Corporation, 1961), 34. The *Annual Report* cites budget reductions as the reason for the cancellations.

11. "1960 Joint Report," 6.

12. House of Commons, *Debates* 2 ,1960-61, 1630.

13. *Globe and Mail* (Toronto), 7 July 1965.

14. Statement by Hon. Paul Martin, Secretary of State for External Affairs, 24 January 1964; in Canadian Broadcasting Corporation, Montreal, Central Registry File no. IS2-2-25, vol. 1.

15. Blair Fraser, "Last Chance for the CBC's $2-million Voice of Canada," *Maclean's*, 22 February 1964.

16. Editorial, *Journal* (Ottawa), "Canada's Voice Abroad," reprinted in *Journal-Pioneer* (Summerside, Prince Edward Island), 20 February 1964, in Files, Publicity and Audience Relations,

17. Editorial, *Daily Times* (Victoria, British Columbia), 10 March 1964. International Service, Montreal.

18. Editorial, *Examiner* (Peterborough, Ontario), 21 January 1964.

19. Fraser, "Last Chance."

20. *Globe and Mail* (Toronto), 4 March 1964.

21. *Globe and Mail* (Toronto), 7 July 1965; *La Presse* (Montreal), 7 July 1965; *Daily Star* (Toronto), 7 July 1965; *Journal* (Ottawa), 6 July 1965. Clippings in Files, Publicity and Audience Relations, International Service, Montreal.

22. Canadian Broadcasting Corporation, *Annual Report*, 1964-65 (Ottawa: Canadian Broadcasting Corporation, 1965), 18.

23. *Globe and Mail* (Toronto), 7 July 1965.

24. Statutes, *Broadcasting Act, 1958*, 7 Elizabeth 2, chap. 22.

25. Committee on Broadcasting, *Report* [Fowler] (Ottawa: 1965); for a detailed discussion of the events which led to the formation of the Fowler Committee, see Toogood, "The Canadian Broadcasting Corporation," 205-46.

26. In 1965, there were 4,582,000 television households in Canada.

27. Honourable Judy LaMarsh, Secretary of State, *White Paper on Broadcasting* (Ottawa: Queen's Printer and Controller of Stationary, 1966), 18.

28. Morton, *A Short History of Canada*, 240.

29. *New York Times*, 23 January 1967.

30. *Newsweek*, 1 May 1967, 34.

31. *New York Times*, 28 April 1967.

32. Canadian Broadcasting Corporation, *Annual Report*, 1967-68 (Ottawa: Canadian Broadcasting Corporation, 1968), 34.

33. Ibid.

34. *Gazette* (Montreal), 31 November 1967.

35. *Montreal Star*, 1 December 1967.

36. John C. Ward, Acting Executive Vice-President, Association of Radio and Television Employees of Canada, letter to numerous reporters and government officials, 2 December 1967.

37. *Gazette* (Montreal), 5 December 1967.

38. Canadian Broadcasting Corporation, "The International Service of the Canadian Broadcasting Corporation" (Montreal: CBC-IS, 1967, mimeographed), 1.

39. Telegram to Prime Minister of Canada, The Right Honourable Lester B. Pearson, Parliament Buildings Ottawa, from Yvon Cherrier, national president, Association of Radio and Television Employees of Canada, Montreal, and George Frajkor, national councillor, Canadian Wire Service Guild, Montreal, dated 30 November 1967. Also, this telegram was sent to: Minister for External Affairs, The Honourable Paul Martin; Secretary of State, The Honourable Judy LaMarsh; Minister of Labour, The Honourable John Nicholson; and Minister Without Portfolio, The Honourable John Turner.

40. House of Commons, *Debates 5*, (30 November 1967), 4875.

41. Ibid.

42. *Gazette* (Montreal), 2 December 1967.

43. *Montreal Star*, 2 December 1967.

44. *Globe and Mail* (Toronto), 4 December 1967.

45. Charles R. Delafield, interviewed by the author, audiocassette, 7 July 1971.

46. House of Commons, *Debates 5*, (4 December 1967), 4982.

47. *Gazette* (Montreal), 5 December 1967.

48. Editorial, *Globe and Mail*, 4 December 1967.

49. Editorial, *Montreal Star*, 4 December 1967.

50. Ibid.

51. Editorial, *Star* (Toronto), 4 December 1967.

52. Editorial, *Star* (Toronto), 6 December 1967.

53. Editorial, *News* (Wallaceburg, Ontario), 19 December 1967, clipping.

54. Letters to the Editor, *Gazette* (Montreal), 6 December 1967.

55. *Chronicle Herald* (Halifax, Nova Scotia), 9 December 1967, clipping.

56. Cited in *Gazette* (Montreal), 7 December 1967.

57. Telex Message PST102, from Department of External Affairs to C. R. Delafield, 8 December 1967.

58. Order in Council P.C. 1968-525, 19 March 1968; Statutes, *Broadcasting Act, 1968*, 16-17 Elizabeth 2, chap. 25.

59. Ibid.

5 ACHIEVING STABILITY, 1967-70

ORGANIZATION AFTER INTEGRATION

In 1963, the CBC conducted a feasibility study for possible integration with the International Service. When the government called for total integration in 1967, many of the preliminary consolidation plans had been completed by the corporation. Guy Coderre, the vice president for administration at CBC headquarters in Ottawa, wrote to the president of the corporation recommending "the adoption of a firm objective for the establishment of an external services division."[1]

Coderre attached a summary of his initial findings and analysis. According to Coderre, the external activities of the corporation involved the International Service, the three national domestic networks, and corporate relations, and were subdivided into the following categories: short-wave program service, program exchanges, export sales, external relations, and foreign offices. He suggested that a policy objective to integrate the external services be written that would take into account the interrelationships of the five categories of services. In 1963, Coderre had listed five general objectives for an external services division and he included them in his 1968 analysis:

(a) To arrange for access to foreign programming required by the national service.
(b) To reflect Canada's image and views abroad.
(c) To obtain revenue by the sale of CBC programs abroad.
(d) To provide for general relationships with foreign broadcasters, societies, etc., and for assistance to emerging nations.
(e) To provide a focal point within the Corporation for the coordination and management of activities listed in Items (a) to (d) through a combination of direct operating and service responsibilities and for coordinating related activities and requirements of the operating divisions.[2]

123

Coderre defended his objectives by observing that "The cohesiveness of the area [international division] is ensured by the specialization inherent to its non-domestic character."[3]

Prior to 1968, the International Service had performed these same tasks. What Coderre actually proposed was another bureaucratic layer, a separate division within CBC structure.

Figure 3 International Service Organizational Chart: 1962

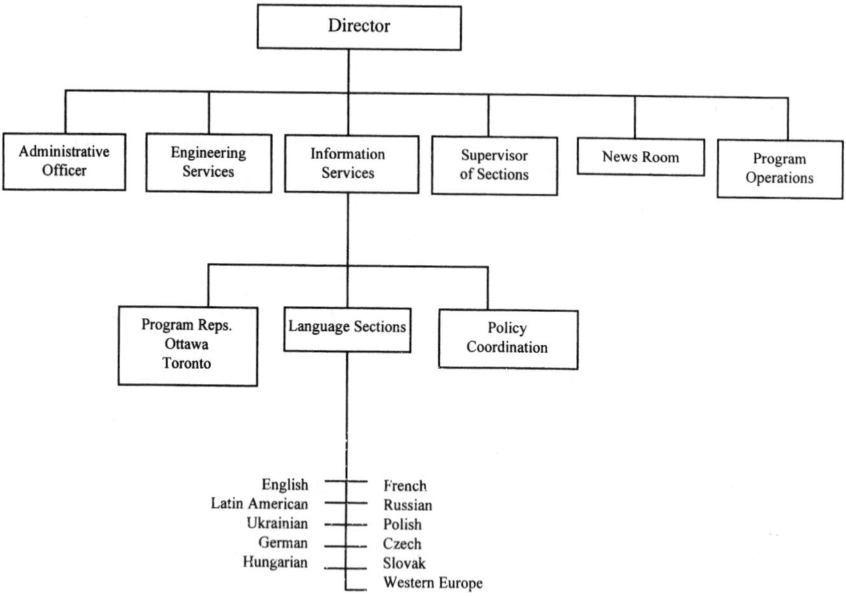

CORPORATE STRUCTURAL CHANGES

In 1963, the International Service was a separate division within the CBC with the director, CBC-IS, reporting directly to the vice president of the corporation (see fig. 3). After integration the Corporation rearranged the organizational structure by adding the new designation, External Services Division, which included the International Service (see fig. 4) . Following Coderre's lead, the primary purpose of the new division was to coordinate all CBC broadcast operations and exchanges with foreign offices.

Figure 4. International Service Organizational Chart, 1968.

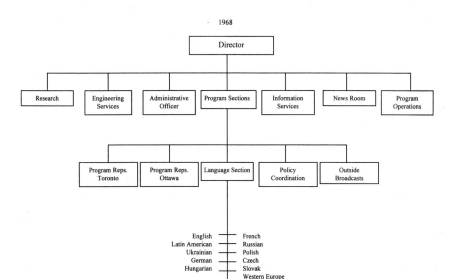

Lines of authority were modified as well. The director of the International Service now reported directly to the head, External Services Division, who, in turn, reported to the executive vice president of the corporation. The added layer of bureaucracy was in place.

Positions beneath the upper levels of management, although rearranged from earlier organizational structure, kept their traditional lines of authority and remained essentially the same as the 1959 example (see fig. 2). A new position, research, was added to the International Service in 1968. This officer was responsible for conducting and monitoring audience research. Another new section, outside broadcasts, was created to coordinate external broadcasting activities for the External Services Division. The supervisor of sections title was deleted from the organizational chart, but there was an officer in charge of the language sections, under the program sections designation. Since the lines of authority for this position were unchanged, this was a change in title only.

These organizational changes were minor. The major change occurred with the establishment of the External Services Division which became an "organizational mediator" for the International Service. Instead of the director of CBC-IS reporting directly to the vice president of the Corporation, he had to report to the director-general, External Services Division. The integration notion had little to do with administrative change; it was done for budgetary reasons. The integration of all broadcasting activities that were concerned with overseas operations (e.g., International Service, production liaisons in foreign offices) saved the corporation money because the inclusion of all the organizational elements under one budgetary category (External Services Division) prevented unnecessary duplications.

1963 POLICY STATEMENT AND PROGRAMMING POLICY

During the 1960s, the overall operational policy statement had become more general. In 1963, for example, the International Service intended "to provide an international broadcasting service, now supplemented by related transcriptions and television activities for the dissemination of Canadian news, views and information."[4] The statement recognized the importance of international shortwave radio broadcasting in projecting "information which helps to present and explain Canadian policies abroad" and "is a useful instrument of foreign policy." In simple terms, the International Service's basic task was "to present abroad an objective picture of Canada in all its variety and of Canadian points of view on national and international affairs" (1).

The significance of the 1963 policy statement is the lack of differences in general policy toward broadcasts beamed to Eastern Europe and those directed to the other target areas. For Canada, the Cold War era had begun to wane in the 1950s. As indicated in the policy statements for the 1960s, the International Service broadcasts were intended to present an objective reflection of the Canadian identity without any reference to a need for special ideological content in the programs beamed to Eastern Europe.

Program elements at CBC-IS followed a strict format policy that required each language service to follow three basic guidelines: 1) give "a clear account of what is going on in Canada and elsewhere through a news service which is comprehensive, accurate, and objective"; 2) include "explanations of Canadian policies and their background"; and 3) "present a picture of Canadian life in all its variety" (1).

For most international shortwave radio broadcasting services, the programming of the 1960s was categorized underneath broad headings of news, information, and entertainment. Talk radio programming was the predominant element. The International Service, according to the policy statement, relied heavily on talks covering "economic and cultural affairs, press reviews, profiles, actualities, interviews, mailbags (listener response to programming), and occasional music" (1).

The budgetary reductions and subsequent consolidations that were experienced during this decade affected the International Service programming by demanding more diversification. Sharing transmitter time with the Northern Service, for example, required greater use of supplementary broadcasting activities. The programming policies at CBC-IS were reflected in all aspects of the operations—shortwave services, transcriptions services, and relays.

REVIEW OF SHORTWAVE SERVICES

During the 1960s, the International Service broadcast in eleven languages. Although the number of languages used in the transmitted shortwave services stabilized during this period, there were modifications made in target areas. In 1961, an African service in English and French was inaugurated. This addition to the transmitted services was in line with Canada's interest in the emerging nations of Africa. Canada wanted to make its presence known to the younger nations of Africa and the International Service, sensitive to this need, broadcast a total of one hour and thirty minutes in English and French to the Dark Continent.[5]

By 1966, another consolidation effort brought about the inauguration of an Afro-European service. The distance from Sackville to Africa posed a transmission problem. The strength of the signal emanating from the Sackville transmitters proved inadequate for good reception. The CBC-IS transmitted the Afro-European service to Europe, then rebroadcast the program via rented BBC transmitters that were beamed to Africa. A total of 8:45 hours of weekly broadcast time in English and 7:00 hours in French were directed to audiences in Africa and Europe during this period (see table 9).

Table 9. Total Hours Broadcast Weekly to Africa from Sackville and via BBC Relays, 1966-70.*

Language	From Sackville	1966-1970 via BBC relays
English	5:15	3:30
French	5:15	1:45
Total	10:30	5:15

*These times were taken from the December program schedules or the nearest available month.

After 1966, the daily transmission schedule from Sackville commenced at 2:45 A.M. eastern standard time with the Afro-European service. The South Pacific service in English began at 3:25 A.M. The next transmission, from 7:15 A.M. to 8:43 A.M., provided programming in English and French to North America, Europe, the Caribbean, and parts of the United States (see table 10).

Table 10. Total Hours Broadcast Weekly in English and French to World Areas, 1960-70*

World Area	1960	1961	1962	1963	1964	1965	1966	1967	1968	1969	1970
Australasia	:30	:30	:30	1:30	1:30	1:10	1:00	1:00			
South Pacific**									1:00	1:00	1:00
Europe, U.S.A., Caribbean Area						1:00	1:00	1:00	1:00	1:00	1:00

*These times were taken from the December program schedules or the nearest available month.
**Directed to Australia, New Zealand, the South Pacific Islands, and the west coast of the U.S.A. and Mexico. Note: From 1960 to 1964, the hours broadcast were only in English; from 1965 to 1970, English and French each broadcast 30 minutes.

The first transmissions beamed to the Central and Eastern European target areas started at 8:45 A.M. when the Ukrainian broadcasts went on the air. The remainder of the Central and Eastern European services were described as follows:

The Ukrainian Service is followed by Czech and Russian, following which there are six minute news bulletins aimed at Europe in both French and English at mid-morning. The foreign language transmissions are resumed at 10:30 A.M. when the first Polish broadcast goes on the air. This is followed by the second segment of the Russian transmission, a 15-minute Slovak transmission beamed to Czechoslovakia, another Polish transmission, the second 30-minute Czech transmission, a 30-minute German-language transmission, and a 15-minute Hungarian broadcast.[6]

The budget reductions of 1961 did not affect these services; consequently, the total weekly hours did not vary much over the decade (see table 11).

Table 11. Total Hours Broadcast Weekly to Eastern Europe, 1960-70*

Language	1960	1961	1962	1963	1964	1965	1966	1967	1968	1969	1970
Czech	8:45	7:00	8:45	8:45	8:45	7:00	7:00	7:00	7:00	7:00	7:00
Slovak	1:45	1:45	1:45	1:45	1:45	1:45	1:45	1:45	1:45	1:45	1:45
Polish	7:00	7:00	8:15	8:15	8:15	5:15	7:00	7:00	5:15	5:15	5:15
Russian	6:15	7:00	7:00	7:00	7:00	5:15	5:15	5:15	5:15	5:15	5:15
Ukrainian	4:30	3:30	3:30	3:30	3:30	3:30	3:30	3:30	3:30	3:30	3:30
Hungarian	1:45	1:45	1:45	1:45	1:45	1:45	1:45	1:45	1:45	1:45	1:45
Totals	30:00	28:00	31:00	31:00	31:00	24:30	26:15	26:15	24:30	24:30	24:30

*These times were taken from the December program schedules or the nearest available month.

Similar to the arrangement with the BBC for the Afro-European service the International Service rented BBC transmitters beginning in 1968 that were used to rebroadcast Eastern European services beamed to the target area. This rental arrangement with the BBC provided the International Service with an excellent signal into Eastern Europe. Prior to this arrangement, the International Service had difficulty reaching many areas in Eastern Europe from the Sackville transmitting site. There were 22:45 hours of weekly broadcast time via BBC relay transmissions to Eastern Europe (see table 12).

The English service increased its total broadcast time from 11:40 hours in 1960 to 16:15 hours in 1966, and, the French service increased from 3:30 hours in 1960 to 11:15 hours in 1966. Both increases reflected new beam directions which included more than one area of the world in a transmission (see table 13). For example, beginning in late 1965 the English and French transmissions from Sackville were directed to the Caribbean, the United States, and Europe, and included another transmission to Europe later in the day. The Afro-European service, implemented in 1966, added to the area duplication, making the total hour count to Western Europe much higher.

Table 12. Total Hours Broadcast Weekly to Eastern Europe via BBC Relays, 1968-70*

Language	Length of Program	Broadcasts Per Week	Transmission Type	Total Time
Czech	:30	Daily	Simultaneous	3:30
Slovak	:15	Daily	Pre-recorded	1:45
Polish	:30	Daily	Simultaneous	3:30
	:15	Daily	Pre-recorded	1:45
Russian	:15	Daily	Pre-recorded	1:45
	:30	Daily	Simultaneous	3:30
Ukrainian	:30	Daily	Simultaneous	3:30
	:15	Daily	Pre-recorded	1:45
Hungarian	:15	Daily	Pre-recorded	1:45
Total Time				22:45

*These times were taken from the December program schedules or the nearest available month.

Table 13. Total Hours Broadcast Weekly to Western Europe, 1960-1970a

Language	1960	1961	1962	1963	1964	1965	1966	1967	1968	1969	1970
English	11:40	6:15	10:30	14:15	13:00	12:05	16:15	16:15	16:15	16:15	16:15
French	3:30	6:00	6:00	6:00	6:00	11:15	11:15	11:15	11:15	11:15	11:15
German	3:30	3:30	3:30	3:30	3:30	3:30	3:30	3:30	3:30	3:30 3:30[b]	3:30 3:30[b]
Totals	18:40	15:45	20:00	23:45	22:30	26:50	31:00	31:00	31:00	34:30	34:30

[a]These times were taken from the December program schedules or the nearest available month.
[b]Same broadcast, but different time, via BBC relay.

The German service broadcast hours remained constant throughout the period with 3:30 hours. The summary totals for Western Europe reflect the changes in priorities after the inauguration of the CBC Northern Service in 1961. In 1960, for example, 18:40 hours per week were beamed to Western Europe. This was decreased by nearly three hours in 1961. By 1966, however, through the use of rebroadcasting agreements with the BBC and duplication of services to certain areas, the CBC-IS overcame this loss and actually increased the total output to Western Europe by approximately 55 percent. The strategy for reaching maximum audience size in Western Europe included the scheduling of programs during the mid-afternoon so that the transmissions could be received during peak evening listening periods beginning at nine o'clock (8).

Finally, to complete the daily schedule, the Caribbean and Latin American service in Spanish, Portuguese, and English was broadcast during the evening hours (see table 14). Spanish was broadcast 5:15 hours per week and Portuguese, 3:30 hours. From 1960 to 1964, the average English weekly total was 3:30 hours. Because of area duplications from 1965-70, an average of 6:27 hours were added to the English-language broadcast time.

Table 14. Average Total Hours Broadcast Weekly to Caribbean Area, U.S.A., Latin America, 1960-70*

Language	From Sackville
Spanish	5:15
Portuguese	3:30
English	3:30
	6:27**
Total	18:42

*These times were taken from the December program schedules or the nearest available month.
**Europe, U.S.A., Caribbean Area, 1965-70.

The programming patterns for all transmitter services remained relatively unchanged from those patterns in the late 1950s. Primarily the programs were topical, which meant that whatever was news in Canada, or whatever theme was planned to illustrate an aspect of Canadian life and culture, was broadcast to the world audience. Essentially, all transmitted services consisted of the following:

> . . . news bulletins, commentaries, news reports, features, actualities, interviews, music, and replies to audience mail. They . . . [attempted to] include contributions by Canadians in many walks of life who report on and interpret the Canadian scene or who, as personalities, or experts, have something to say of interest to our listeners (8).

The English- and French-language sections could rely on program material from the CBC domestic services, or from outside contributors such as reporters or academicians the foreign language staffs then had to translate and adapt the material for broadcast. As a way of projecting Canadian opinion, outside contributors often read their own material for the English and French services.

In the preparation for programming, all language sections could call upon several sources for information. The CBC-IS newsroom, for example, provided all services with news reports for all transmitted services. In 1968, the International Service broadcast twenty-two news bulletins daily in various languages Monday through Friday, eighteen news bulletins on Saturday, and eleven on Sunday (8).

The policy coordination section supplied all language sections with commentaries, news reports, and talks on a variety of subjects. These scripts were written in English or French and subsequently translated or adapted where necessary. The French coordination section also transcribed broadcasts from the English and French domestic networks and circulated this material among all CBC-IS language sections for possible use (8).

The concern over duplication of services among all corporation broadcasting operations was virtually eliminated after integration. The CBC-IS, as a more directly appended division of the corporation, could rely more heavily upon all CBC programming activities. This cooperation was extremely useful in coordinating an objective presentation of the Canadian identity via the International Service.[7]

TRANSCRIPTION SERVICE

There was a significant increase in the shipment of spoken-word transcriptions in English, French, Spanish, and Portuguese during this period, with the largest increase occurring in 1967.

In 1966, 9,859:10 hours of program time were distributed while in 1967, largely because of the centennial celebration and Expo '67, the hours of program time distributed increased to 14,346:10.[8] In 1969, approximately 11,000 program hours of spoken-word transcriptions were shipped to foreign domestic services.[9]

Shipments of music transcriptions and tape increased more than the spoken-word transcriptions during the same period. In 1966, for example, 11,924:41 hours of music programs were shipped abroad while 46,523 program hours were shipped in 1967, the highest in the history of the International Service.[10]

In 1967, the International Service distributed free programs to any broadcasting service that requested them. The only stipulation was: "CBC-IS transcriptions may be broadcast any number of times, but they may not be commercially sponsored or used in television broadcasts. Unless specified, there is no expiry date."[11]

For the most part, the 1967 transcriptions were related to the centennial celebration and Expo '67. A series of eighteen thirty-minute programs for radio entitled "The Expo Lectures" were prepared for distribution. These lectures were given by internationally known scholars and experts at the Expo site and included Dr. Barbara Ward, Dr. John Kenneth Galbraith, and Dr. Linus Pauling, among others.[12]

Beginning in 1963, the CBC International Service presented a series of fifty-two thirty-minute programs on Canadian history as a part of the pre-centennial observance. There was a laudatory response to the series from the audience and from foreign broadcasting services requesting the programs. Mail responses indicated that the audience wanted printed material they could read and study. The International Service published the texts of the fifty-two programs in four paperback volumes and made the series available to the audience free of charge.[13]

A collaboration with RCA Victor Company, Limited, resulted in the commercial release of "Music and Musicians of Canada," a seventeen-record collection of Canadian music; a nine-record album of folk music entitled "Canadian Folk Songs"; a recording of Calixa Lavallee's "The Widow" by the CBC Symphony Orchestra of Winnipeg; and the first commercial recording by the Montreal Symphony Orchestra.[14] This was, by any standard, an important element in the "projection of Canada" theme, and one that reached a wider audience than shortwave radio broadcasting. In 1969, the International Service distributed more than 49,000 program hours of music to some 130 countries and territories of the world.

A year earlier the International Service had distributed only 15,000 programs. This increase of more than 300 percent represented a considerable
investment in musical programming which included both transcriptions,
featuring Canadian composers and performers in both quarter-hour and
half-hour formats, and higher quality pressed recordings of both
Canadian folk and classical music performances.[15]

The transcription service evolved into an important operation of the
International Service. For information dissemination, the transcription
service provided foreign domestic broadcasting services with program
material about Canada. Since these transcribed programs were broadcast
on medium wave frequencies (standard AM broadcast band) by the foreign services, it was possibe that they were reaching larger audiences than
they would on the international shortwave radio broadcasting frequencies. The response to these transcriptions was highly favorable.[16]

RELAYS

Another supplementary operation, relays, was used extensively during
this period. A relay was defined as "a special program or program item
based on a Canadian event of probable interest to a particular country,
and prepared for release on the domestic service of that country."[17] Relays
were requested by target country broadcasting services and were delivered
by transoceanic cable or by tape via airline shipment. For example, in
1969, the German section of CBC-IS, a frequent user of relays, provided
German-language stations with 359 items which were broadcast over
more than a dozen stations for a total of ninety-four broadcast hours.
Typical items were topical news reports, actualities, talks, interviews, and
analyses of Canadian current events in a magazine format. They were
rarely timely, giving the target broadcasting service ample time to schedule them on the domestic networks.

As with the transcription service, the relays provided foreign broadcasting services with program material about Canada. Since the relays were
often fed directly into the foreign domestic network via undersea cable or
satellite, numerous network affiliates broadcast the item simultaneously,
thereby insuring even greater timely audience coverage and better information dissemination. In West Germany, for example, an International
Service item broadcast via a domestic radio network during the traffic rush
hours, morning and afternoon, would reach thousands of listeners.

OTHER BROADCASTING SERVICES

Since the late 1950s, the CBC-IS had the responsibility for distributing television programs to foreign networks. The CBC *Annual Report* of 1967-68 observed that the International Service "regularly" distributed its video program *Canada Magazine* to more than thirty countries.[18] By 1970, however, the use of television for foreign distribution was discontinued because of the high production costs.[19]

In 1963, another broadcasting operation for the shortwave hobbyist was added to CBC-IS programming: the Radio-Canada Shortwave Club. Club membership was open to shortwave listeners (SWLs) anywhere in the world:

> The Club is intended for that large body of people who are interested in international shortwave broadcasting and who wish to keep in touch with technical developments in telecommunications in Canada.
>
> To qualify for Club membership, applicants must send in five different reception reports of any Radio Canada shortwave broadcast.
>
> . . . each reception report must include the frequency and wavelength, time and date of transmission as well as some program details. . . . to continue as a member in good standing, each member must send in at least one reception report each month.[20]

The Radio-Canada Shortwave Club was an effective means for keeping in close contact with a certain segment of the international shortwave broadcasting listening audience. The reception reports were invaluable to the engineering section of the International Service for frequency management; program comments were important to the producers of the various language sections; and club correspondence increased the number of letters received by the International Service. All club members were welcomed visitors at Radio-Canada whenever they traveled to Montreal. In short, the Radio-Canada Shortwave Club was an effective public relations tool. By the end of 1969 club membership was 8,452.[21]

In retrospect, CBC-IS program operations in the 1960s followed a strict format policy that placed certain requirements on each language service: to provide a comprehensive, accurate, and objective news service; to explain Canadian policies; and to present a picture of Canadian life. Yet the budgetary reductions and subsequent consolidations at the International Service demanded more diversification in the use of shortwave services, transcriptions, and relays.

By 1970, the CBC-IS had achieved a greater degree of stability as an international broadcasting operation. The total budgetary and administrative integration with the corporation gave the International Service constitutional and financial stability. The troubling times of near-abolishment had faded, offering the hope of a brighter, more secure future.

NOTES

1. Internal Memorandum from Guy Coderre, vice president, administration, to president, CBC, 15 January 1968.
2. Ibid.
3. Ibid.
4. Canadian Broadcasting Corporation, "International Service: Policies and Practices," (Montreal: International Service, 1963 mimeographed), 1.
5. CBC International Service Program Schedule, September-October, 1961 (Montreal: Canadian Broadcasting Corporation International Service, 1961), 1.
6. "International Service, 1968," 8. 7. Brian Townsley, interviewed by the author, Montreal, 5 November 1971.
8. "International Service, 1968," app. no. 6.
9. Canadian Broadcasting Corporation, Annual Report, 1968-69 (Ottawa: Canadian Broadcasting Corporation, 1969), 59.
10. "CBC International Service, 1968," app. no. 6.
11. Catalogue entry, Transcription Service.
12. Ibid.
13. Charles R. Delafield introduction to The Ordeal of New France: The French Colonial Period, by W. J. Eccles, (Montreal: Pierre Des Marais, Inc., for the C.B.C. International Service, 1969), v. The titles of two volumes written by Laurier LaPierre were: Genesis of a Nation: The British Colonial Period; and The Apprenticeship: The Dominion of Canada's First Half Century. D. C. Masters authored the final volume, The Coming of Age: The Modern Era, 1914-1967.
14. Canadian Broadcasting Corporation," Annual Report, 1967-68 (Ottawa: The Canadian Broadcasting Corporation, 1968), 45.
15. Canadian Broadcasting Corporation, "CBC International Service Annual Report, 1969," (Montreal: International Service, 1968, mimeographed), 1.
16. Ibid.
17. Ibid.
18. Annual Report, 1967-68, 45.
19. Brian Townsley, interviewed by the author, 8 July 1971.
20. Canadian Broadcasting Corporation, "Radio-Canada Shortwave Club Information" Montreal; International Service, n.d., mimeographed).
21. Canadian Broadcasting Corporation, Annual Report, 1968-69 (Ottawa: Canadian Broadcasting Corporation, 1969), 38.

6 TRANSITIONS, 1971-74

As THE INTERNATIONAL Service moved into the 1970s, its primary operational policy continued to be the "expression of Canadian identity by means of shortwave broadcasting, supplemented by relays, transcriptions, and sound and visual recordings."[1] To aid implementation of that policy, the following subgoals were established:

1. *Content.* Programming is to be primarily Canadian content and character.
2. *Quality.* Programming for international broadcasting and distribution is to be of an expert quality suitable to the target audience.
3. *Balance.* Balance is to be maintained between information, enlightenment and entertainment.
4. *Recognition of Canadian Talent.* The International Broadcasting Service is to contribute to the international recognition of Canadian talent.
5. *Scope.* The International Broadcasting Service, in consultation with the Department of External Affairs, should be extended or revised, in time, languages and areas covered in accordance with changing priorities, available facilities and financial resources (1-2).

From its inception, the International Service had pursued similar objectives and since World War II, the "projection of the Canadian identity" was the underlying theme of all programming broadcast by the International Service. During the transitional phase, 1971-74, the CBC-IS staff implemented its operational objectives according to an organizational structure which included a director, assistant director, and a manager of information programming.

The director held the highest level of responsibility within the International Service. The official duties and responsibilities of this position included planning, organizing, directing, and controlling the activities of the International Service by reporting and maintaining liaison with government

137

departments "to secure or exchange information and data required for the formulation of I.S. policy."[2]

Since the director was directly responsible for following Department of External Affairs policy guidelines, an examination of government involvement is essential in discovering precisely how and to what degree the International Service was advised by government in the broadcasting operations. In 1971, Charles Delafield explained the degree of involvement with government in the following manner:

> . . . once a year . . . we review with External Affairs what we are currently doing and what our plans are; what we think we should be doing. This is usually done by . . . letter, saying to External Affairs, here is where we are now, these are the areas of the world that we think should be covered, and this is the way we see Canadian interests developing.
>
> We're not the final experts in this of course . . . External Affairs, representing all government departments, is the key department in terms of overseas projection of Canada by any form, whether it's films, or whether it's trade fairs, or whatever.
>
> We put down on paper our own thinking and send this to External Affairs and say, "Appreciate your comments." This usually seems to be a more satisfactory way of doing it than to say to them, "Let us have your views," because you make the thing more precise this way . . . you can put down what you want and get specific comments. So, obviously enough, we talk in terms of areas of the world we're not covering . . . we review what we are doing and ask them comments on: Are we less concerned about, let us say, South America than we are concerned about the Caribbean? What are your order of priorities? Can we get some idea of whether we should be doing more to the Caribbean and less to Latin America? I just use this as an example.
>
> So they reply to this after it has been circulated in the various areas of the Department. The Deputy Minister has a look at it and it may be, if he isn't satisfied with it, he will obviously refer it to the Minister. But the reply we are going to get back is a pretty complete indication of their thinking.
>
> . . . they may say we should be doing this in the space of the next two or three years. *We still have the right to decide what we are going to do* [italics mine]. We don't necessarily have to follow their guidelines. On the other hand, we would be stupid if we did something entirely different which they thought was of no particular significance or rather low on the priority list. We've got a perfect right to do it but after all, we wouldn't be terribly responsible if we did.

That is the way it works. They don't tell us what sort of program service we should provide. They don't tell us what sort of transcription service, what sort of projection of Canada, in terms of programs, we should be doing.[3]

What deserves attention is the sequence of events related to the consultation with External Affairs. First, once a year, Delafield *initiated* the consultation with a letter outlining CBC-IS views concerning target audiences and programming goals. Second, External Affairs replied in the form of a letter, making comments about priorities of programming directed to different areas of the world. In short, External Affairs staff members offered "their thinking" about the CBC-IS proposal. Third, External Affairs never suggested programming styles or supervised programming content. Strictly speaking, the "projection of Canada" was an International Service interpretation. Finally, Delafield asserted the right to broadcast independently from government control:

> You can put out government propaganda if you want to, but if no one listens to it or no one believes in it, the whole thing is self-defeating. And, this is well understood by the Department [of External Affairs]. That's the strongest argument we have: "You want people to listen, you have to leave it to us; we are the broadcasting experts. And, we can only promise you that we'll do a responsible job. . . ."[4]

ORGANIZATIONAL STRUCTURE

Although the director was responsible for the entire operation of the International Service, he had assistance in policy formulation and implementation from two other key managerial posts: assistant director and manager of information programming (see fig. 5). Under the guidance of the director, the assistant director planned, organized, directed, and evaluated the operations of the International Service. The job classification document outlined the duties and responsibilities of this position:

> . . . assists the Director in developing objectives by formulating or recommending changes in I.S. policies; maintains liaison with Government departments in order to exchange information and data required for the operation of the Service.[5]

Figure 5. Organizational Chart

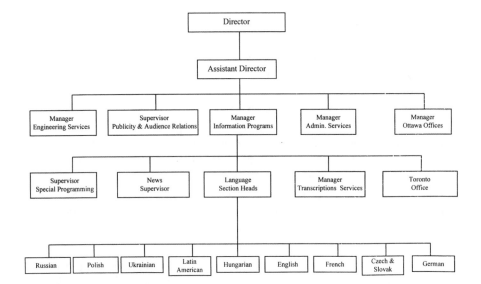

Whereas the director and assistant director had the responsibility for the formulation of operational policy, the manager of information programming assumed the job of implementing the policy in the daily broadcasting activities of the International Service:

> [The Manager] plans, organizes and directs the programming of the language sections, including news, current affairs, and special events distributed by shortwave, tapes, transcriptions and films.[6]

More specifically, the manager of information programming had the responsibilities and authority for providing guidance and direction to:

1. . . . the Heads of the foreign language sections in all matters relating to their sphere of activity.
2. . . . the Newsroom Supervisor regarding the operation of the news services and their relationship to the language sections.
3. . . . the provision of suitable talks, press reviews and comment for the use of the language sections.[7]

In addition he was responsible for planning, developing, and supervising the music and transcription department and its distribution activities; for arranging coordination of outside events; for supervision of the program output of the Ottawa and Toronto production offices; and for providing other program resources as required.[8]

In 1971, Lucien Coté, manager of information programming, commented on the responsibilities of Manager. Regarding the supervision of the section heads, Coté revealed:

> Policy is very simple. We're not sub-stations for any foreign radio. We tell about international affairs and we insist that they look closely at the Canadian news to help us meet the objectives about the reflection of Canada. So, if some section forgets about Canadian content, we try to see that this is changed.[9]

Since Coté supervised the newsroom staff and helped select stories for broadcast, he served as a primary "gatekeeper" for all news reports broadcast on CBC-IS. As chief editor of all programming content, Coté was also concerned with the commentaries broadcast from all sections. According to Coté, listeners preferred four-to-five minute newscasts followed by commentaries embellishing the background of featured news items to lengthy newscasts which he maintained "were tedious" and failed to retain the interest of listeners. These uncensored commentaries, written by both CBC-IS and outside writers (newspaper and magazine reporters, or university professors), were intended "to reflect a variety, an objective balance, of Canadian opinion about a topic."[10]

Under the 1971 organizational structure, a current affairs officer assisted Coté in the preparation of commentaries for broadcast. He reported directly to the manager of information programming and held additional responsibilities for talks and feature programs on current national and international matters. The current affairs officer also hired journalists and economists for the writing of commentaries.[11]

The manager of information programming was also assisted in the maintenance of high-quality production standards through listening sessions with the director, assistant director, and supervisor, publicity and audience relations. The listening sessions, held once a week, analyzed the content and the production quality. The content analysis, for example, determined whether or not the news bulletins on a particular topic were consistent among all language sections. The production quality represented the overall "sound" of the program, e.g., the program format, pacing, and announcing style. After the listening session, a production critique was sent to the producer for review. The primary objectives of the critique sessions were to maintain standards and to offer constructive criticism.[12]

To aid in the implementation of policies the manager of information programming was assisted by four staff members: the supervisor of special programming, the news supervisor, the manager of the transcription services, and the International Service representative stationed in Toronto.

The supervisor of special programming coordinated all external activities of the International Service in both radio and film for overseas relay transmissions or shipment. The news supervisor directed the daily newsroom operation and its relationship to the language sections. The planning, direction, coordination, production, and distribution of both music and spoken-word transcriptions of the International Service were the responsibility of the manager of transcription services. The International Service representative in Toronto established and maintained contacts with governmental, cultural, educational, institutional, and religious groups. This figure also represented CBC-IS with the ethnic communities in the Greater Toronto area and advised section heads on current and future events. Toronto, a cosmopolitan center of numerous ethnic organizations, provided program ideas to augment the "projection of Canada" theme.

The manager of information programming held the key position of overseeing the entire operations of CBC-IS. Those responsible for the daily broadcasting activities, however, were the heads of sections. The heads of sections were subordinate to the manager of information programming. The foreign-language section heads were responsible for planning and coordinating production of daily programs; for shortwave broadcasting; and for planning, coordinating, and providing programs (audio tape, film, or transcriptions) to foreign broadcasting organizations within the geographic target area.

The duties of the English- and the French-language section heads were similar, except that they held additional duties of negotiating terms with the CBC domestic network authorities for joint-program exchanges with foreign services.

The four main managerial positions for the daily operations were director, assistant director, manager of information programming, and the heads of sections. Subordinate to these four managerial posts in the administration were the managers of engineering services, administrative services, and the Ottawa offices, and the supervisor of publicity and audience relations.

The manager of engineering services was responsible for planning and evaluating aspects of shortwave operations to ensure optimum effectiveness of high-frequency transmissions and reception. He recommended the broadcast times, frequencies, and antenna beam directions for optimum coverage of current or projected target areas.[13]

The manager of administrative services was in charge of all budgetary and contractual matters, and also supervised personnel, industrial relations, office services, and finances.

The manager of the Ottawa office was a new position. As the representative of the International Service, he was a key advisor to the director and was responsible for maintaining liaisons with Canadian government departments, agencies, and organizations, and with diplomatic missions in Ottawa. A source of information, particularly concerning activities and programs of Parliament having a bearing on operational policies of the International Service, his sphere of influence included Canadian policy projects in the external, political, economic, social, and cultural areas.[14]

An administrative officer stationed in Ottawa was appropriate for policy formulation. The geographic separation between Montreal and Ottawa had been cumbersome for International Service managers. The daily presence of a CBC-IS administrative officer working in Ottawa was undoubtedly useful in discerning governmental policies.

The supervisor of publicity and audience relations was responsible for publicity and listener correspondence. He supervised the administration of the Radio-Canada Shortwave Club, initiated, organized, and supervised International Service participation in listener polls and surveys, special publicity events, exhibitions, and conferences. The supervisor also distributed publicity materials to the press, established and maintained contacts with representatives of the press, government departments, and Canadian overseas missions for CBC-IS promotional purposes.[15]

In 1971, the International Service added only two new positions to the administrative structure: manager of information programming and manager of the Ottawa office. In reality, the manager of information programming was simply another name for what had been called supervisor of sections, although additional lines of authority were now placed under the Manager's jurisdiction, since he became responsible for all programming output via shortwave, relays, and transcriptions.

The other new position, manager of the Ottawa office, was an important addition to the CBC-IS staff. Housed in Ottawa, across the street from the Parliament buildings, the manager maintained close contact with government officials and advised the director, of the Service on policy matters. In the past, the mechanics of liaison had been a point of considerable discussion for the International Service; placing a staff member in Ottawa was a positive step toward strengthening its position with governmental agencies.

OVERVIEW OF OPERATIONS

In July 1971, the CBC-IS shortwave services to Europe were greatly improved with the installation of two new 250-kilowatt transmitters at Sackville. This new equipment, the subject of much discussion since the Fowler Report of 1965, together with the original three fifty-kilowatt transmitters, substantially increased the operating efficiency of the International Service.

In 1971, the International Service broadcast a total of 138:36 hours to six areas: Western Europe, Eastern Europe, Caribbean-U.S.A., Latin America, Africa, and South Pacific.

There were 33:08 weekly hours (24 percent) broadcast to Western Europe with the following breakdowns: English, 15:10 hours; French, 10:58 hours; and German, 7:00 hours weekly. Eastern Europe was again the most important single world area with a total of 50:45 hours broadcast weekly (37 percent). Russian and Ukrainian languages received the majority of broadcast time for Eastern Europe, (19:15 hours), with Czech and Slovak second (17:30), Polish third (10:30), and Hungarian last, with 3:30 hours each week.

The CBC-IS broadcasts in English and in French to the Caribbean-United States totaled 19:50 hours weekly. Although prior to 1971, the English and French transmission paths from Sackville actually covered states along the U.S. eastern seaboard, it was not until 1971 that the United States was officially recognized as a broadcast target area; in this year16:34 hours were broadcast weekly in English, and 3:16 hours in French. In 1971, Latin America received transmissions from three language services: English (3:30), Spanish (5:22), and Portuguese (3:30), for a total of 12:22 hours weekly broadcast time.

Beginning in 1970, transmissions in English and in French broadcast to Africa totaled 15:31 hours with the former receiving one and a half hours more broadcast time than the latter. Interestingly, Africa received more than three hours more broadcast time each week than Latin America. Lucien Coté, manager of information programming, explained why such a high priority was placed on Africa: "[Our broadcasts are] a part of Canada's aid to Africa. The African is curious. He wants to know what's going on in the rest of the world. He wants to know about various ordinary matters . . . this is enough to justify our service to Africa."[16]

The final target area, South Pacific, received 7:00 hours weekly broadcasting time in English. This area includes Australia and New Zealand with which Canada has Commonwealth interests.

PROGRAMMING PATTERNS

The general goal of the International Service programming was to project the Canadian identity to the world radio audience. Therefore, each of the eleven language services planned programming to fit this operational goal.

WESTERN EUROPE

English

The English Section beamed four transmissions to Western Europe for a total of 15:10 hours each week. Two of these daily transmissions were relayed to additional target areas, e.g., Afro-European and Europe-North America, and two were directed exclusively to the European continent. The programming continued to follow the broadcasting magazine format. The daily program, "Today's Magazine," for example, was designed to feature various topics chosen to represent Canadian life, focusing on culture, economics, or government. A sample week from 1971 broadcasts, 18-24 July, illustrates an example of programming patterns (see Appendix C for the complete weekly report). During that week, "Monday Magazine" contained the following topics: Morocco's future under King Hussan; interview with Dr. Ray Lawson on traditional treatments for breast cancer; and a talk on diamonds.[17] Other programs, such as "Aspects of Canada," and "Focus," were similar in format and content.

The following items from the current affairs officer are representative of the special features broadcast by the English section to Europe during the same week:

COMMENTARY: Soviet View of Mr. Nixon's China Visit
                 By: Axel Krause, *Business Week*, correspondent, Moscow

PRESS REVIEW: President Nixon's Planned Visit to China
                     By: V. I. Rajewsky, CBC-IS Staff
TALK: Oil Exploration Threatens Sable Island Wild Horses
                     By: Bill Hammerhand, Halifax
INTERVIEW: Transportation of Oil Through Arctic Water
                     Interview with Dr. B. R. Pelletier, Marine Ecology
                     By: Ron McInnes, CBC, Halifax[18]

During this same period, the English section sent recordings of the "Canadian Press Review," a compilation of opinions from the various newspapers across Canada, to domestic services in Europe. Similar arrangements were made for "The World of Science," "l'Attitude," and "Forum."[19]

French

The French section programming beamed to Europe was via three 45-minute transmissions for a total of 10:58 hours per week. Two of these transmissions included additional world areas in the beam pattern, Africa and U.S.A.-Caribbean, and one was directed exclusively to Europe.

The French Section Weekly Report for the period 18-24 July shows that the programming patterns in French closely resembled those in English. For example, daily newscasts were followed by special reports, commentaries, or features. On Monday, 19 July, a Canadian press review, prepared by the public affairs staff, was broadcast in French. Moreover, the all of weekly programming contained numerous "projection of Canada" subjects such as travel to the Klondike, Arctic exploration, theatre notes, and pipeline construction.[20]

German

The thirty-minute German program, "Hier Sprict Kanada," was broadcast twice daily to Europe. Gerd Pick, head of the German section, reported that the broadcasting magazine format was selected after he had made several field trips to West Germany.[21]

According to Pick, music was selected for a young audience and was used mostly as thirty-second transitions between program segments. Classical music was not programmed because of the fading and interference problems associated with shortwave broadcasting.

Pick stressed that the most important elements of the programming were news and information about Canada. Following the newscast, vari-

ous talk shows were broadcast to project the Canadian identity. During
the sample week, for example, the following items were broadcast on
Monday, 19 July:

NEWS BULLETIN:	Packing for Peking
NEWS COMMENTARY:	Opportunity for Youth Programme
TALK:	Young Canadians Travel and Learn
TALK:	Life in Isolated Village Faces Industry Change
	Stock Market Report.[22]

Pick believed that information programs could also be entertaining. He
observed that a short talk entitled "Pedal Power," basically a report on the
rise of bicycling in Canada, was also entertainment because of the writer's
slant. Another information-entertainment program segment broadcast 25
July 1971, "Red Carpet Dog Centre," was a short news item about a dog
"hotel." The primary sources for these features were newspaper and magazine articles.[23]

The German section did not produce a transcription service because
West German domestic stations preferred short program segments. Thus,
live relay transmissions via transatlantic cable to the German networks in
Austria, West Germany, and Switzerland were broadcast simultaneously
by all affiliates. This mode of transmission could include all networks in
West Germany and Austria, or of them, subject to prior negotiations. The
telephone cable-network transmissions were of three types: a two-way
talk report between a German section staff member and a reporter from a
network; a direct news report to a network; and a relay for delayed transmission. The length of the program items varied but the typical length was
about two minutes. If, for example, there was an important news event in
Canada, a network representative in West Germany telephoned Pick and
asked for a detailed report for a newscast. At a predetermined time, Pick
broadcast direct to the West German network and to its station affiliates,
either from his home or from his office. The source of the report, Radio
Canada, was identified at the beginning and at the end of the news item.
A much larger radio audience was reached using direct broadcast reporting than would have been possible via shortwave broadcasts. Unlike the
other language services, the German section made extensive use of direct
broadcast feeds to the West German networks and affiliate stations.[24]

Although the German section broadcast from Sackville only thirty minutes daily (with an additional delayed BBC relay later in the day), it con-

sistently received more mail than the other language services beamed to Western Europe. Pick attributed much of this popularity to the fast pace of the program and the imitation of the West German AM broadcast station programming.

The programming patterns of the English, French, and German sections beamed to Western Europe reflected the basic operational goal of the "projection of Canada" theme. The question remained: What type of broadcasts were beamed to Eastern Europe?

EASTERN EUROPE

Czech

Unlike the decade of the 1950s, at which time the Czech section was broadcasting polemic political commentaries on the news, the operational policy in 1971, according to Walter Schmolka, head of section, stipulated that the programming in Czech should project the Canadian identity.[25] To accomplish the operational policy, two thirty-minute programs were broadcast via four transmissions daily for a total of 14:00 hours per week.

Each transmission began with a news report covering international and Canadian news. The balance of the program consisted of various features depicting Canadian life to the Czech listeners. On Tuesday, 20 July, for example, the following segments were included in the Czech transmissions:

NEWS BULLETIN NO. 2

NEWS COMMENTARY:	Soviet Views of Mr. Nixon's China Visit
	By: A. Krause, *Business Week Magazine*
	Correspondent, Moscow
PRESS REVIEW:	Looking Through the Canadian Newspapers:
	Canada and the East Pakistan Tragedy
	By: R. Olynk
SPORTS TALK:	Sports Review:
	1. The Women's British Amateur Athletic Association Championship in London
	2. Inglesais Captures Swim
	3. Atlanta Chiefs Win Over Montreal Olympics
	4. Tour de la Nouvelle France
	By: M. Vitek[26]

The Czech section programmed a wide variety of topics to fit the "projection of Canada" theme: cultural and economic news, sports, and philately. This programming pattern was followed throughout the broadcast week.

Slovak

Broadcasting a total of 3:30 hours per week (including BBC relays), the Slovak section programmed only one fifteen-minute daily transmission. Although limited in time, the Slovak service broadcast a daily program which contained a newscast, a commentary, press reviews, and music. Different days of the week were scheduled with different topics. For example, Sundays were devoted to listener requests for music; Mondays were reserved for special features and music; Wednesdays concentrated on sports, and so on. The following is representative of the programming content for Saturdays:

LETTERBOX:	Answering Listeners' Questions on: Canadian Dollar and the Development of Canada's Currency
	By: I. Trevichavsky
TALK:	International Stamp Corner:
	1. British Columbia Centennial Stamp
	2. Philatelic Contest
	By: I Trevichavksy[27]

Hungarian

The Hungarian section broadcast 3:30 hours weekly. According to audience mail, the program reached not only the target country, Hungary, but also minorities in Czechoslovakia, Romania, Yugoslavia, and Hungarians in Sweden, Israel, and Australia.[28]

About one-third of the Hungarian-language program was devoted to news; one-third focused on commentary or press review; and the remaining segments consisted of features on Canadian life. Following is a description of the 1971 Hungarian service:

> Recording tours, interviews with prominent Canadian-Hungarians, press clippings, help us to prepare "city roundups." A great number of listeners have family ties with Canada. (Relatives and friends of the 1956 Hungarian refugees—37,500—create a large listener's camp.) Interest in Canada is

growing year by year. Cultural exchange between the two countries is the most important (music, sport, sciences) but also in trade, Canada is considered a good Western trade partner. Canadian experience in modern production reported on in our programs, is followed with interest, especially since the Hungarian Government started a new economic system in which foreign experience and personal contacts could be used by individuals.[29]

The Hungarian section's programming closely followed the patterns of other Eastern European services. Polemic broadcasting was a thing of the past.

Polish

In 1971, the Polish section broadcast, including relays, a total of 10:30 hours per week. Programming one thirty-minute and one fifteen-minute transmission daily, the Polish service resembled the other Eastern European broadcasts. On Wednesday, 21 July, for example, the following items were broadcast:

> NEWS BULLETIN:
> TALK: The Mariposa Folk Festival
> FEATURE: Canadian Chronicle:
>   1. Canada-Peking Air Link
>   2. Ants May help Fight Forest Pests
>   By: V. Rjewsky.

Similar programs were scheduled on the rest of the days during the sample week.[30]

Russian

Carroll Chipman, head of the Russian section, reported that the basic purpose of the Russian broadcasts was to project Canada. Through a programming total of 11:45 hours weekly, the Russian section attempted to satisfy the projection theme by conveying Canadian interests to the Russian audience. Chipman characterized the Russian service as: ". . . radio people and operate much the same way as any local broadcasting station. We want to broadcast and have a dialogue with our listeners."[31]

Because the transmissions were received in Moscow before most people arrived home from work, Chipman believed that most of his listeners were professionals:

. . . we get the intelligentsia, the academician, the musician, and so on. These are the people we count as our listeners. And we've really shaped our program to meet the needs of people we know listen to us, not just from letters we get but from people we speak to who come here. . . .[32]

To meet the needs of the Russian audience, Chipman reported that he was free to select any topic for broadcast:

We deliberately do not interfere in their domestic affairs. As a matter of policy . . . we are free to make radio decisions. Twenty years ago we had to ask if it were wise to criticize this or that. We were thinking in political terms. Now, since we are not allowed to speak about domestic affairs, we ask, is this interesting? Or, in other words, we make radio decisions.[33]

The Russian section broadcast a magazine format similar to other CBC-IS language services. On Friday, 24 July 1971, for example, the following was broadcast in Russian:

	NEWS BULLETIN:
NEWS TALK:	Chou En Lai's Eight-Point Plan for Better
	Relations with U.S.A.
	By: Colin Godbold
FEATURE:	Ideas and Action No. 127
	Slavic Conference in Montreal.[34]

The subject matter for this sample broadcast was not unlike the programming for other Eastern European Countries: it was directed toward the interests of the audience but did not attempt to project Canadian government views on international issues. In this way, Russian broadcasts reflected the overall operational objective of projecting things Canadian.

Ukrainian

The programming in Ukrainian consisted of three thirty-minute daily transmissions. In 1971, J. B. Wesolowsky, head of the Ukrainian section, reported that the major target audience was located in Poland, Yugoslavia, Czechoslovakia, and the Soviet Union. With more than 700,000 Ukrainians living in Canada at that time, the Ukrainian section drew from an abundance of programming sources. For example, Ukrainian musicians and choirs in various Canadian cities performed religious programs for CBC-IS broadcasts to Eastern Europe.[35]

The Ukrainian section's programming pattern deviated from the other Eastern European sections with only two regularly scheduled features, both of which were broadcast on Sundays—"Sundays Prayer" and "International Letter Box." Wesolowsky reported that he usually planned programming on a day-to-day basis and used topical items that were requested by listeners via mail.[36] Nevertheless, a copy of the Ukrainian Weekly Report, from 1971 shows that the programming content of the Ukrainian transmissions were similar to the other Eastern European services.[37]

LATIN AMERICA

English

The English section programmed only 3:30 hours per week to Latin America. The basic program format for all English-language services was abbreviated to accommodate the shorter program length to this world area. The following items, broadcast Monday through Friday, were illustrative:

Radio Canada News
Today's Magazine
Sports, Stocks, Weather & News Headlines

Saturday and Sunday programs deviated slightly from the pattern:

Saturday	Sunday
Radio Canada News	Radio Canada News
Focus	Listeners Corner Part II
Radio Canada Shortwave Club	The In Bit
Sports & News Headlines	Sports & News Headlines[38]

A comparison of weekly reports for all English-language services shows there was a high degree of similarity in the programming content.[39]

Spanish

The Spanish section broadcast 5:32 hours to Latin America weekly. An excerpt from a 1971 the weekly report demonstrates that the Spanish section employed a forty-five-minute magazine program format comparable to the services discussed above.

Wednesday, 21 July 1971

NEWS BULLETIN:	National and International News for the Spanish-speaking Audience
NEWS COMMENTARY:	The Review of the Federal Labor Code By: Wilfred List
CULTURAL TALK:	Philately - A Series of Programmes on New Stamps By: Carlos Davila
INFORMATIONAL TALK:	Canadian Cities - Yellowknife By: José Barrio
MUSICAL INTERLUDE:	Pete Fountain, Clarinet Solo[40]

J. J. Rodriguez, head of the Spanish section, emphasized the importance of information programming beamed to Latin America. Citing two instances which illustrated that CBC-IS programming fostered trade agreements between a Latin American country and Canada. When a news feature on Canadian locomotive manufacturing was broadcast in Spanish, he received a letter from a Latin American company executive requesting more information. After reviewing the information, the Latin American company initiated an order to purchase railroad locomotives from the Canadian manufacturer. A similar situation involving a news feature on sewing machine needle manufacturing in Quebec also led to a Latin American-Canadian trade agreement.[41]

The Spanish section made extensive use of transcriptions, including a series of thirty-minute programs on Shakespearean drama, and several musical selections. In 1971, the transcriptions were shipped to more than 200 domestic services in Latin America.[42]

Portuguese

E. O. Butcher, head of the Portuguese section, reported that the half-hour program beamed to Brazil was a broadcast magazine format, i.e., different program topics were broadcast by days of the week. The weekly report shows that the programming was similar to that on the Spanish service.[43]

CARIBBEAN-U.S.A., AFRICA, AND SOUTH PACIFIC

Since only two languages, English and French, were broadcast to the diverse areas of the Caribbean-U.S.A., Africa, and the South Pacific, they are discussed as one.

The English section broadcast 16:34 hours to the Caribbean-U.S.A., 8:31 hours to Africa, and 7:00 hours to the South Pacific in 1971. The English section used the same program format as the services beamed to Europe and the numerous duplications of English-language program content were without a doubt reflective of the need for cost effectiveness. The differences in programming content that was more appropriate for one target area than for another. For example, on Sunday, 18 July, only the Afro-European service offered the following special features:

AFRICA COMMENTARY: P. Keatly - Assesses the Possibility of British Warships Purchase by One of South Africa's Most Important Military Figures

CROSSROADS: H. Windsor - Annual Grants to Students from Africa, and the Changing Procedure.[44]

The French Section programmed 3:16 hours to the Caribbean-U.S.A., and 7:00 hours each to Africa and the South Pacific areas. Frequent program duplications noted in the weekly report for, 19-23 July 1971, illustrated once again the amount of format and content coordination among all language sections.[45]

The overview of 1971 programming reveals that under the supervision of Lucien Coté, manager of information programming, there was uniformity in program content among all eleven language services. All services used the broadcast magazine format and the principal segment of the magazine format—news—originated from the central newsroom; the commentaries and features were distributed to all section heads by the current affairs staff. Consequently, news, commentaries, and topical features provided by the current affairs staff frequently were broadcast by all language services, providing a homogeneous program output.

The predominance of talk over musical entertainment was also evident among all language services. As a primary medium for *information* dissemination, the CBC-IS programs condensed as much news and information as possible to fit the short time allotted for each transmission.

An examination of the programming patterns of 1971 reveals heavy reliance on Canadian sources for newscasts, commentaries, and features. The daily projection of the Canadian identity transmitted to the world radio audience via the International Service was an important part of the total Canadian information dissemination effort. On at least two occasions, the information dissemination of CBC-IS helped in completing trade agreements between Canada and at least one Latin American country.

NOTES

1. Secretariat D'Etat Radio-Canada, "Provisions Des Programmes 1971-72, Programme: International Broadcasting Service, Program Memorandum," (Montreal: CBC, n.d., mimeographed), 1.
2. Canadian Broadcasting Corporation, "Report on Organization and Job Classification in the International Service," (Montreal: Canadian Broadcasting Corporation, 1971, mimeographed), 2.
3. Charles R. Delafield, interviewed by the author, audiocassette, Montreal, 7 July 1971.
4. Ibid. A. L. Hicks, Information Division, Department of External Affairs, agreed with this view in an interview by the author, Ottawa, 30 July 1971.
5. "Report on Organization," 1971.
6. Ibid.
7. Ibid.
8. Ibid.
9. Lucien Coté, interviewed by the author, audiocassette, Montreal, 12 July 1971.
10. Ibid.
11. "Report on Organization," 1971.
12. Coté interview.
13. Ibid.
14. "Report on Organization," 1971.
15. Ibid.
16. Coté interview.
17. CBC International Service, "Weekly Report: English Section," 18-24 July 1971, mimeographed.
18. Canadian Broadcasting Corporation International Service, "Weekly Report: Current Affairs Officer," Montreal, 19-23 July 1971, mimeographed.
19. CBC International Service, "Weekly Report: English Section," 18-24 July 1971, mimeographed.
20. CBC International Service, "Weekly Report: French Section," 19-26 July 1971, mimeographed.
21. Gerd Pick, interviewed by the author, Montreal, 27 July 1971.
22. CBC International Service, "Weekly Report: German Section," 18-24 July 1971, mimeographed.
23. Pick interview.
24. Ibid.
25. Walter Schmolka, interviewed by the author, audiocassette, Montreal, 14 July 1971.
26. CBC International Service, "Weekly Report: Czechoslovakian Section," 18-24 July 1971, mimeographed.

27. CBC International Service, "Weekly Report: Slovak Section," 18-24 July 1971, mimeographed.
28. Letter, John Mezei, head, Hungarian section, International Service, to the author, 18 February 1972.
29. Radio Canada International, "Highlights: 15 Years of the Hungarian Section," Montreal, 12 November 1971, mimeographed.
30. CBC International Service, "Weekly Report: Polish Section," 18-24 July 1971, mimeographed.
31. Carroll Chipman, interviewed by the author, audiocassette, Montreal, 28 July 1971.
32. Ibid.
33. Ibid.
34. CBC International Service, "Weekly Report: Russian Section," 18-24 July 1971, mimeographed.
35. J. B. Wesolowsky, interviewed by the author, audiocassette, Montreal, 9 July 1971.
36. Ibid.
37. CBC International Service, "Weekly Report: Ukrainian Section," 18-24 July 1971, mimeographed.
38. Radio Canada International, *Program Schedule*, no. 4 (Winter 1971).
39. CBC International Service, "Weekly Report: English Section," 18-24 July 1971, mimeographed.
40. CBC International Service, "Weekly Report: Spanish Section," 18-24 July 1971, mimeographed.
41. J. J. Rodriguez, interviewed by the author, audiocassette, Montreal, 1 July 1971.
42. See "Weekly Report: Spanish Section."
43. E. O. Butcher, interviewed by the author, Montreal, 13 July 1971.
44. "Weekly Report: English Section."
45. "Weekly Report: French Section."

7 INTROSPECTION

IN JUNE 1969, Charles Delafield wrote a lengthy memorandum to CBC management posing general questions about future activities in shortwave radio broadcasting. Leading the list of questions were those concerning the responsibilities of CBC-IS outside the purview of External Affairs. Did the International Service have "a role in French and English broadcasting to Canadians serving and living abroad?" Should CBC-IS broadcasting in English and in French present a "Canadian service overheard" or a "foreign service from Canada"? "How serious are we," Delafield wrote, "in our external broadcasting planning"?[1]

Delafield inquired into the future of international shortwave radio broadcasting over a ten-year period. As television satellite transmissions became more commonplace, a concerned Delafield asked: "What will be the place of international television as a world medium in ten years and what will be its relationship to I.S. and their specialized language personnel"? (176)

The Delafield memorandum of 1969 focused on a wide range of difficult questions he believed needed attention if the International Service was to continue as a viable communications medium for External Affairs and for Canada. Delafield's memorandum was timely, because the corporation was receptive to change. Approval of new transmitters at Sackville offered additional broadcasting opportunities, and heeding the advice of the 1965 Fowler commission, the board of directors of the CBC officially implemented the name change from the International Service of the Canadian Broadcasting Corporation to Radio Canada International (RCI) in 1972 (46). Later that year, a special task force assigned to study many of Delafield's earlier questions, which was another indication of corporation interest in innovation and change. The creation of a task force was an important development at the Radio Canada International head office. For the first time in its history, RCI conducted a comprehensive self-study.

On 11 September 1972, the RCI task force was established by the CBC board of directors. Chaired by Betty Zimmerman, the RCI Task Force,

157

included Alan Brown, Jean-Lucien Caron, and Brian Townsley, all long-time CBC employees. The task force undertook a comprehensive self-study "to recommend, through the President to the CBC Board of Directors, broad policies for . . . [the] international broadcasting service, and to outline the management consequences and areas of decision that would result from these policies, if adopted" (see pg. i in this work). The study was broadly based and attempted to project RCI needs over the next five to ten years. The board approved four major responsibilities for the task force undertaking:

1. To study the background and development of the CBC International Service up to the present time, including its relations to other parts of the Corporation;
2. To determine the international needs of the Canadian Government Departments in the area of broadcasting: External Affairs, Trade and Commerce, Information Canada and CIDA, to seek their views on how these could best be attained;
3. To compare the objectives and functioning of other world broadcasting organizations in the field;
4. To elicit informed outside-CBC opinion on the different areas of the Study

By any standards the task force investigation was an enormous undertaking and most imporant, it was a first attempt at a sanctioned self-study. Other governmental agencies had investigated the International Service in the past, but the task force convened, supported by a budget of approximately $20,000, it marked the beginning of a new era of internal questioning with the specific goal of answering queries regarding policy formulation and program implementation. The Delafield memorandum in 1969 had asked questions which attempted to probe the future of Canadian short-wave broadcasting, but the corporation at that time failed to respond; by 1972, however, the corporation was ready to formulate a ten-year plan.

The RCI staff, which in 1972 numbered 180, contributed to the study as well as corporation management personnel who worked in international areas. Other participants from outside RCI and the CBC included the following: the departments of External Affairs, Industry, Trade and Commerce; the Canadian International Development Agency, Information Canada; shortwave broadcasting operations of the British Broadcasting Corporation, Deutsche Welle, ORTF, Voice of America,

Radio Japan, Radio Nederland, Radio Sweden, Radio Belgrade; consultants from various universities, journalists; directors from the Institute of International Cooperation and the Canadian Institute of International Affairs, and the Information Advisor to the Quebec Delegation in Brussels.

The task force discovered that outside contributors were in agreement regarding Canadian endeavors abroad; these efforts were hampered by the lack of extensive knowledge about Canada among foreign nationals. The consultants believed that international shortwave radio broadcasting made an essential contribution to purveying information about Canada to key world areas (52).

"If RCI did not exist," the task force committee asked, "would you create it?" If the answer was affirmative, "How would you set it up?" These were the main questions put to the people interviewed for the study. The subsequent answers reaffirmed the need for a Canadian international shortwave radio broadcasting service and the belief that it should be independent of any government department. Consequently, the task force recommended the following:

> That the Canadian Broadcasting Corporation continue to have sole responsibility for Radio Canada International's activities; that RCI remain as CBC's international broadcasting service; and that CBC management provide guidance to make RCI an effective service as an integral part of the Corporation.
>
> That there be regular consultation between the CBC, represented by Radio Canada International, and the Department of External Affairs, for the purpose of determining target area and broadcast language priorities (8-10).

Although the status quo remained, the overall purpose of the Canadian international broadcasting service needed clarification. A "strategic objective approved by CBC management, and communicated and applied within Radio Canada International," the task force observed, would serve "as a source of policy for programming and . . . for planning, setting standards and evaluating performance" (76).

The task force submitted the following strategic objective statement for approval or revision by CBC management:

> Radio Canada International is directed by the CBC to provide a program service designed to attract an international audience with the purpose of fur-

ther developing international awareness of Canada and the Canadian identity by distributing, through shortwave and other means, programs which
reflect the realities and quality of Canadian life and culture, Canada's
national interests and policies and the spectrum of Canadian viewpoints on
national and international affairs (78).

The task force extrapolated planning guidelines and program policies
from the strategic objective statement. While most of the statement was
directed toward the Canadian identity elements, one phrase needed clarification: " . . . by distributing, through shortwave and *other means* [ital-
ics mine] . . . ." The task force noted that shortwave radio was the
principal distribution method for RCI but recommended a development of
"other means" to augment broadcasting operations. In fact, the task force
went so far as to explain that the present percentage of shortwave use at
RCI accounted for 85 percent of the total distribution while other means
represented 15 percent of the total programming output. Future percent-
ages, the task force explained, should be 75 percent via shortwave and 25
percent via other means. The task force pointed out that the two distribution methods, if distinctively different, are complementary elements of a
single process of communicating the Canadian identity to the world audience (97).

The task force explained how RCI should "attract an international
audience." For shortwave broadcasts, the task force suggested following
a "very flexible and approximate guideline": information about Canada,
60 percent; international information, 20 percent; target area concerns, 20
percent. "Actual proportions of these elements to be included in programs," the task force continued, "would be secondary to their judicious
use. The aim is towards impact of the elements in proportion to their priorities, not a rigid quantitative or percentage or percentage presence"
(98).

The task force recommended a "program mix" aimed at achieving an
accurate reflection of Canadian life and culture by covering the following:

> linguistic dualism and cultural pluralism; regional diversity; overall econ-
> omy, including trade concerns, technical, industrial and agricultural capa-
> bilities and natural resources; heritage, history and traditions, including
> religion; sports; cultural interests and achievements (including music, drama
> and letters, etc.); science interests and achievements (102).

As to possible polemic broadcasts, the task force wrote pointedly:

> Newsworthy events in any country are legimate [sic] subjects for accu-
> rate reporting and forthright "pro and con" commentary. It is, however,
> contrary to RCI's objectives to indulge in gratuitous attacks (in single pro-
> grams) or gratuitous campaigns (over a period of time) against the domes-
> tic policies of other countries (104).

The task force recognized that an international broadcaster must give
priority to target areas and broadcast languages and must annually review
and update them. There were two primary factors which affected RCI
rankings of targets and languages: the needs of the Canadian government
in disseminating information abroad, and the capabilities with the imposed
limitations of existing broadcasting equipment (106).

RCI "country plan" priority listing was determined by External Affairs
and embraced Canadian foreign policy, trade, tourist, immigration, and
aid interests. The way in which RCI implemented its strategy depended
upon whether or not shortwave was a suitable medium of distribution. If
shortwave radio broadcasting was not an appropriate medium to reach a
target country, other means such as transcriptions, topical discs, tapes, or
relays were used (108).

Distributing television programs was a limited activity of RCI, and the
task force recommended no extension of this outreach element to developed
countries. The task force wrote that CBC should undertake "a subsidized
distribution of its television programming to the emerging nations" (17).

In the early 1970s, a growing number of Canadians were traveling and
working abroad. To provide broadcasting to Canadians abroad, the task
force proposed a new objective: to program special news and information
for Canadian citizens in target areas (20).

The task force addressed the question of geographic placement of the
RCI studios. Over the years, the task force observed, questions regarding
the location of RCI in Montreal were posed and discussed. The most frequently mentioned alternatives to Montreal were Ottawa, Toronto,
Vancouver, and Winnipeg. There were seven criteria for meeting location
needs:

> 1) Availability of adequate production and technical skills and facilities; 2)
> Availability of personnel, program material and commentators, for produc-
> tion in Canada's two official languages, in conjunction with . . . 3) program

material and commentators for production in foreign languages; 4) Availability of program material to reflect the regional diversity of Canada; 5) Centre of high financial and industrial activity, providing trade and economics expertise; 6) Immediate access to Government information; 7) Availability of a CBC national newsroom (32).

Comparison of the competing cities revealed that Montreal satisfied all but two of the location criteria—availability of material to reflect Canada's regional diversity and immediate access to government information. The task force determined that Montreal remained the best choice of a location for RCI's studio facilities. To aid the programming of Canadian material, the task force strongly urged closer working relationships with the CBC domestic radio English Service Division (ESD) and French Service Division (FSD) (83).

The Task force also stressed the need for additional transmitters. In July 1971, two new 250-kilowatt transmitters were added to the existing three, albeit aging, fifty-kilowatt transmitters.[2] Certainly, the acquisition of two transmitters each generating five times the power output of the older models helped increase target coverage but not without inherent limitations. The Sackville transmitters and antennae had an effective signal-strength radius of about 3,000 miles, placing within range the United States, the Caribbean, Mexico, Central America, and the northern rim of South America; and eastward, the western rim of Europe. Any target countries beyond that radius received substandard signal strength, making listening difficult. For example, to reach Eastern Europe, the USSR, and Africa with a competitive signal, RCI negotiated rental or use exchanges with the BBC and Deutsche Welle. Inherent limitations imposed on the Sackville transmitting site were identified. A single language program required two to three transmitters for delivery because the target audience needed different frequencies to counter unfavorable atmospheric conditions. RCI had a total of eight transmitters available for eleven language services with a daily average hours broadcast per language of 1.5 hours. Compared with the transmitting facilities of other Middle Powers, Australia and Holland, for example, RCI broadcast more language services. Australia used fifteen transmitters to broadcast eight languages while Holland targeted eight languages and used nine transmitters. The average daily hours per language broadcast for Holland (6.25) and Australia (6.7) were substantially higher than that for RCI (1.5).

The task force , indicating that eleven language services spread technical resources very thin, concluded that a "solution (fewer languages") to the technical dilemma ("too few transmitters") also leads to a higher program productivity and better use of transmitter facilities."[3] Since External Affairs dictated language and target country priorities, it was obvious to the task force that more transmitters were needed to adequately meet the operational requirements. Furthermore, the report concluded, if technical expansions were not approved, a reduction in the number of language services was indicated.

The task force compared RCI with two international broadcasting service size categories—"large" and "small to medium" based on target audiences, transmitter count, languages, shortwave weekly program hours, staff, and budget. The large category included the BBC, Voice of America, and Deutsche Welle, and the small to medium services compared were Radio Belgrade, Radio Sweden, Radio Nederland, ORTF, Radio Japan, and Radio Australia. The task force recognized a third category, "giant," which included the USSR and China, both broadcasting close to 2,000 program hours per week. The other shortwave comparative data for the USSR and China were not available. RCI fell within the "small to medium" category of shortwave broadcasting services. The task force believed that RCI could continue to operate within the limits of the "small to medium" category, but concluded that improvements were needed to meet operational objectives over the next ten years (128-29).

Following guidance, of the External Affairs RCI pressed for new resources which would enable Japan and China to be included within the target zones. The geographic distance from Sackville to Japan and China presented nearly impossible technical problems. Relays would have to be negotiated with Radio Japan to reach east Asia and beyond. The rationale for the proposed targeting of the Pacific Rim was that it paralleled Canadian foreign policy interests in that world area (130).

In summary, the RCI task force attempted to project a ten-year course of action. There were a total of thirty-one recommendations covering key aspects of RCI operations, including new recommendations for additional transmitting equipment and a recognition of the need to reach large numbers of Canadians visiting or working abroad. During the investigation, hundreds of interviews were conducted and the resulting data were compiled and analyzed, giving CBC management considerable information about future Canadian competitiveness in international radio broadcasting. The task force stressed the need for RCI to continue under the guidance of External Affairs in the areas of languages and target areas, with a more complete integration into CBC by utilizing programs produced by both the English Service Division and the French Service Division of the domestic broadcasting operations. There was renewed interest in seeking "other means" of distributing information about Canada to the world audiences. Submitted 9 May 1973, the task force report was an important first step toward evaluative introspection.

MANAGEMENT CONSEQUENCES

The retirement of Charles Delafield in August 1973[4] ended his extraordinary leadership tenure at RCI. No previous Director of RCI had held the directorship position as long. His exceptional career at CBC and at RCI spanned more than thirty years of service. Delafield's leadership tenure provided needed continuity, especially during the stressful times of near-abolishment. It was Delafield, an established, dedicated corporation man, and member of the CBC old guard, who held the Canadian international shortwave radio broadcasting operation together.

In January 1974, Alan Brown, a member of the task force committee, was named director of RCI. A long time CBC employee, Brown was a professional broadcaster who joined RCI after a nine-year assignment with Canadian Armed Forces Radio in West Germany. Taking the idea from a German radio network program, he had earlier helped create the popular CBC radio show, "As It Happens."[5]

Under Brown's leadership RCI attempted to follow the recommendations of the task force. One notable move toward fulfilling the task force recommendations occurred in 1974 when RCI improved poor signal strength into Western Europe by renting Montreal-London transatlantic cable, sharing costs on a pro rata basis among three users: RCI, CBC English Services radio, and the BBC World Service. The result was a greatly improved signal into both Eastern and Western Europe.[6]

The task force report indicated a need for programming expansion in east Asia, and in 1974, RCI moved quickly to implement the recommendation. RCI management personnel visited Japan to explore interest there in topical or cultural recorded programs for broadcast by NHK national radio. Alan Yates, assistant program director, recorded programs, a key player in the RCI-Japan inquiry, noted that the purpose of the visit was "to assess present Japanese use of our recorded program material, to evaluate the potential market for material specifically tailored to Japanese requirements and, . . . to help RCI determine the feasibility of shortwave transmissions to Japan."[7]

Yates concluded there were "no glowing prospects" for any substantial airtime on Japanese domestic stations for RCI recorded materials. He recommended one twelve-inch disc per month for a minimum list of 150 users or "a limited tape service."[8]

Another development in the distribution of programming via *other means* was the use of topical discs. Yates decided to provide medium wave radio stations with smaller discs, with one or two segments on each side of the record, instead of a complete fifteen- or thirty-minute program. Produced in a high quality format, the 33 1/3 rpm discs contained segments ranging from one minute and thirty seconds to seven minutes and thirty seconds. Each week approximately 2,000 radio stations in more than 100 countries received, at no cost, topical discs in English, French, and Spanish for use in local programming. In 1976, more than 68,000 topical discs were shipped to foreign subscribers; in 1977, nearly 119,000; and in 1978, more than 132,000 RCI topical discs were broadcast regularly on foreign domestic radio stations.[9]

For the first time, promotional announcements about the operations and services of RCI were broadcast via CBC television on a trial basis. This exposure prompted more than 1,500 letters of inquiry from Canadian viewers. In addition, the RCI schedules were distributed to CBC offices, to Canadian embassies and consulates abroad, and to passport offices in Canada. Passport offices reported a distribution of 10,000 RCI schedules to traveling Canadian citizens (38).

RCI programming closely followed the 1971 patterns with the noble expectation of ". . . increased effectiveness in the three areas of programming, operations and administration" (38). In 1975, a new position was created which called for a graduate engineer—supervisor of frequency management. Paralleling this development, RCI began installing computerized technical operations at the Sackville site in 1976.[10]

In 1978, John Akor, director of Radio Nederland, initiated a cooperative group effort with three international broadcasting services from the Middle Powers position along the world power continuum: Radio Canada, Swiss Radio, and Radio Sweden. The purpose of the Group of Four, as it became known, was to share information concerning aspects of mutual interest. Members of the Group of Four were similar in several respects: they were in the small-to-mid range of international broadcasting; they were allocated similar budget amounts; and they broadcast under similar mandates. The Group of Four met biannually and discussed problems of mutual interest. One outgrowth of this association was the establishment of a radio committee in the European Broadcasting Union (EBU) which included international shortwave radio broadcasting service representatives. Another accomplishment credited to the Group of Four participation was program evaluations. Meeting as a group, the representatives discussed program objectives for a particular area of the world, and then each service representative played a tape of a show previously broadcast. The programs were evaluated for news coverage, the tone of the language, pacing, and overall merit of the content. On one occasion, after listening to an RCI program, one colleague decided his service was not meeting operational goals as well as RCI. The Group of Four was a cooperative venture which helped each service solve problems of mutual interest.[11]

RCI underwent reorganization in the mid-1970s in response to the need for more efficient staffing of management personnel. While RCI was attempting to follow the task force recommendations, there was another government call for austerity. In 1978, CBC budget cuts caused the abolishment of forty-one RCI positions with an actual reduction of thirty-eight personnel.[12]

Brown resigned the RCI directorship in 1979. He was replaced by Betty Zimmerman, the task force committee chairperson and only female member of UNESCO's prestigious MacBride Commission for the Study of Communications.[13] Two significant developments were associated with the Zimmerman appointment. She was the first woman to head any international radio broadcasting service; and she reexamined the CBC-RCI-External Affairs liaison and reestablished closer linkage and better understanding between them. An underlying characteristic of the Zimmerman tenure was purposeful management. She demanded and received a clearer operational mandate from CBC management and External Affairs. Once she knew the mandate, Zimmerman attempted to dispel any misconceptions of RCI purposes by sharing programming policies with CBC management. Subsequent to CBC management approval of RCI policies, Zimmerman required that all RCI programs be evaluated periodically for an assessment of quality and policy fulfillment.[14]

In the spirit of the task force , both Brown and Zimmerman reexamined operational goals and attempted to evaluate RCI's effectiveness. They were both cognizant that any broadcasting organization has two communities of concern—the internal staff and the external audience. Maintaining effectiveness, always a constant threat to any broadcaster, remained a daunting task for RCI management. With Brown and Zimmerman, research was the key to its discovery.

EFFECTIVENESS: RESEARCH STUDIES

In 1973, sensitive to the effectiveness issue, RCI employed a Gallup Associates audience survey to determine the extent of shortwave listening in the United States and to discover the frequency of listening to six of the shortwave services beamed to North America: BBC, Voice of West Germany, Radio Moscow, Radio Nederland, Radio Canada International, and Radio Havana. Gallup found that one out of every eight adults (13 percent) in the United States owned a shortwave radio receiver. The demographic distribution of set ownership was skewed toward higher education. Among the respondents reporting shortwave set ownership, 21 percent had attended college, 12 percent had completed high school, and 8 percent had grammar school education. Ownership of shortwave receivers was somewhat greater among respondents in the 30-59 age group (16 percent) than among those 18-29 years of age (12 percent) or among those 60 years of age or older (8 percent).

Gallup asked the respondents to identify the frequency of listening to the six shortwave radio services received in the United States. Of the respondents polled, 6.1 percent listened to RCI within one month. Listeners in the United States preferred the BBC World Service over RCI. The Gallup Organization projected this percentage to 900,000 people listening to RCI each month. More people aged 18-29 listened to RCI than within the older age categories, yet all age categories reported they preferred to listen to the BBC World Service.[15]

RCI commissioned a Gallup follow-up study two years later. The research data indicated RCI increased its share of radio listenership in the United States by almost 3 percent while the audience share of the BBC World Service increased by 1.3 percent. RCI was named the preferred international shortwave radio broadcasting service among U.S. listeners with a two percentage point lead over the second-place service, the BBC.[16]

In 1973, another RCI commissioned study investigated the shortwave listeners (SWLs) in the United States. The SWL was a *regular* shortwave listener and was, according to the researchers, "a more discriminating, sophisticated auditor than the casual, infrequent listener of international broadcasting services."[17]

Among the 304 respondents (45 percent return rate) to a mailed questionnaire to the Newark News Radio Club membership (675 members), there were ten favorite international broadcasting services cited. RCI ranked fourth with eighty-six mentions (28.3 percent of all respondents). The top three were Radio Nederland, Radio Australia, and the BBC.[18]

A survey conducted in West Germany by CBC Research found that 350,000 people listened to RCI's "Hier Spricht Kanada" once a week or more. Additionally, 150,000 West Germans listened to RCI once a month or more. These figures reflect an improvement in signal strength, indicating RCI was more competitive in Western Europe in 1974 than the task force reported in 1973. The improved signal strength was the result of the COTC Montreal-London transatlantic cable.[19]

Research projects were expensive, and RCI budget realities precluded any regular participation in audience surveys. Yet RCI used more quantitative research data during the 1970s than in any previous period and began a more organized, systematic evaluation process of programs broadcast to the world radio audience. International shortwave radio broadcasters need research for basic information guidance, and RCI sought answers to questions which probed: "audience size; the extent of Canadian listenership abroad (and at home); RCI policies and Canadian viewpoints"; appropriateness and uses of programs; and Who's listening and why?; Who's not [listening] and why?" RCI attempted to find answers through selected quantitative methods of survey research and analyses of received mail. The qualitative methods used at RCI were focus groups, anecdotal material, expert evaluation, and listener panels.[20]

Survey research methods for international broadcasting services are inherently complicated. Typically, the researcher investigates a nonprobability sample drawn randomly from a mailing list and extracts restrictive generalizations from the findings. The generalizations are limited to the population under investigation and any extrapolation to the general radio audience is an inappropriate procedure. When the general population is sampled randomly (a probability sample) to determine audience size and listening preferences, the results can produce generalizations applicable to all radio listeners. Of the two, the second is the most difficult and the most expensive. RCI "piggybacked" its research questions with major audience studies conducted by the BBC research department on two occasions during the 1970s.

One of the duties of the Research and Audience Relations Department at RCI was to examine and quantify the characteristics of the listener mail. Although sketchy at best, an analysis of the mail attempts to characterize the RCI listener without making any projection of audience size. This research technique is probably the oldest and most widely used among international radio broadcasters. One of the earliest practices was the QSL card. A QSL, the international Q-signal meaning "acknowledge receipt thereof," is sent to a listener upon receipt of a card or letter noting the date, time, program elements heard, and signal report of the transmission. Requests for a QSL card are routine, and many SWLs collect the cards as a record to show when and how often they listened to an international broadcasting service. The signal reports also help the broadcast engineering department track signal strength patterns, and any additional comments in a letter may assist in characterizing the audience. Since the letter analysis is applicable only to people who take the time to write, the comments about the program content are not representative of the larger audience. RCI used the QSL card activity to aid engineering, tabulated the number of letters received each year, and passed any evaluative comments or criticisms about programming to the appropriate language section.

Since 1945, the primary qualitative evaluations of RCI programming were conducted by the heads of language sections, resulting in a coordinated, concerted effort toward program quality supervision. As in most broadcasting operations, professionalism was emphasized, but RCI had no systematic, organized method of evaluation other than periodic reviewing of programs for constructive criticism and evaluation.

By the early 1980s, RCI adopted the use of a standardized evaluation form for shortwave programs. Using the operational objective statement as a guide, the listener completed the form by assigning percentage points to each evaluative category. The three overall program criteria were taken directly from the official goal statement: a) "to attract an international audience; b) for further developing international awareness of Canada and the Canadian identity by reflecting the realities and quality of Canadian life and culture; c) to reflect . . . Canada's national interests and policies and the spectrum of Canadian viewpoints of national and international affairs."[21]

According to Alan Familiant, the director of programming and operations during the Zimmerman tenure, the review process was held twice a year and consisted of two activities. The head of a language section and the personnel responsible for the production of a particular thirty-minute program marked the evaluation form and made written comments. Simultaneously, at another location in the studios, a program evaluation committee made up of seven staff members, including the director of RCI, the director of programming and operations, and other management members, evaluated the program. Then they met together and compared scores and comments. If the scores were approximately the same and there was little disagreement, there was no need for further discussion. If there was a wide disparity of scores between the two evaluation groups, discussion ensued and adjustments in program production were made. Subsequent to this joint evaluation procedure, "management listened, management judged, management passed the results to the section heads."[22] With the new procedure, the production staff evaluated programs alongside the management personnel, providing a healthy balance of opinion and constructive criticism. No records of the discussions were kept and the evaluation sheets were later destroyed. Job performance was never measured on the basis of program evaluation.[23]

During the decade of the 1970s, RCI management attempted to evaluate internal operations and to measure audience reactions to programming. There was never enough money allocated to maintain a continuing audience research effort yet RCI did participate with the BBC, the VOA, and the CBC head research office for an occasional survey of target audiences in Western Europe. The key to maintaining high standards at RCI was the concerted effort to make periodic introspective examinations of both the mandate and the programming broadcast daily to the world radio audience. RCI management, came to understand this need.

CONTINUING CONCERNS: A QUESTION OF CENSORSHIP

In 1976, Tom Cossitt (Leeds), a Progressive Conservative member of Parliament, together with others on the Hill, expressed concern that censorship and "influence" by External Affairs personnel over RCI Russian-language broadcasts had been documented "in certain internal CBC documents" brought to their attention. Cossitt charged that RCI broadcasts "critical of the Communist system on such matters as persecution of Jews in the Soviet Union" were censored by External Affairs, and there had been "a direct attempt to silence comments by CBC Russian language commentator Dr. F. Yaroshevsky." In the House of Commons, he called for an "immediate parliamentary inquiry" to determine the degree of censorship exercised by the Department of External Affairs. His motion for parliamentary inquiry did not receive the required unanimous consent in the House and the motion was not passed.[24]

The primary concern of Cossitt and others focused on the principle of independent journalism, a foundational precept of CBC and government relations.[25] The government of the day was never to interfere with CBC journalistic and overall programming integrity. Were the daily broadcasts to the Soviet Union censored in any way?

The commentator in question, Dr. F. Yaroshevsky of Toronto, was a freelance contributor to RCI. Since 1975, RCI held extensive evaluations of all language sections. In 1976, Yaroshevsky's freelance contributions to the Russian section were evaluated for compliance with the 1973 CBC strategic objectives mandate of projecting "the realities and qualities of Canadian life and culture, Canada's national interests and policies and the spectrum of Canadian viewpoints on national and international affairs."[26]

Cossitt asked in the House of Commons: "Did Radio Canada International censorship have removed from newscasts in the Russian language two items made by Dr. F. Yaroshevsky on May 19, 1976?" The two items in dispute were: "(a) a demonstration by Jewish women in Canada protesting against treatment of Jews in the USSR; and (b) a report on the opportunities and the difficulties which doctors from the Soviet Union have encountered in settling in Canada."[27]

Carroll Chipman, head of the Eastern European section, indeed had deleted the two items. His action was explained as follows: "No one instructed Mr. Chipman to impose censorship or to delete particular items from RCI's programming or to forbid particular subjects being treated. The deletion was Mr. Chipman's correct interpretation of the instructions regarding the ordering of commentaries. . . ."[28]

In other words, RCI editors attempted "to reflect major developments in Canada in proportion to their importance to the average Canadian, comparable to what might be found on the front page of a major Canadian newspaper."[29] RCI management categorically denied any act of censorship. A. W. Johnson, president of CBC, declared on national television, "There is no censorship policy and never has been."[30]

Cossitt was not easily convinced. A year later he charged that RCI and External Affairs were guilty of a "cover-up operation." He asserted that after his initial inquiry into the Yaroshevsky matter, M. Mogilansky, then head of the Russian section, was "ignominiously and unwarrantly demoted, along with certain others. . . ."[31]

When two Russian journalists visited RCI in August, 1975, Cossitt inquired in the House of Commons whether the purpose of the visit was "to discuss the content of programming to the Soviet Union by CBC?" Further, he asked: "Was an attempt made by these visitors to persuade members of the Russian section of Radio Canada International to eliminate any political events or comments from coverage of the Canadian scene in Russian language broadcasts?" Ralf Goodale, parliamentary secretary to the president of the privy council, acknowledged that the visit took place but stated that there was "no attempt by the Russian visitors to influence or to persuade about program content."[32]

Controversy in the Eastern European section was not new. As was the case during the Kesyerlink affair ten years earlier, news commentaries beamed to the Soviet Union were easy targets. The notion of broadcasting under a "one-voice" policy, that is, all language sections were to "reflect Canada," was easily mandated but was difficult to implement, especially with freelance contributors writing in Russian and Ukrainian languages. In fairness to RCI, specific instructions and rules pertaining to proper subjects for commentaries broadcast to Eastern Europe were given to the freelance contributors, including Dr. F. Yaroshevsky. RCI and Chipman came under attack for exercising editorial functions.

Although the use of freelance contributors probably added breadth of opinion to the Russian language commentaries, the Cossitt inquiries uncovered at least one problem associated with an outsider failing to follow the spirit of the 1973 "projection of Canada" mandate. To prevent further problems, RCI established a Central Talks Division which coordinated news backgrounders and commentaries for all language sections.[33]

In a submission to the Canadian Radio-telvision and Telecommunications Commission (CRTC) in May 1978, relations between RCI and External Affairs were described as "cooperative in a variety of ways." Concerning "influence" by External Affairs on RCI programming, the report stated: ". . . it should be stressed that RCI progams are not shaped or influenced by that Department [External Affairs] or any other part of the Canadian government."[34]

On the matter of program criticism, the CBC submission to the CRTC observed:

> Complaints from foreign governments do not disturb RCI's management or working newsmen as long as the material in question was accurate and relevant. The editors are not bent on attacking any government, damaging anyone's reputation or threatening any foreign government's power. Bad governments make their own bad news, and RCI simply reports it. This is quite a different thing from proselytizing for a particular point of view— which some critics accuse RCI of doing; and what others say RCI should be doing. The trick is to be a good journalist and prove them both wrong.[35]

Prime Minister W. L. Mackenzie King opened the inaugural broadcast of the Canadian Broadcasting Corporation's International Service, February 25, 1945.

CBC International Service transmitting facility at Sackville, New Brunswick, c. 1960s.

Delegates to the 1932 International Radio Conference, Madrid, Spain, include Donald Manson, Canadian Broadcasting Corporation, at far left on rear row. Standing next to Manson is Lt. Col. W. A. Steel, a key figure in Canadian telecommunications development.

Ottawa, 1951: Rt. Hon. Louis St. Laurent with key executives of the Canadian Broadcasting Corporation: left to right, Donald Manson, Augustin Frigon, St. Laurant, and Davidson Dunton.

Peter Aylen, the first supervisor of CBC-IS.

Ira Dilworth

Betty Zimmerman

Charles R. Delafield

RCI Reception honoring Margaret Schweykowsky, German Section: left to right, Schweykowsky, Betty Zimmerman, director, and Alan Familiant, program director.

CBC President A.L. Johnson, third from left, meets with RCI Director Alan Brown, fourth from left. RCI personnel, left to right: Alan Yates, John Ramsey, and Axel Thogersen, far right. Also pictured is Pierre Desroches of Radio-Canada.

Jean Désy in 1951.

Any questioning of the Eastern European operations prompted inquiry into the External Affairs-RCI working relationship. The task force report had specified a closer tie with External Affairs. After her appointment as RCI director in 1979, Betty Zimmerman attempted to clarify the relationship between External Affairs and RCI. Although the so-called liaison had existed since 1942, Zimmerman noted problems, particularly with what she termed "a very loose relationship," despite the fact that the 1968 Order in Council had reinforced the mandate that consultation should be undertaken. Moreover, Zimmerman recalled that External Affairs had been unsure about what the relationship actually was or should be, and observed that RCI had independence in program and editorial policies. In effect, External Affairs was "a little nervous about interfering in any way."[36]

Although External Affairs and RCI had established a working relationship over many years, it is significant to note that upper-level CBC management had never been involved in the liaison. In October 1979, a meeting with the undersecretary of state, the president, and the executive vice president of CBC was held, and according to Zimmerman, "a very sensible agreement" was reached stipulating that RCI would be editorially responsible only to the CBC and that External Affairs would be consulted regularly concerning target areas and languages.[37]

Letters of clarification concerning liaison and editorial responsibilities were passed between A. W. Johnson, president, Canadian Broadcasting Corporation, and Undersecretary of State A. E. Gotlieb.[38] Zimmerman had accomplished her goal of obtaining a written statement, indeed a letter of understanding between both parties. Similar letter transmittals occurred on an annual basis.[39]

The liaison focal point at External Affairs was the External Communications Division which is part of the Communications and Culture branch. By 1987, Gaston Barban from the External Communications Division reported consultation was occurring "almost on a bi-weekly basis."[40]

BUDGET PROBLEMS: A QUESTION OF EFFICIENCY

The CBC submission to the CRTC placed RCI in a comparative perspective with other international broadcasting services, calling the RCI budget "modest." In 1977, "the United States, the United Kingdom (through the BBC) and West Germany," the report declared, "each spent about $100 million a year on their shortwave operations." RCI, the report observed, spent a total of $9.6 million dollars.[41]

Broadcasting less than 200 hours per week in eleven languages, RCI struggled to compete for international shortwave radio audiences due to the imposed financial limitations. For example, using five transmitters, with two of them described as obsolete, the RCI shortwave broadcasts were no match for the BBC, with its forty language services and eighty transmitters. Yet RCI management argued that it had overcome financial limitations by improving operational efficiency.

During the five years from 1973 to 1978, RCI doubled the production and distribution of recorded programming and tripled its export of recordings while the proportion of spending on shortwave programming was reduced by 5 percent and shortwave program-hours were increased by 25 percent.

"Now, given the present economic climate and the public demand for improvements in the CBC's domestic service," the report concluded, "RCI cannot realistically expect to be given the funds for a major expansion of its service. It's one of the big disadvantages of working in a service most Canadians are barely aware of."[42]

In October 1977, RCI engineering attempted to determine an overall efficiency rating of the shortwave services to the five target areas. Using an elaborate scoring system, the engineering department established points for program timing (number of hours or minutes broadcast), number of frequencies used, and transmitter distance from target area. Overall efficiency of total RCI output was found to be 45 percent. RCI management, then, attempted to demonstrate that the overall efficiency rating would be improved to 94 percent if the following options were implemented: add five new transmitters and antennas at the Sackville site; reduce the number of languages to four; and add an additional one-half hour to the prime-time broadcasts in the remaining seven languages.[43]

This was a bold admission of inefficiency. Alan Brown wrote the following in the introduction to the report:

. . . of the $75 million spent on operations from 1944-1974, from one third to one half was wasted on programming that did not reach its destination with a competitive signal or did not (in a given language) spread over an adequate daily period to catch those interested listeners who might otherwise have been available.[44]

The report was an RCI management scheme to emphasize the importance of operational efficiency and to argue for more facilities. The formulaic constructs were complex, however, and for non-engineers, undoubtedly difficult to understand and highly questionable.

Efficiency and effectiveness were two bothersome problem areas for RCI management and unquestionably affected annual budget allocations. By 1980, the overall Canadian economic climate was far from healthy. Following its southern neighbor, the United States, into a deep recession, Canadian interest rates soared to a record 19 percent. Unemployed Canadians numbered one and one half million by the end of 1982.[45]

The CBC, a bewilderingly expensive organization, came under fire. RCI was totally integrated with the CBC and so was caught in a web of budget cutbacks aimed mostly at the domestic services. Despite the predictions of economic hard times, there were glimmerings of improvement at RCI. For example, the CBC board of directors recognized that millions of Canadians were traveling or living abroad. The board approved a new policy directive asserting that RCI broadcasts should also serve Canadians abroad. English and French programming from the domestic networks such as "The World at Eight," "Sunday Morning," "The House, le Monde ce matin," Antenna 5," and "l'Evénement" were broadcast via shortwave to the United States and the Caribbean.[46] While reaching a substantial number of Canadians in these areas, the new policy authorizing the use of existing programs saved RCI production costs.

Boldly, RCI management and External Affairs proposed a ten-year plan of target areas and language priorities. Despite budget problems and a questionable financial future, RCI went forward and did so with government endorsements.

In 1982, for example, the Federal Cultural Policy Review Committee (Applebaum-Hébert) endorsed RCI broadcasting efforts (175 hours weekly), recommending continued editorial independence and supporting the addition of service to the Pacific Rim and Asia "as soon as possible."[47] By the next November, a weekly fifteen-minute program in Japanese covering trade news and issues between Canada and Japan was produced in Vancouver, relayed by satellite, and broadcast Saturdays via Radio Tanpa, a shortwave station in Tokyo.[48] Although off to a modest start, the new Japanese-language service, first proposed in 1974, finally served Canadian interests in the Pacific Rim area.

By 1985, RCI broadcast 188 hours per week, including fifty-eight hours targeted to Canadians living abroad. Three new 100-kilowatt transmitters replaced the outmoded fifty-kilowatt units at Sackville giving RCI a total of eight transmitters (three 100-kilowatt and five 250-kilowatt), including two dedicated for Northern Service use.[49]

In 1986, the Task Force on Broadcasting Policy (Caplan-Sauvegeau) reported that RCI broadcast in twelve languages (160 hours weekly, again reflecting budget cuts) and proffered a well-meaning recommendation that "the cost of operating Radio Canada International should be assumed by the Department of External Affairs, with the department deciding on the scope of the service provided."[50]

The task force recognized the importance of RCI programming:

> We believe this is money [$16 million] well spent, given how widely it allows informative programming about Canada and world events to be broadcast. We further believe that two changes are called for . . . RCI should be allowed to expand its services . . . we are persuaded that to protect the future of the service, RCI should be included in the formal mandate of the CBC.[51]

During some difficult economic times, from 1972 to 1985, introspection of purpose, efficiency and effectiveness underscored RCI managerial tactics. Beginning with Delafield, and continuing with the Brown and Zimmerman directorships, RCI weathered the economic difficulties and continued achieving its mandate. No longer the illegitimate child of a troubled marriage between External Affairs and CBC, RCI made the transition into adulthood carefully, fulfilling its operational mandate with all available means. Although shortwave broadcasting was the common staple for the dissemination of Canadian news and views, RCI moved into a higher technological era utilizing non-shortwave means, e.g., satellite relays for rebroadcasting by a foreign national radio system.

RCI management's dedication to meeting operational goals was symptomatic of its directors' understanding of purpose—to project the Canadian identity to the world radio audience. Certainly no one can fault RCI's attempts to fulfill that mandate.

NOTES

1. Memorandum from Charles R. Delafield to Canadian Broadcasting Corporation Management, Montreal, 11 June 1969, in Radio Canada International, "Report of the Radio Canada International Task Force," Betty Zimmerman, chairman, Montreal, 9 May 1973, Appendix J, 175-76.

2. Canadian Broadcasting Corporation, *Annual Report*, 1971-72 (Ottawa: Canadian Broadcasting Corporation, 1972), 65.
3. "Report of the RCI Task Force," 124.
4. Letter from Brian Townsley, supervisor, publicity and audience relations, RCI, to the author, 18 December 1973.
5. *Gazette* (Montreal), 23 August 1975.
6. Canadian Broadcasting Corporation, *Annual Report*, 1974-75 (Ottawa: Canadian Broadcasting Corporation, 1975), 21.
7. Canadian Broadcasting Corporation, "Radio Canada International and Japan: A Survey of the Broadcasting Scene in Japan and as Assessment of Potential RCI Service in and to that Country" (Montreal: International Service, 1975, mimeographed).
8. Ibid.
9. Canadian Broadcasting Corporation, *Annual Report*, 1976-77 (Ottawa: Canadian Broadcasting Corporation, 1977), 38.
10. Ibid.
11. Betty Zimmerman, interviewed by the author, audiocassette, Montreal, 17 December 1987.
12. Canadian Broadcasting Corporation, *Annual Report*, 1978-79 (Ottawa: Canadian Broadcasting Corporation, 1978), 25.
13. Gordon Black, "Shortwave Survives at RCI," *Broadcaster* (March 1980): 38.
14. Zimmerman interview.
15. The Gallup Organization, Inc., "Shortwave Listening in the United States," cited in "Report of the Task Force Report," 172-73.
16. Canadian Broadcasting Corporation, *Annual Report*, 1974-75 (Ottawa: Canadian Broadcasting Corporation, 1975), 21.
17. James L. Hall and Drew O. McDaniel, "The United States' Shortwave Listener Audience for International Broadcasts" (Montreal: International Service, October 1973, mimeographed), 2. See also James L. Hall and Drew O. McDaniel, "The Regular Shortwave Listener in the U.S.," *Journal of Broadcasting* (summer, 1975): 363-71.
18. Hall and McDaniel, "The U.S. Shortwave Listener," 23.
19. *Annual Report*, 1974-75, 21.
20. John E. Hamilton III, "'We Know They're Out There Somewhere,' Evaluating the Audience Research Methods of International Radio Broadcasters: A Case Study of Radio Canada International" (master's thesis, University of Windsor [Ontario]), 1987), 65-85; for an overview of research methods employed by international broadcasters, see, Browne, *International Broadcasting*, 319-35.
21. "RCI Program Evaluation Form," Montreal, 1984.
22. Alan Familiant, interviewed by the author, audiocassette, Montreal, 3 December 1987.
23. Ibid.

24. House of Commons, *Debates*, vol. 14, 1976, Standing Order 43, 14929.

25. Frank Ward and Helen Koshits, "Radio Canada International and Broadcasting Over the Iron Curtain," in *Western Broadcasting Over the Iron Curtai,* K. R. M. Short ed. (London: Croom Held Limited, 1986), 26.

26. House of Commons, *Debates,* 8, 6 July - 17 October 1977, 8089.

27. Ibid.

28. Ibid.

29. Ibid.

30. Short, *Western Broadcasting,* 27.

31. House of Commons, *Debates,* 3, 1978-79, 2441.

32. Ibid.

33. Short, *Western Broadcasting,* 27.

34. Canadian Broadcasting Corporation, "The CBC - A Perspective," vols. 1 - 3, Submission to the Canadian Radio-television and Telecommunications Commission in Support of Applications for Renewal of Network Licenses" (Ottawa: Canadian Broadcasting Corporation, 1978), 359.

35. Ibid.

36. Zimmerman interview.

37. Ibid. A followup letter was sent to A. W. Johnson, president, CBC, from A. Van, undersecretary of state for External Affairs on 31 October 1979 that confirmed the department would provide consultation under Order in Council P.C. 525 of 1968 and "that such consultation would not refer to programming and editorial policies. . . ."

38. Letter from A. W. Johnson, president, Canadian Broadcasting Corporation to A. E. Gotlieb, undersecretary of state for External Affairs, 29 October, 1979, in RCI Files, Montreal. This was the first exchange of letters between the CBC presidential level and External Affairs concerning the liaison.

39. Zimmerman interview.

40. Gaston Barban, interviewed by the author,audiocassette, Ottawa, 8 December 1987.

41. "The CBC - A Perspective," 360.

42. Ibid., 362.

43. Radio Canada International, "An Efficiency Formula and Its Consequences," Montreal, 31 October 1977, 4, 9, 35.

44. Ibid., 1.

45. Morton, *History of Canada,* 279.

46. Canadian Broadcasting Corporation, *Annual Report,* 1980-81 (Ottawa: Canadian Broadcasting Corporation, 1981), 23.

47. The Federal Cultural Policy Review Committee, *Report,* Louis Applebaum, chairman and Jacques Hébert, co-chairman (Ottawa: Information Services, Department of Communications, Government of Canada, 1982), 295.

48. Canadian Broadcasting Corporation, *Annual Report*, 1982-83 (Ottawa: Canadian Broadcasting Corporation, 1983), 28.
49. Canadian Broadcasting Corporation, *Annual Report*, 1985-86 (Ottawa: Canadian Broadcasting Corporation), 18.
50. The Task Force on Broadcasting Policy, *Report*, Gerald Lewis Caplan, co-chairman and Florian Sauvageau, co-chairman (Ottawa: Minister of Supply and Services, 1986), 317.
51. Ibid.

8 MESSAGES FROM THE PAST

WHY DOES CANADA, a Middle Power, broadcast via shortwave to a relatively undefined international radio audience? Throughout the period under study, 1945-85, the International Service, and later RCI, was questioned repeatedly by government officials, the press, and parliamentary committees as to *why* Canada should support an international broadcasting operation. A central theme emerged: the importance of daily information dissemination about Canada because of possible benefits associated with national sovereignty, the promotion of trade and, to some extent, tourism and possibly immigration.

Canadian mass media, dominated by the CBC with its numerous services, the private broadcasters, the press, the publishing companies, and the National Film Board, all contributed greatly to the promotion of national unity. But Canada had never been well-known internationally. For example, there were no Canadian periodicals with large international circulations to reach large segments of the world's population. Coverage of Canadian news and information was never extensive in the foreign press. Even the American press covered news and information about Canada in a sporadic manner. Admittedly, the Canadian embassies and consulates distributed information about trade, industry and culture. Typically, however, this was *requested* information from interested parties. Simply put, Canada never had an international information agency.

International shortwave radio broadcasting, a medium that can cross national boundaries with minimal interference, had the capability of reaching large segments of a population, not only in a single country, but worldwide. And unlike print media, radio broadcasting was not affected by literacy. Thus, international shortwave radio broadcasting met the criteria for widely disseminating information on a daily basis that could be beneficial to Canada, particularly since Canadian print media were not extensively circulated abroad and printed materials were usually valuable only for the literate.

181

There remains the notion that international shortwave radio broadcasting may not have universal audience appeal. One theory posits that international radio broadcasting tends to reach middle to upper-income levels and the more educated members of a society. Even if the theory were to be substantiated by scientific audience research, such a discovery would not undermine international radio broadcasting. Quite the contrary, it would mean that a more elite segment of society—opinion leaders, perhaps—would be receiving news and information about Canada and could, therefore, disseminate the broadcast content to a wider group, either through the media or via interpersonal communication.

Any qualitative judgment about the value of RCI programming operations must focus on the goals or the purposes for broadcasting to an international audience. A corollary condition concerning operational goals of any international shortwave radio broadcasting service is the degree of government involvement in formulating policy. For Canada, the principal purpose for broadcasting to the world radio audience was to project various elements of Canadian culture. In its early wartime broadcasting, CBC-IS was involved in "psychological warfare." From 1948 to 1955, during the intense years of the Cold War, the political commentaries beamed to Eastern Europe took a hard-line stance toward the Soviet bloc. Yet the degree of government involvement with CBC-IS operations was negligible. A crucial question surfaced: Was the International Service the official voice of the Canadian government? The Department of External Affairs, the only governmental agency even remotely connected to CBC-IS, was concerned with long-range policy including target areas and languages broadcast, and served as a *consultant* on broadcast content which dealt with matters of state. The final responsibility for broadcasting, however, rested with the International Service of the Canadian Broadcasting Corporation. The Department of External Affairs never dictated how the service should broadcast or what programming material should be included. Thus, the International Service, never an official arm of the government, represented *all* of Canada.

The Cold War presented a dilemma for CBC-IS. Criticism of a foreign country's domestic affairs was expressly forbidden by policy yet the mood of North America during the late 1940s and early 1950s was aggressively anti-Communist. The Voice of America and the BBC World Service were actively asserting the ideological differences between East and West. In the United States Senator Joseph M. McCarthy was preaching the fear of Communist takeover of government through subversive infiltration of key government agencies, including the Voice of America. In Canada, paralleling the political alarmists in America, Robert Keyserlingk employed McCarthy tactics and attacked the CBC, the National Film Board, and the International Service by asserting, largely through innuendo and emotionally charged accusations, that they were soft on Communism. Although Keyserlingk did not receive as much attention and notoriety in Canada as McCarthy did in the United States, his criticisms undoubtedly caused some members of Parliament to question the supervision of the International Service in Cold War broadcasting. It was this questioning that subsequently led to the secondment of Jean Désy, a Foreign Service officer, as director of CBC-IS.

The Désy appointment, allegedly temporary since he was actually on loan to the International Service from the Foreign Service, was an interesting contradiction of Canadian concerns that government should not be directly involved with any activities of the Canadian Broadcasting Corporation. Prior to the Désy appointment, all of the directors of the International Service were employees of the corporation with no government connection. Evidence in *The Hansard* (*Supra*, p.59) indicates his "temporary" posting was a direct result of troubling worries among some members of Parliament over the External Affairs-Corporation-International Service liaison.

The Désy tenure at CBC-IS was fraught with management problems and generated considerable confusion over the degree of government involvement with the Canadian Broadcasting Corporation. Although Désy strengthened the External Affairs-International Service liaison to the satisfaction of Parliament and the press, he was, at best, an iconoclast, representing a political ploy intended to satisfy troubling concerns over any attempt to propagandize the Canadian position to Eastern Europe. Both Parliament and the press failed to realize that when compared with the total CBC-IS weekly broadcasting output of ninety-hours, all the fuss was over a minor amount of "controversial" material embedded in political commentaries beamed to Eastern Europe.

The multilingual nature of international broadcasting was the chief determinant in molding the organizational structure of the International Service. The first organizational chart was subdivided into geographic target areas and language services for the programming elements and remained the basic structure of the International Service throughout its history. The need for specialized programming beamed to foreign audiences fostered organizational autonomy at CBC-IS since its operation did not fit the pattern of the CBC domestic services.

Still another factor which fostered autonomy for CBC-IS operations was financial. Prior to total budgetary merger with the corporation in 1969, the International Service had been financially independent, receiving annual government grants. The Government also allocated funds to purchase the Radio-Canada Building in Montreal for the housing of CBC-IS staff and studios which, through leasing arrangements with CBC domestic services, helped finance the shortwave broadcasting activities. Both of these financial provisions—direct parliamentary grants and the rental of Radio-Canada Building—were separate from the corporation, providing monetary independence for the International Service. After the merger, the tax money was still provided by the government specifically for the International Service but was attached to the annual budget of the Canadian Broadcasting Corporation. While the new funding procedure probably diminished some of the autonomy, the fact remains that no direct CBC funds were used for International Service broadcasts.

Although the main managerial positions remained essentially unchanged, the International Service continued to explore its organizational structure and personnel posts for possible improvement. By 1971, the director, his assistant, and the manager of information programming were responsible for policy formulation while the heads of language sections were the implementors of policy. With the exception of the manager of the Ottawa office, all of the managerial positions were present throughout the period under study. The addition of an Ottawa-based manager was an important development, especially in providing information about government actions which might affect programming policy.

The manager of information programming (formerly supervisor of sections), a position established in 1971, incorporating more duties and responsibilities, was the primary gatekeeper of news and programming and helped achieve uniformity in expression by coordinating all programming elements. The position closely resembled the duties and responsibilities of a general manager in commercial broadcasting stations.

The heads of sections held a great deal of responsibility in deciding which program content best suited the target audience. The International Service utilized native speakers from target areas to program in eleven different languages with authority and with precision in meeting the needs and wants of the audience.

The 1971 programming elements, shortwave services, transcriptions, and relays seem to have satisfactorily reflected the "projection of Canada" goal. The overview of transmitted services indicates that with the addition of the English- and the French-language broadcasts to Africa, the International Service reached five world areas. In fact, Asia was, at that time, the only area not covered by direct CBC-IS beam patterns.

The implementation of the "projection of Canada" operational goal demonstrated an interesting approach to international broadcasting. Recognizing that the precise size and demographics of the target audiences were indeterminable, the International Service used two additional media forms to insure greater coverage: transcriptions and relays. Both services were transmitted over foreign medium-wave stations or networks and undoubtedly reached large segments of the general population in a target country. The transcriptions and relays were the first International Service attempts at reaching audiences via "other means." In 1978, transoceanic cable was rented to insure that a more competitive signal reached Western Europe; a direct program feed via satellite to Hong Kong in the 1980s helped augment the over-the-air shortwave broadcasts.

CBC-IS management consistently maintained that the primary purpose of its broadcasting activities was to project Canada to the world radio audience. With such a general goal, the value of the International Service broadcasts was difficult to demonstrate with conventional research methods. When asked about the effectiveness of the broadcasts, CBC-IS management explained that one directional beam from the Sackville-based transmitters covered several different countries, making any attempt to sample the general audience for research purposes difficult and expensive. Occasional audience studies conducted by the BBC World Service include a few questions about CBC-IS programming . In the main, audience size documentation for CBC-IS broadcasts was largely unsupportive, relying on audience mail, infrequent surveys, and making references to "potential audiences" in world areas vis-à-vis the number of receivers. When staff members at CBC-IS discussed research evidence, they qualified the value of these "measurements of effectiveness."

The issue of effectiveness plagued the International Service periodically throughout its history. In the name of austerity, the International Service was nearly abolished in 1964 and 1967. There were echoes of abolishment in the mid-1980s as well. Each time a crisis developed over the International Service, the press spoke predominantly in favor of the shortwave broadcasting operation, while certain elements of government called for abandonment. The evidence indicates there was a lack of knowledge and awareness of International Service operations among the press corps, members of Parliament, and the Canadian taxpayer. Without public relations efforts directed at important government officials, disaster was almost inevitable. Common ground awareness and relational communication was needed but did not occur. This is not to suggest that government should have been more involved in CBC international broadcasting activities. Quite the contrary; the lack of government participation in supervisory capacities made impartiality in programming possible. But as the Fowler committee warned in 1965, all elements of Canadian society should be informed about CBC-IS operations, including government.

The question of value for international broadcasting is not easily answered. In 1972, not long after the official name change from the International Service of the Canadian Broadcasting Corporation to Radio Canada International (RCI), the corporation established a task force to probe the question of value. One major finding was the unanimity of opinion expressed by outside consultants that RCI was a worthwhile endeavor that should be retained because of its unique value for purveying the Canadian identity to the world radio audience.

The RCI task force was a first effort to bring together for an exchange of ideasrepresentative of several different groups: the corporation, RCI, External Affairs, and professional consultants. In retrospect, the RCI task force was an important milestone for Canadian international broadcasting, resulting in a ten-year plan of action that featured continuing introspection.

Following the spirit of the task force report, RCI management reexamined operational goals and attempted to evaluate effectiveness. In the 1970s, cognizant that any international broadcasting organization had two major communities of concern, the internal staff and the external audience, RCI examined each with renewed vigor. Pursuing the elusive effectiveness issue, RCI participated in periodic quantitative audience research surveys, and in 1983, began using a more organized, systematic evaluation of program content and production style.

All of these activities were threatened by continued allocation shortfalls and budget cuts. High inflation gripped North America in the early 1980s, resulting in a government call for wider austerity. The Canadian Broadcasting Corporation, a bastion for the preservation of the Canadian identity, fell onto hard times. RCI, then fully integrated into the Crown corporation, felt the economic crush as well.

Despite the budget slashes of the early 1980s, one fact prevailed: the basic goal of disseminating news and information about Canada to the world radio audience was met daily in the shortwave broadcasts of RCI. Since 1945, Canada, a leader among the Middle Powers, has been represented by the International Service and later, RCI, to assert national sovereignty and to inform other nations about Canadian interests abroad.

The future of international shortwave radio broadcasting as a communications medium remains an open question. With the end of the Cold War, most of the hard-line political uses of international shortwave radio broadcasting faded into history. The Soviet bloc versus the Western powers confrontation that generated so much broadcast program content of questionable propagandistic tones is now silent. Instead, the now familiar news, commentary,and radio broadcasting magazine-format programs can be heard across the HF spectra.

One important by-product of the Soviet Union collapse is a reshuffling of positions across the imaginary world power continuum. The Great Powers, the United States and the United Kingdom, remain strong while Russia struggles with economic recovery. China, with its explosive population growth (one in five humans in the world is Chinese), is attempting to adapt a predominantly agrarian economy to an internationally competitive business economy. Doubtless, the reshuffling of world powers will continue as global economics evolve.

The Middle Powers—Canada, France, the Netherlands, Sweden, Japan, Germany, among others—remain securely placed between the two world power continuum extremes, Lesser and Greater. The Middle Powers, allegedly content with political allegiances to the Great Powers, may grow stronger economically but probably without major global political influences. Yet, all would powers continue to need electronic media.

Communication may be a crucial factor for international relations in the future. Although CNN can be seen worldwide via satellite transmission, in the Third World only the urban centers have access to television sets. Beyond the urban areas, radio broadcasting is a citadel of hope for millions of people around the world.

International shortwave radio broadcasting is not outdated. As new technologies improve, there may be direct broadcasting satellite use dedicated to radio as well as to television transmission delivery systems. But the majority of the rural, uneducated, and widely scattered world populations will continue to rely on shortwave radio broadcasting for news, information, and entertainment programming.

Canada's radio broadcasting presence among the community of nations is essential. More than 140 international shortwave radio services, representing a wide range along the world power continuum, agree. Without a radio "voice" reaching millions of curious listeners across the globe, the goal statement, "This is Canada," could generate a troubling question: "What is Canada?"

In the 1930s, early Canadian Broadcasting Corporation proponents of shortwave radio broadcasting, such as Donald Manson, L. W. Brockington, E. L. Bushnell, and Rene Morin believed the prestige of Canada was at stake. They viewed international shortwave radio broadcasting as a means for "advertising Canada." Little has changed since then. There remains a continuing need for world awareness about Canada.

Transnational communication is the cornerstone of RCI operations. No other Canadian media has the potential to reach vast populations across the globe on a daily basis. Despite this fact, budgetary uncertainty has plagued RCI. Perhaps the key to overcoming an unpredictable future is making sure RCI is not an "invisible service."[1]

NOTES

1. James Careless, "Making Waves Abroad," *Maclean's*, 19 October 1987,81.

A APPENDIX

Transmissions to Great Britain and Europe: November, 1946

GMT	SUNDAYS	MONDAYS	TUESDAYS
1600-1615	Program Preview	Program Preview	Program Preview
1615-1630	Musical Program	Musical Program	Musical Program
1630-1645	Hier Spricht Kanada	Hier Spricht Kanada	Hier Spricht Kanada
1645-1700	Hier Spricht Kanada	Hier Spricht Kanada	Hier Spricht Kanada
1700-1715	Kanada Vola Ceskos	Kanada Vola Ceskos	Kanada Vola Ceskos
1715-1730	Kanada Vola Ceskos	Kanada Vola Ceskos	Kanada Vola Ceskos
1730-1745	Canada Roept Nederland	Canada Roept Nederland	Canada Roept Nederland
1745-1800	Verietes Musicales	Verietes Musicales	Verietes Musicales
1800-1815	La Voix du Canada	La Voix du Canada	La Voix du Canada
1815-1830	La Voix du Canada	La Voix du Canada	La Voix du Canada
1830-1845	Kanada Vola Ceskos	Kanada Vola Ceskos	Kanada Vola Ceskos
1845-1900	Kanada Vola Ceskos	Kanada Vola Ceskos	Kanada Vola Ceskos
1900-1915	Heritage of Music	Latin American Serenade	Dance Music
1915-1930	Heritage of Music	Latin American Serenade	Dance Music
1930-1945	Canadian Commentary	Canadian Chronicle	Canadian Chronicle
1945-2000	News	News	News
2000-2015	Program Preview	Program Preview	Program Preview
2015-2030	Hier Spricht Kanada	Hier Spricht Kanada	Hier Spricht Kanada
2030-2045	Hier Spricht Kanada	Hier Spricht Kanada	Hier Spricht Kanada
2045-2100	Canada Roept Nederland	Canada Roept Nederland	Canada Roept Nederland
2100-2115	La Voix du Canada	La Voix du Canada	La Voix du Canada
2115-2130	La Voix du Canada	La Voix du Canada	La Voix du Canada
2130-2145	Canadian Drama	Distinguished Artists	Western Trails
2145-2200	Canadian Drama	Distinguished Artists	Western Trails
2200-2215	Concert Orchestra	Dance Music	Dance Music
2215-2230	Concert Orchestra	Dance Music	Dance Music
2230-2245	Canadian Commentary	Canadian Chronicle	Canadian Chronicle
2245-2300	News	News	News

WEDNESDAYS	THURSDAYS	FRIDAYS	SATURDAYS
Program Preview Musical Program Hier Spricht Kanada Hier Spricht Kanada	Program Preview Musical Program Hier Spricht Kanada Hier Spricht Kanada	Program Preview Musical Program Hier Spricht Kanada Hier Spricht Kanada	Program Preview Musical Program Hier Spricht Kanada Hier Spricht Kanada

Kanada Vola Ceskos
Kanada Vola Ceskos
Canada Roept
  Nederland
Verietes Musicales
	Kanada Vola Ceskos
	Kanada Vola Ceskos
	Canada Roept
	  Nederland
	Verietes Musicales
		Kanada Vola Ceskos
		Kanada Vola Ceskos
		Canada Roept
		  Nederland
		Verietes Musicales
			Kanada Vola Ceskos
			Kanada Vola Ceskos
			Canada Roept
			  Nederland
			Verietes Musicales

La Voix du Canada La Voix du Canada Kanada Vola Ceskos Kanada Vola Ceskos	La Voix du Canada La Voix du Canada Prairie Schooner Prairie Schooner	La Voix du Canada La Voix du Canada Kanada Vola Ceskos Kanada Vola Ceskos	La Voix du Canada La Voix du Canada Kanada Vola Ceskos Kanada Vola Ceskos
Old Songs Canadian Composers Canadian Commentary News	Radio 1946 Chotem Trio Canadian Chronicle News	Music for You Music for You Canadian Chronicle News	Hockridge Show Hockridge Show Canadian Chronicle News

Program Preview
Hier Spricht Kanada
Hier Spricht Kanada
Canada Roept
  Nederland
	Program Preview
	Hier Spricht Kanada
	Hier Spricht Kanada
	Canada Roept
	  Nederland
		Program Preview
		Hier Spricht Kanada
		Hier Spricht Kanada
		Canada Roept
		  Nederland
			Program Preview
			Hier Spricht Kanada
			Hier Spricht Kanada
			Canada Roept
			  Nederland

La Voix du Canada La Voix du Canada Drama Series Drama Series	La Voix du Canada La Voix du Canada Canadian Composers Old Songs (Repeat)	La Voix du Canada La Voix du Canada Hit Tunes Hit Tunes	La Voix du Canada La Voix du Canada Variety Program Variety Program
Dance Music Calypso Songs Canadian Commentary News	Dance Music Dance Music Canadian Chronicle News	Dance Music Dance Music Canadian Chronicle News	Dance Music Dance Music Canadian Chronicle News

B APPENDIX

FROM A DIABOLICAL PAST TO THE PRESENT
By O. Sosula

WHAT CAN BE SAID about my present life, when compared with my socialist life of the past?

For instance, before the war I was occupying, in Kiev, a small room in a co-operative tenement, and I was envied by many people. And my wife was feeling lucky to be able to use the hall to heat her coffee on the kerosene lamp. On account of the exiguity of my room, I was not wasting time in tidying up my place of abode and I had very little to spend for furniture and fuel. I was then realizing economies and could buy state bonds.

For want of a compulsory National Loan, we have been obligated to buy a home and a new car. My wife who has her own bank account, has bought a number of bourgeois trifles, as, for instance a chesterfield, a refrigerator, a washing machine, a television set, a toaster and a lot of the gadgets, the names of which I don't even know. Our floors are covered with carpets, just like the Sultan's place.

And to activate all this machinery, if the authorities would allow us only 16 kilowatts of power as the Kiev municipal council used to do, there would not be too much difficulty. But, it is not the case and that, precisely, is the cause of our present troubles. As soon as evening comes, in one room we have a television, in another our radio howls, in a third one my daughter plays the piano. Under such circumstances, try to write or read or go to sleep. Such an uproar could not have taken place in Kiev. Our neighbors would have soon pulled down the partition if he had not called the police. But, here, I have no close neighbors, I am the owner of an individual house. I really regret my co-operative room.

In the past, on Saturdays, my wife would drive everybody out of the room to proceed to her weekly washing. Now, the contrary happens. She invites me in the house to clean the carpets with the vacuum cleaner.

My wife has become such a "bourgeois" that she refuses to walk half a kilometer to the grocery story to buy our food. I have to drive her to the store. In the days of yore, she would numbly job on from the Podal Ward to the Passarabka Ward in Kiev, and remain for ten hours in line to buy a herring or a pound of sugar. And the stores here have nothing in common with the Kiev co-operative. They are chuckfull of goods. One has only to make his choice and proceed to the cash girl, who makes up the bill. For such a shop, the quinquennial plan would have assigned at least 35 employees. Really, this kind of doing business is unpleasant.

When I used to go shopping in Kiev, I would queue up and wait until my turn would come to buy a pound of cereals or a can of something. That gave me a chance to learn the latest news. I knew exactly whose dirty linen had been stolen during the night, how much water was added to the wine sold in the store or which cabinet minister would be the next victim of the Department of the Interior.

However, we, city people, can put up with the situation. But as for the farmers, it is a real catastrophe. Take, for instance, my friend Seman Wus who comes from a village of the Louhenstakynen Province. The poor fellow has saved $7,000, which he has recently invested in a farm.

There was a time when Seman Wus was living on a so-called collective farm, or holkhoz, called "Death to Capital" and he had no worries. When he was back from work, it was absolutely immaterial to him to hear that the farmhouse was burning, that the seeding was being done or that the cattle were fed.

Now, poor fellow, he is worrying all the time. Here, it is not the same as the holkhoz, where, as soon as the crop was gathered in, the Soviet officials would immediately collect, CC bit of it so that the holkhoz people were left absolutely carefree. Now Seman Wus has more worries than the director of a whole group of holkhozes. He has 150 acres under cultivation, 20 acres in forest, a 5-acre orchard, farm buildings and machinery. He has about 200 pigs, a good stock of cows and a poultry-yard with thousands of hens, ducks and geese. He bought recently a new Cadillac for 5,000 dollars. If comrades Kornijtchuk and Korotchenko and even the famous Melnikov would see him drive his car, they would be green with envy.

SECTION: Ukrainian   DATE: Unknown (1950s)
ORIGINAL LANGUAGE: Ukrainian   BROADCAST NO.: (1950s)
TRANSMISSION BY: CBC-IS   SCRIPT NO.: 383

A MESSAGE TO MY FRIENDS IN UKRAINE
By Nestor Horodovenko

Dear Friends, composers, orchestra conductors, choir directors and singers now living in Ukraine.

I cannot write to you, neither in my own name nor on behalf of my other Ukrainian artists who have chosen freedom, because a letter from me would bring you nothing but misfortune. We know what you can expect when you receive a letter from abroad, especially if that letter comes form someone who has chosen freedom. It is therefore, on the free waves of Canadian radio that I send you this message on the other side of the Iron Curtain, for we have not ceased to love you and to appreciate the talents with which you have been so generously endowed by our dear Mother Ukraine.

It is only since we live on this free land of Canada, where the dignity of man is respected and one can think and create freely, that we have realized with horror the degree of moral oppression to which we, Ukrainian musicians, have been subjected for two decades by the Soviet regime.

Those who have reduced Ukraine to colonial status have made her music an instrument of propaganda. They have tied the wings of her songs, and the unexcelled music of our fatherland, which used to dispense light, happiness, and purity and beauty has been reduced to the shameful role of a vulgar street organ. And we have been compelled with you to crank that barbarous instrument.

There were not enough composers to write hymns and cantatas in honour of those who have succeeded in climbing to the top of the Stalinian ladder and maintaining themselves there in an unstable equilibrium. Remember how many pieces you have composed for such a purpose and how often we have been conducting the singing of those infamous songs in honour of "the wise Stalin, the father of his people," in honor of Dzerzhysnki, Boudenny, Vorochilov, Jakir, Toutchatchevsky, Yagoda, Kotowski, Schors, the insignificant Tchapaiew, and many others. When you have composed a song in honour of a leader and the conductors had directed its execution, the object of your homage had sometimes been eliminated by the Stalinian crushing machine. And, as a result of that accident, the composers were embarrassed on account of their faux pas and the conductors were not very proud of their achievement. As for the singers of those compulsory praises, we had to simulate on the stage, in the presence of thousands of spectators, by our forced smiles, signs and gestures, a spontaneous and exuberant admiration for a silly ignoramus such as Adjutant Simon Boudenny. What a sinister comedy!

Here in Canada, we, Ukrainian musicians, can relax after such a severe strain. Here, in Canada, a panegyric in honour of the leaders of the nation is inconceivable. It would only provoke mirth and ridicule. Here music soars in a different atmosphere. Here we keep and revive and broadcast the masterpieces that the Soviet regime persecutes so systematically in Ukraine in order to procure its complete annihilation.

When the happy hour shall come, we will be ready to contribute our stone to the reconstruction of the ancestral mansion. Believe in us, we are still your friends, our longing eyes are wistfully turned toward the fatherland, but we heartily dislike Bolshevism which has covered our country with tears and blood.

Au revoir!

SECTION: Ukrainian   TIME: 9:45 a.m.
TRANSMISSION BY: CBC-IS   BROADCAST NO.: 236
DATE: February 21, 1953   SCRIPT NO.: 569

FORMER SOVIET CITIZEN IN A CANADIAN FACTORY
By M. I. Kazanetzky

Entering the factory my first thought was that I came to the wrong place. Cars were driving into the wide yard and well-dressed men and women were getting out. All the women wore expensive fur coats, had beautiful hair-does, and were powdered and rouged. "These are probably all office workers," I thought. I came early, for fear to be late, and now I remained at the entrance waiting for the women workers to appear. But they did not come. The same elegant young ladies continued to enter through a wide glass door. I felt conspicuous in this well-dressed crowd, even if before coming to Canada I thought I looked quite presentable.

Taking the elevator to the fourth floor I entered a large light room with fluorescent lights over each table. It was filled with these neatly dressed women and girls I noticed earlier. Each of them had her own locker in an adjoining room in which they hung their street clothes, taking out their work clothing, consisting of a blue coat with white collar and cuffs. Nearly all the girls removed their dresses, putting on their work coats over their underwear. When I saw the underwear they had on I was flabbergasted. "Some working women," I thought. Back home even the kommissars' wives do not have such underwear.

The room was filled with talk, laughter and jokes, until the moment a bell sounded and everyone took her place behind the table. I was working in a chemical factory packing the finished products. The work was light, but since I was not accustomed to it, my first attempts failed. The bottles and jars did not find their proper places and the wrapping paper crumpled. The girls sitting next to me did their work quickly and accurately and the number of finished packages grew beside them. I worriedly looked at the little I had done, comparing my few packages with the number others had. "I'll get fired," I thought unhappily.

Suddenly everyone left their places of work and went towards a door opposite of the entrance. One of the girls in passing me said "break." By her voice and the gesture she made I understood that I must get up and follow her, but I did not know why. Later I found out what the word "break" meant. It was ten o'clock by my watch. In the next room which we entered there were tables, benches and chairs, as well as a strange box I never saw before. It had glass windows through which one could see candy, chocolate and biscuits. Nearby another box was standing. I saw the necks of various bottles, inscribed "Lemonade," "Coca Cola," and "Seltzer." Above each item there were slits for money. The girls put small change into these slits and, having pressed the corresponding lever, pulled out the chocolate, candy or biscuits.

The break lasted ten minutes, after which everyone went back to their places and work continued until 12 o'clock. Five minutes before noon the girls stopped and went to wash and dress in the next room. At 12 o'clock sharp all were in the streets or in the factory canteen. There I saw a counter, with various sandwiches under glass. Girls in clean white coats poured coffee, tea, cocoa, and milk, and served the workers. The whole lunch at the factory cost about 50 cents. This included soup, meat vegetables and coffee or tea. Everything was very tasty and so plentiful that I could not eat it all. After lunch some girls went down town and some remained in the building, reading, knitting or just talking.

Summoning my memory and reaching into my scant supply of English words I asked one of them: "How many packages are we supposed to do in a day?" Astonished, she looked at me and replied: "As many as you can." "How? There is no norm?" "And what is norm?" she asked. "Well, a norm is the minimum you must do to fulfill the plan." "A norm, a plan?" The girls looked at me as if I was out of my mind. No, everyone was doing as much as she could. For my part I was flabbergasted and must confess now that I did not believe her.

The lunch break lasted one hour. And at three o'clock came another 10 minute rest period, filled with talk and joking. Five minutes to five all girls stopped work, washed, changed and sharp at five were already in the street. This was my first day in a Canadian factory.

To my surprise I was not fired. With every day I saw that my work was becoming better and faster. During the whole week no one came up to me telling me to hurry. Friday night we were given envelopes with money. There was no queuing up before the cashier's window and no signing for loans or subscriptions. Then I found out the astonishing fact that we do not work on Saturdays. "But why," I asked, "is there a holiday tomorrow?" "Oh no," I was told, "we never work on Saturdays. We have a five-day week." Here you have a five-day week promised by the communists. But it prevails not where they are in power, not in the countries of People's Democracy, but in capitalist Canada. We have two days of rest every week, which we can use as we like. There is no shock-work, Saturday work or Sunday work. You are free and can do what you please.

My first week's pay was $28. My room cost four dollars and food about seven to eight. In this way I still had 16 dollars left at the end of the week. For this sum of money I could buy four dresses, 16 pairs of silk stockings, or three pairs of good shoes, i.e., things which in the Soviet Union I would not be able to buy for a whole year's work.

After three months I received my first raise. I learned a lot during those three months. I noticed that there were practically no elderly women working in the factory. The girls were about 18-25 years old, as elderly and married women very seldom hold jobs in this country. After one year the girls were earning 35-40 dollars a week. They all, without exception had bank accounts. Many come to work driving their own cars.

I was greatly astonished by this prosperity and once I asked one of them," Why do you work? That is, you do not need to, since you are well-off?" Came the answer: "But what else should I do? Life without work is a bore. Everybody is working here." "Very well," I continued, "but would you have enough to eat, if you would not be working?" "To eat?" And she looked at me, greatly intrigued. "Do people in your country work so as not to be hungry?" I was ashamed to admit that sometimes there was not enough even for food.

During these first three months I caught a cold and stayed at home for two days. In the evening of the second day I went to a doctor and asked him: "Please give me a certificate stating that I am really sick." "What for?" he asked. "For the factory, of course." He tried to tell me in vain that this was not necessary, but I insisted. With a shrug he wrote it out for me. Going to work I thought: "I'll be fired for sure. I haven't been there even for three months, and already I have missed work." The certificate in my pocket did little to quiet me. How great was my wonder when nobody even asked me why I did not come to work. "I'm glad to see you again," my boss told me. No one is forcing you to work here. But, of course, one does not get paid for days missed. Everyone is working in this country, because in a free country like Canada, work gives you all the things which make life more comfortable.

SECTION: Russian   TRANSMISSION BY: CBC-IS
ORIGINAL LANGUAGE: Russian   DATE: Unknown (1950s)

NEW YEAR'S MESSAGE FOR CZECHOSLOVAK LISTENERS
By Rev. A. Cameron
Church of The Messiah, Montreal

It is my privilege on the occasion of the New Year to extend fraternal greetings and best wishes to the Czech people. In so doing I know that I am speaking for the entire Canadian people. The unhappy divisions which now separate the peoples of the world are unable to cut off entirely the deep flow of human goodwill and fellow feeling which unites all the people of the earth in one human family. This profound current of human unity and fellowship is continually seeking means of expression and at no time more sincerely than during this holiday season.

As one enters a New Year, it is customary to take stock of the present and look towards the future. Let us admit that for many of us these are dark days. For those who still cherish deeply the sentiments of humanity, decency and goodwill—it would seem that a blight has fallen on the world, and that the best hopes of men are everywhere in retreat. It has become very difficult to maintain our belief in the dignity of man and our faith in the unity of mankind. We have seen so many high hopes blasted, and so many noble ideals prostituted.

At such a time I can think of no better affirmation of faith and confidence than that conveyed by Thomas Masaryk's personal motto—"Truth Prevails." This is really a statement of faith in the moral structure of things. It expresses the conviction that in the very nature of reality, the truth will ultimately prevail, and that untruth, no matter how powerfully supported, cannot finally maintain itself. The lie will be found out. The lie cannot for long support a truly human structure.

This conviction is a beacon of hope to the religious man. It is a faith which carries him through, not this year alone, but through the entire pilgrimage of life. "Truth Prevails"—this is a statement of fact about the nature of reality. It is the solid foundation upon which the human spirit can stand.

Many of the assumptions on which men base their lives today are simply not true. One of these assumptions, and a very powerful one, is that material well being is the end of life: that man's individuality, his personality, his very soul are subordinate to the quest for material things. From this it follows quite logically that in human relationship physical force should be the final arbiter.

Any religious message that speaks to the deepest intuitions of our humanity must repudiate this untruth. It must assert that man is a spirit, and that ultimately, he lives by the things of the spirit. This truth must be understood, not as mystical sentimentality, but as an inescapable fact. When an individual or a nation makes material ends the highest goal in life, when they are seen as ends in themselves, and not as means of the fulfillment of man's true life of the spirit—something in man's true centre has been violated.

Man is more than an economic machine, more than a producer and consumer of material goods. Man is a spirit and if this be denied then that which is distinctively human disappears, and the fruits of the spirit "love, joy, peace, patience, kindness, goodness, faithfulness, gentleness, self-control," wither away. Human life then recedes to the level of the jungle where strong men dominate, until they in turn are overthrown by superior force or subtle trickery.

But the truth has a way of asserting itself and history provides us with innumerable illustrations. A few weeks ago, Benedetto Croce, the Italian philosopher, died in his bed at the age of 86. During the years of the Mussolini regime, little was heard of this world-famous scholar. Mussolini was much in the news, and a speech by him was an international event. Men analyzed his utterances for portents of the future. But Croce, in social and political isolation, was writing. He was allowed to write because Mussolini scornfully said that nobody would understand him. In 1933, Croce published a book in which he quoted the following words of John Milton: "to suffocate, not matter where or in whom, a truth, or a germ or a possibility of truth, is far worse than to extinguish a physical life, because the loss of truth is often paid for by the human race with tremendous calamities and the truth brought back for unspeakable sufferings."

These words were prophetic. The truth was extinguished for a time, so thoroughly that men seemed not to question what was taking place. But the truth was resurrected and with terrible travail. The Italian dictator came to an inglorious end, but Croce, the man of truth, fulfilled his days, and died in the honour of the human spirit.

"Truth Prevails" the personal motto of Thomas Masaryk was no mere slogan for him. It was a working philosophy of life. When knowledge of the facts convinced him that truth and justice were at stake, he felt himself committed to the cause of truth. It is heartening to remember that there have been such men as Croce and Masaryk among us. It revives our sense of human dignity and reminds us that in all ages, and under the most difficult circumstances, the cause of truth and justice has not wanted for worthy champions.

Men who long for truth feel the oppression of a world which seems eager now to destroy what men live by. But men of truth must keep the faith. They know that even if they should perish, the verities of human spirit will prevail.

Each of us must keep faith in his or her own way. For the individual to maintain his integrity and keep intact the inner citadel of the spirit is no easy task. Let us not waste our resources by cursing our lot, or blaming the travail of our time. Each of us has a part to play, however small, in maintaining human dignity and decency. There is an Arab proverb: "It is better to light a candle than to curse the darkness." Each one of us has it within his or her power to keep our own spirit alive, and be a witness to the serene and quiet light of truth.

Let us pray: Make our hearts thy dwelling place, O Lord, that we may go forth with the light of hope in our eyes and the fire of inspiration in our lives; that, thy word on our tongues and thy love in our hearts, we may do they will this day and evermore. Amen.

SECTION: Czech   DATE: Unknown (1950s)
ORIGINAL LANGUAGE: Czech TRANSMISSION BY: CBC-IS

POSSIBLE SUCCESSOR TO U THANT
By Michael Littlejohns
Correspondent, United Nations

INTRO: Commentary on the possible successor to U Thant. The possible candidates now are from Ethiopia, Finland and Ceylon.

LITTLEJOHNS: Africa has a rare opportunity to add to its lustre by supplying the United Nations with its next Secretary-General. So, for that matter, Asia, Europe and Latin America. But an African with the right credentials probably would have a distinct edge. The main credential is the support of the major powers which have the right of veto.

Though several names from virtually all of the continents have been mentioned in public and private speculation, so far none of them has this crucial backing. There's only one officially declared African candidate, Mr. McKonnen, the Minister of Communications of Ethiopia. Mr. Jacobson, Finland's Ambassador to the U.N., is an announced candidate, supported also by the Nordic group of countries, and the latest diplomat to throw his hat into the ring is Mr. Amora Singh, the U. N. Ambassador of Ceylon, whose name is said to be the one most often mentioned by the Russians, though neither they nor the Americans have yet come out with a formal commitment to anyone.

U Thant, who has been Secretary-General of the U. N. since November, 1961, has said repeatedly that he has no intention of serving beyond the expiration of his current term at the end of the year. Still, a large body of members has refused to take him seriously, believing that he could be persuaded to carry on if it became difficult or impossible to find a successor on which all might agree. U Thant suffered a dizzy spell in his office the other day and his doctors diagnosed extreme exhaustion and sent him off on a rest-cure to Bermuda, from where he's not due to return until well into July. The episode has made many governments realize that they must look seriously for a new Secretary-General, but it still hasn't dissuaded all that he can't ultimately be drafted especially as his health is essentially good.

Mr. McKonnen told reporters recently that he doesn't doubt U Thant's retirement decision but he and the other announced candidates have all been a bit inhibited by the fact that there are so many members who do. The name of Mr. Robert Gardner of Ghana keeps coming up but he's the Executive-Secretary of the U. N. Economic Commission for Africa, and there's a traditional reluctance to appoint from within the secretariat. President Nyerere of Tanzania has been mentioned often as the sort of man the U. N. would be glad to have, but there's no hint that he's interested, though the office of Secretary-General is considered to rank with that of a Head of State of government.

The tantalizing thought is that before the end of the year, a person will appear who's not even been thought of now, and that he or she—there's not sex discrimination—will become the new U. N. leader. U Thant, the late Dag Hammerskjold, and the first Secretary-General Trygue Lie, all emerged in that way.

Michael Littlejohns at the United Nations.

DISTRIBUTED BY: Current Affairs Officer International Service
NUMBER: 1013   DATE: July 5, 1971
USE: All Sections   CATEGORY: Commentary

INDICATION OF NEW U.S. POLICY FOR CHINA'S U.N. ADMISSION
By Colin Godbold
CBC Correspondent, Washington

INTRO: In Washington, there's an indication that a new policy toward the admission of Peking to the United Nations will be announced within a few days. Colin Godbold reports:

GODBOLD: This is the time to place your bet. Officialdom may know what it's going to do but it is not saying anything worthwhile. The majority of speculators are convinced that the solution to the Peking versus Taipei problem will be this: The United States will not, this year, sponsor a preliminary vote requiring a two-thirds majority of the member nations to permit the admission of China into the United Nations. Such a roadblock has usually spelled death for any such attempt.

Since last year, there was a simple majority vote in favour of admission killed by the two-thirds majority requirement, it seems certain that China will be in this year. So what happens to Taiwan? The theory, the gambling, is that the United States will back a vote calling for two-thirds majority vote for the expulsion of the regime of Generalissimo Chiang Kai-shek. In other words, while China is certain to be voted in, Taiwan is certain to be retained, if they want to stay.

The issue, then, is entirely between the two regimes. If Peking and Taipei don't pack off, there is a possibility of having two nations in the World Body—China and Taiwan. The trouble is that so far both nations have adamantly refused to countenance such an arrangement. So the side bets are on Taiwan walking out of the U. N. General Assembly, resolving to go it alone.

It may be that Mr. Nixon has resigned himself to this idea, although he said he won't desert his friends. Allowing Taiwan to go it alone would not amount to that since there are always the nuclear umbrella the tacit and formal agreements between Washington and Taipei to fall back on. Chiang Kai-shek won't be deserted but the old dreams of reconquering the mainland will.

The visit to China of the Canadian Opposition Leader, Mr. Stanfield, has had wide publicity here, in particular, his defence of the people and government of the United States. And there's a growing belief that the Chinese ambassador to Canada, Huang Hua, is probably going to become Peking's major contact with the United States. One speculator suggests that the talks between Peking and Washington, conducted in Warsaw for the past fifteen years, may be transferred to Ottawa, if they are resumed.

In summary for the moment, all is floating in a wonderland of speculation with mild optimism as the predominant element.

This is Colin Godbold in Washington.

DISTRIBUTED BY: Current Affairs Officer, International Service
DATE: July 8, 1971   NUMBER: 1166
USE: All Sections   CATEGORY: News Report

SITUATION IN COLOMBIA AS PAN-AM GAMES OPEN
By Jim Reed
Cali, Colombia

INTRO: Students are threatening to disrupt the Pan-Am Games due to start in Cali, Colombia, on Friday. The story from Jim Reed is a familiar one from Latin America.

REED: As I speak now standing in the simple square of Colombia's third largest city, Cali, the site of this year's Pan-American Games. While this four hundred and thirty-four year old city is engaged in a massive cleaning and painting programme, business men here are cleaning up in other ways. Motel and restaurant prices have risen an average of twenty-five percent, and Colombia entrepreneurs are flocking here to take advantage of gullible tourists.

At the same time, the authoritarian government had vowed that Cali will not become another Mexico City, and soldiers are very much in evidence ready to quell predicted student protests.

Colombia, like many other Latin American nations, is feeling the pressures of a growing and increasingly well organized left-wing movement. The present government is a coalition of traditional right-wing Conservative and Liberal parties, and in the last election it was almost defeated by the Socialist party, in that vote led surprisingly enough by former dictator Rojas Pinilla and his daughter Maria.

After a month in Colombia and conversations with people from all walks of life, I feel that it is clear that many Colombians believe that the last election was a fraud and that Rojas Pinilla in fact won it, but because of the many socialist reforms that he had promised was not allowed to assume the presidency. Colombia suffers from the traditional Latin American ailments of poverty, of a too rapidly expanding population, and of massive unemployment. Almost fifty percent of the population of twenty million live on an income of less than two hundred dollars per year, and in large segments of the population, tuberculosis and other diseases are endemic. Education is expensive here and it's available only to a very few. Consequently, fifty percent of the population is illiterate. Agrarian reform has been attempted, but it is generally felt to be almost totally ineffective in solving the problem of land distribution.

Migration to the city is increasing, and the government seems unable to find solutions to the resulting housing crisis. Thus, thousands of houses here contain four and five families each, over crowding is rampant and cities are growing at the rate of three, four, to five percent per year. Colombia is the home of the radical priest, Camillo Torre who identified himself with Colombian guerrilla movements and who was killed by government soldiers in the Colombian Andes. Father Camillo and Che Guevara have become popular heroes here, and student groups openly acknowledge their devotion to these two revolutionary leaders. Students and left-wing movements see the government's recent purchase of Mirage fighters from France, and the vast expenditure on this year's Pan-American Games as irrelevant, and against the best interest of the people.

At the moment Cali is full of rumours of mass demonstrations protesting government policy, and attempts to disrupt the games while the attention of the western hemisphere and much of the world is focused here.

The Government determination to prevent any such disturbances may well lead to violence and perhaps bloodshed. Already this year at least one student has been killed in Colombia, and most of the nation's universities are now closed. But in spite of the rumours, in spite of the presence of soldiers, the city of Cali remains for the most part calm, and so far, the only people taking a real beating here are the tourists.

This is Jim Reed speaking from Cali, Colombia.

DISTRIBUTED BY: Current Affairs Officer, International Service
DATE: July 26, 1971   NUMBER: 1151
USE: All Sections   CATEGORY: Commentary

THE SITUATION IN NORTHERN IRELAND
By Michael Maclear
CBC Correspondent, London

In the shopping area in the slummy Catholic ghetto of Londonderry called "The Bog Side," there is a simple stone cross placed right on the sidewalk. This grim memorial commemorates the killing by British troops of a young nineteen-year-old during some recent riotings. His death was special because, according to the local people, the dead man had carried no weapons when shot down at almost blank range.

For once the people here cannot feel the acceptance of death; it is part of any war; cannot forget this one shooting as any different from all the others, and so have created a martyr among martyrs, have placed a stone cross where it is hauntingly inescapable—outside a butcher shop.

But this memorial very special, for it records not just the death of a man, but of a parliament or of the parliamentary system. As a consequence of this shooting, there is no longer a parliamentary opposition in Ulster and this means that the Catholic community is no longer participating in the running of the province. It means that the moderates have lost all patience and that all political action must not take place on the streets.

While the opposition MP's don't quite admit to that, they talk of forming an alternative assembly. In effect, a second rival administration, so that more than ever, the Catholic community would become a state within a state. But this alternative assembly can have no muscle except for that of the I.R.A. and if it uses the illegal Republic Army to get its way, then street politics be the only kind.

The feeling of the Catholic leaders I've talked to in recent days is that a grim new course has been embarked upon. The new horrors felt that events have an inevitability of arms showdown at the end. There are two major factors that influence this pessimistic outlook: one is the apparent change of attitude in the Irish Republic; the other, the changed appearance of Ulster's parliament. And these changes were triggered by the rifle shot that killed the allegedly unarmed Londonderry rioter.

The British government refused an official inquiry. Why? Only the Lord and the London government can explain, because, of course, such silence encourages more violence. This refusal seems the more extraordinary because the British government had been warned that opposition MP's in Ulster would quit, unless there was an inquiry. And that meant, if there was to be no effective parliament in Northern Ireland, there could only be, instead, indefinite British military rule.

Well, London's readiness to run this risk has convinced the Ulster Catholics that Britain is backing the Protestant Unionists, come what may, to achieve a hairline solution. At the same time, recent statements by the Dublin government, of bleakly condemning the partition of Ireland, have encouraged belief that the Irish Republic won't stand idly by in any major fighting. The outcome, anyhow, is the conscious demise of the parliamentary system in the north. In not preventing this, the British are taking a terrible risk. Lord O'Neil, the former Ulster Prime Minister, exactly described the risk in a recent CBC interview when he talked of the danger of the worse civil war Europe has ever seen.

Meantime, the Catholics, or their leaders, have knowingly sacrificed the legal means of ensuring steady, if gradual equality. The Ulster parliament, of course, still nominally exists. It will reassemble in October. But twelve of the thirteen opposition MP's will be missing. All the Social Democrats and Independent Labour members will be gone. Instead, just one representative of the official Labour Party will have the entire opposition benches to himself. Yet, in political terms, it would not be him but the thirty-six members who confront him who will be like lepers. They may continue to believe in their own credibility, but as the Unionists reassemble on what will be the party's fiftieth anniversary of continuous rule, the occasion may read to outsiders not so much like a jubilee as an obituary.

This is Michael Maclear reporting.

DISTRIBUTED BY: Current Affairs Officer International Service
DATE: July 27, 1971   NUMBER: 1158
USE: All Sections   CATEGORY: Commentary

C APPENDIX

CBC International Service Weekly Report

CURRENT AFFAIRS OFFICER

DATE: July 19, 1971 to July 23, 1971

MONDAY:

PRESS REVIEW: Tour de Presse. De: Jean Claude Daigl
S.I., Montréal.
Sujet: Le Développement de la Baie de James.

NEWS REPORT: International Union of Local Authorities
Annual Meeting in Toronto.

NEWS REPORT: Department of National Defence Tracks
Icebergs. By: Bill Curtin, CBC, Goose Bay.

TALK: Oil Exploration Threatens Sable Island Wild Horses.
By: Bill Hammerhand, Halifax.

TALK: Stage Show Brings Northern Message to the South.
By: Henry Strube, Technical Coordinator of Show.

PRESS REVIEW: President Nixon's Planned Visit to China.
By: V. I. Rajewsky, I.S. Staff.

NEWS REPORT: M. Wilson et le Marché Commun. De:André
Manderstam, Radio-Canada, Londres.

COMMENTARY: Soviet Views of Mr. Nixon's China Visit.
By: Axel Krause, *Business Week* Magazine
Correspondent, Moscow.

209

COMMENTARY: The Future of King Hassan and Morocco.
                         By: William Hampshire, *The London Daily Express*, Rabat.

COMMENTARY: The Review of the Federal Labour Code.
                         By: Wilfred List, Labour Correspondent,
                         The Toronto Globe and Mail.

COMMENTARY: Trade Union Educational Programmes.
                         By: Wilfred List, Labour Correspondent,
                         The Toronto Globe and Mail.

INTERVIEW: Computers Help Preserve Environment in Canada's
                         North. By: Frank Dolphin, CBC, Edmonton.

PRESS REVIEW: Tour de Presse. De: Jean Claude Daigle,
                         S.I., Montréal.
                         Sujets:
                         1. Dernières Propositions du Vietcong.
                         2. Rapport de la Banque Mondiale sur le Pakistan
                            de l'Est.
                         3. Visite de Nixon en Chine; Premières Réactions.
                         4. Conférence des Ministres des Finances à Ottawa.
                         5. Politique étrangère du Canada.

TUESDAY

TALK: Canadian Chronicle. By: Vladimir Rajewsky, I.S. Staff.
                         Topics:
                         1. Canada-Peking Air Link.
                         2. Ants May Help Fight Forest Pests.

NEWS REPORT: Vente d'Aluminium à la Chine. De: James Bamber,
                         Radio-Canada, Vancouver.

NEWS REPORT: Chou En-lai's Eight Point Plan for Better Relations
                         with the United States. By: Colin Godbold,
                         CBC Correspondent, Washington.

FEATURE: The Mariposa Folk Festival. By: Lloyd Halyk,
                         .S., Toronto.

NEWS REPORT: The Sudan Coup. By: Diane Wilman, CBC, Beirut.

COMMENTARY: Prospect for Canadian Wheat Crop. By: Bill Metcalfe, Managing Editor, *The Ottawa Journal.*

TALK: Youth in Canada. By: Gordon Mesley, I.S. Staff.

INTERVIEW: Transportation of Oil Through Arctic Water. Interview with Dr. B. R. Pelletier, Marine Ecology Department, Dartmouth. By: Ron McInnes, CBC, Halifax.

TALK: The Mariposa Folk Festival. By: Margaret Schweykowsky, I.S. Staff.

NEWS REPORT: International Conference of Local Authorities. By: Frank Hilliard, CBC, Toronto.

COMMENTAIRE   Les Relations Canado-Algeriennes. By: Louise De Celles, S.I., Ottawa.

INTERVIEW: Le Problème des Réfugies du Pakistan Oriental. Interview avec M. Georges Lachance, MP, sur sa Visite au Pakistan et en Inde. De: Louise De Celles, S.I.,Ottawa.

NEWS REPORT: The Coup Leaders in Sudan. Leaning to Left. By: Diane Wilman, CBC, Beirut.

WEDNESDAY

FEATURE: The World of Science. Edition 30-71.
Topics:
1. Farewell Gonorrhea.
2. Hello Slowpoke.
3. Seabed Research Capsule.
4. Once Upon a Time There Was a Grizzly Bear.

PRESS REVIEW: The Canadian Press Review. By: David Legate, Associate Editor, *The Montreal Star.*
Topics:
1. Nixon Visit to Peking.

2. Resumption of SALT Talks.
3. The James Bay Project.

TALK: CBC International Stamp Corner, No. 235.
                         By: G. P. Pick, I.S. Staff.
                         Topics:
                         1. Newfoundland's Air Pioneers.
                         2. Good and Bad Cancellations.

NEWS REPORT: Elected Prisoners' Committees in Canadian Prisons.
                         By: Peter Louckes, CBC, Ottawa.

NEWS REPORT: New Soviet Demands for Chinese Admission to U.N.
                         By: Colin Godbold, CBC Correspondent,
                         Washington.

NEWS REPORT: The Situation in the Sudan. By: Diane Wilman,
                         CBC, Beirut.

INTERVIEW: Research into Allergies in Children. Interview with
                         Dr. Collins Williams, Hospital for Sick Children,
                         Toronto. By: Dwight Hamilton, CBC, Toronto.

NEWS REPORT: Chinese Ambassador Arrives in Paris on Way to
                         Canada. By: David Halton, CBC Correspondent, Paris.

THURSDAY

TALK: Radio Canada Shortwave Club. Script No. 440.
                         By: Basil Duke, I.S. Staff.

COMMENTARY: The Coup in Sudan. By: Patrick Keatley,
                         The Guardian, London.

INTERVIEW: The British Columbia Bathtub Race.
                         Interview with Les Montashaw, Race Commander.
                         By: John Herrit, CBC, Vancouver.

PRESS REVIEW: The Prospects for Arab Unity. By: Vladimir
                         Rajewsky, I.S. Staff.

NEWS REPORT: Relations Chine-U.S.A. De: Henri Cruzene,
                          Radio-Canada, Washington.

NEWS REPORT: La Grande-Bretagne et la CEE. De: Andre
                          Manderstam, Radio-Canada, Londres.

TALK: Summer School for Black Children.
                          By: Tom Jagninski, I.S. Staff.

NEWS REPORT: Interview with George Ignatieff, Head the Canadian
                          Delegation, Geneva Disarmament Conference:
                          Nuclear Testing. By: Alex Defontaines,
                          CBC Correspondent, Geneva.

NEWS REPORT: The French Foreign Minister, Maurice Schumann,
                          Visits Canada. By: David Bazay,
                          CBC Correspondent, Paris.

NEWS REPORT: French Foreign Minister to Visit Ottawa.
                          By: Robert Abra, I.S., Ottawa.

FRIDAY

NEWS REPORT: Chinese Grain Mission Arrives in Ottawa.
                          By: Arthur Lewis, CBC, Ottawa.

NEWS REPORT: Another Russian Attack on China But No Mention
                          of Nixon Visit. By: Chris Kaplin, *Reuters*, Moscow.

NEWS REPORT: Visite de Monsieur Maurice Schumann au Canada.
                          De: Lucien Millet, Radio-Canada, Ottawa.

NEWS REPORT: Préparatifs pour Apollo 15. De: Norman Lester,
                          Radio-Canada, Montréal.

INTERVIEW: Canadian Aid to Africa. Interview with Paul
                          Gerin-Lajoie, President, Canadian International
                          Development Agency. By: David Bazay, CBC, Paris.

PRESS REVIEW: Canada and the British Entry into European
                          Common Market. By: Vladimir Rajewsky, I.S. Staff.

INTERVIEW   Livre Blanc Sur l'Entrée de la Grande-Bretagne dans
                             le Marché Commun. Interview avec Henri Mhun,
                             économiste. De: Maryse Reicher, S.I., Montréal.

NEWS REPORT   Décès de Monsieur Ross Thatcher. De: Gilbert
                             Bringué, Radio-Canada, Saskatoon.

NEWS REPORT   British Diplomatic Moves Over Libya. By: Patrick
                             Keatley, *The Guardian,* London.

NEWS REPORT: Sudanese Counter-Coup Not Guarantee of Stability.
                             By: Diane Wilman, CBC, Beirut.

CBC INTERNATIONAL SERVICE WEEKLY REPORT

LANGUAGE ENGLISH I

DATE: July 18, 1971 to July 24, 1971 DAILY TRANSMISSIONS:

AFRO-EUROPE	03:10-03:44 EDT(	07:10-07:44 GMT)
SOUTH PACIFIC	04:25-05:30 EDT	(08:25-09:30 GMT)
EUROPE AND NORTH AMERICA	08:17-09:12 EDT	(12:17-13:12 GMT)
EUROPE II	11:16-11:29 EDT	(15:16-15:29 GMT)
AFRICA II	14:29-15:14 EDT	(18:29-19:14 GMT)
EUROPE III	17:15-17:51 EDT	(21:15-21:51 GMT)
CARIBBEAN AND AMERICAN	18:57-19:29 EDT	(22:57-23:29 GMT)

SUNDAY:

AFRO-EUROPE:

RADIO CANADA NEWS:

AFRICA COMMENTARY :P. Keatley-Assesses the Possibility of British
Warships Purchase by One of South Africa's Most
Important Military Figures.

CROSSROADS:H. Windsor-Annual Grants to Students from Africa,
and the Changing Procedure.

LISTENERS' CORNER I: With Earle Fisher.

SPORTS & NEWS HEADLINES:

SOUTH PACIFIC:

RADIO CANADA NEWS:

LISTENERS' CORNER I & II

ASPECTS OF CANADA: 1. The Adventures of Ookpik, Part 2.
2. North by Sea, Part 2.

EUROPE AND NORTH AMERICA:

RADIO CANADA NEWS:

LISTENERS' CORNER I:

THE IN BIT: 1. F. Peabody-Interviews Zeba Fischer on MILE,
Mobile Intensive Learning Experience.
2. A Visit to the Montreal Youth Clinic.

ASPECTS OF CANADA:Same as SOUTH PACIFIC.

SPORTS & NEWS HEADLINES:

EUROPE II:

RADIO CANADA NEWS:General News for Europe.

AFRICA II:

RADIO CANADA NEWS:

SUNDAY NEWS MAGAZINE   1. Godbold, M. Maclear, D. Halton-World
                              Reaction to Proposed Nixon Visit to China.
                              2. Ronning, A. Harriman, A. Goldberg-S.
                              Relations with Taiwan.
                              3. M. Gorte, D. McNeill-U.S./China
                              Relations in View of U.S. Foreign Policy.

SUNDAY COMMENT   T. Earle-Parliamentary Reporting.

LISTENERS' CORNER II:

SPORTS & NEWS HEADLINES:

EUROPE III:

RADIO CANADA NEWS:

SPORTS REVIEW:

SUNDAY NEWS MAGAZINE: Same as AFRICA II:

SUNDAY COMMENT: Same as AFRICA II, plus:
                              1. G. Pape-British Labour Party's
                              Opposition to ECM Entry.
                              2. Hammerhand-Wile Horses of Sable
                              Island Threatened by Oil Discovery.

LISTENERS' CORNER II:

SPORTS & NEWS HEADLINES:

CARIBBEAN AND AMERICAN:

RADIO CANADA NEWS:

LISTENERS' CORNER II:

THE IN BIT   Same as EUROPE AND NORTH
                              AMERICA.

SPORTS & NEWS HEADLINES:

MONDAY

AFRO-EUROPE:

RADIO CANADA NEWS:
    1. B. Cunningham-Ex-PM Wilson Launches All-out Campaign Against Britain's Entry into ECM.
    2. G. Cochrane-Canadian Fishermen Protest Against Portuguese Fleets.
    3. B. Curtis-Drifting Icebergs a Threat to Oil Rigs Off the East Coast.

TODAY'S MAGAZINE:
    1. A. Krause-Soviet Reaction to Nixon Announcement re Forthcoming Peking Visit.
    2. T. Earle-Parliamentary Reporting.

SPORTS & NEWS HEADLINES:

SOUTH PACIFIC:

RADIO CANADA NEWS:　　　Same as AFRO-EUROPE.

TODAY'S MAGAZINE:　　　Same as AFRO-EUROPE plus: B. Hammerhand-Wild Horses of Sable Island Threatened.

DEAR WORLD:　　　With John Ramsay and Norman Kihl-Highland Games in Canada.

FRED WALKER ON SPORTS:

CROSS CANADA NEWS:

SPORTS & NEWS HEADLINES:

EUROPE AND NORTH AMERICA:

RADIO CANADA NEWS:
    1. D. Willman - Palestinian Guerillas Fleeing into Israel.
    2. M. Maclear—Britons Hope for Tax Cuts in New Budget Today.

                                           3. B. Curtis-Drifting Icebergs a Threat to
              Offshore Oil Rigs.

TODAY'S MAGAZINE: 1. F. Dolphin-Using Computers to Preserve
Our Environment.
2. G. Pape-British Labour Party's
Opposition to Britain's ECM Entry.
3. T. Earle-Parliamentary Reporting.

DEAR WORLD:

FRED WALKER ON SPORTS:

CROSS CANADA NEWS:

SPORTS & NEWS HEADLINES:

EUROPE II:

RADIO CANADA NEWS: General News for Europe.

AFRICA II:

RADIO CANADA NEWS: 1. B. Cunningham-British Mini-budget
Introduced Today in Parliament
2. D. Phelan-Air Canada and Union
Employees Meet in Montreal Today.
3. T. Jagninski-Some Progress on Atlantic
Fares Reported by IATA.
4. Lord Mayor Vogel of Munich-Public
Spending re Cities Must be Doubled.
(ACTUALITY)

TODAY'S MAGAZINE: 1. G. Mesley-Press Attention to the
Activities of Youth.
2. F. Dolphin-Using Computers to Preserve
Our Environment.
3. W. Hampshire-Morocco's Future Under
King Hassan.

CROSS CANADA NEWS:

SPORTS, STOCKMARKET & NEWS HEADLINES:

EUROPE III:

TODAY'S MAGAZINE:
1. W. Hampshire-Morocco's Future Under King Hassan.
2. E. Trepunsky-Interviews Dr. Ray Lawson on Traditional Treatments for Breast Cancer.
3. B. Whitehead-Diamonds.

RADIO CANADA NEWS:
1. B. Cunningham-British Mini-budget Introduced in Parliament.
2. Lord Mayor Vogel of Munich-Public Spending re Cities Must be Doubled. (ACTUALITY)
3. D. Struthers-Air Canada Problems.

COMMENT:
G. Mesley-Press Attention to Youth.

SPORTS, STOCKMARKET & NEWS HEADLINES:

CARIBBEAN AND AMERICAN:

RADIO CANADA NEWS:
1. T. Jagninski-SomeProgress on Atlantic Fares Reported by IATA.
2. Lord Mayor Vogel of Munich-Public Spending re Cities. (ACTUALITY)
3. D. Struthers-Air Canada Problems.
4. C. Godbold-China Prepares Eight-Point Plan for Good Relations Between Washington and Peking.
5. R. Abra-Canadian MP's Call for More Aid to Pakistanis.

TODAY'S MAGAZINE:
1. B. Whitehead-Diamonds.
2. G. Mesley-Press Attention to Youth.

SPORTS, STOCKMARKET & NEWS HEADLINES:

TUESDAY

AFRO-EUROPE:

RADIO CANADA NEWS:

TODAY'S MAGAZINE: 1. G. Mesley-Press Attention to Youth.
                                 2. R. Sinclair-A Visit to a Paper-Making
                                    Plant in Ontario.

SPORTS & NEWS HEADLINES:

SOUTH PACIFIC:

RADIO CANADA NEWS   Same as AFRO-EUROPE.

TODAY'S MAGAZINE: Same as AFRO-EUROPE plus:
                                P. Holting-Waste Disposal.

CROSSTALK:

DISCOTHEQUE:
CROSS CANADA NEWS:

SPORTS, STOCKMARKET & NEWS HEADLINES:

EUROPE AND NORTH AMERICA:

RADIO CANADA NEWS:

TODAY'S MAGAZINE: 1. H. Strube-Touring Show about the
                                    Canadian North.
                                 2. E. Garrity-Interviews J. R. Vallentine on
                                    Pollution in Canada's North.
                                 3. R. Doucette-Air Canada Mediation
                                    Talks Begin.
                                 4. W. Coven-Canada's Peace-Keeping
                                    Image a Fraud.

DISCOTHEQUE:

CROSS CANADA NEWS:

SPORTS & NEWS HEADLINES:

EUROPE II:

RADIO CANADA NEWS:General News for Europe.

AFRICA II:

RADIO CANADA NEWS:
1. D. Struthers-Air Canada Mediation Talks.
2. C. Cathcart-Sale of Alcan Aluminum Ingots to China.
3. F. Hillary-Japanese Delegate to International Conference in Toronto on Pollution in Tokyo.
4. D. Willman-Coup in Sudan.
5. N. Moss-Reaction to British Mini-budget.

TODAY'S MAGAZINE:
1. W. Metcalfe-Canada's Grain Crop and Its Marketing Possibilities.
2. R. Doucette-Air Canada Mediation Talks.
3. W. Coven-Canada's Peace-Keeping Image.

CROSS CANADA NEWS:

SPORTS, STOCKMARKET & NEWS HEADLINES:

EUROPE III:

TODAY'S MAGAZINE:
1. W. Davis-Interviews Joan Sutton on "Fashion Canada," a Federally-Sponsored Program to Develop Canada's Fashion Industry.
2. W. Metcalfe-Marketing Possibilities for Canada's Grain Crop.
3. A. Allen-The Automobile and the Bicycle.

RADIO CANADA NEWS:
1. F. Hillary-Japanese Delegate on Pollution in Tokyo.
2. P. Loucks-Canadian Inmates to be Given More Say in Prison Management and Conditions.
3. D. Willman-Coup in Sudan.

COMMENT:W. Coven-Canada's Peace-Keeping Image.

SPORTS, STOCKMARKET & NEWS HEADLINES:

CARIBBEAN AND AMERICAN:

RADIO CANADA NEWS:
1. F. Hillary-Japanese Delegate on Pollution in Tokyo.
2. P. Loucks-Canadian Inmates to be Given More Say in Prison Management and Conditions.
3. D. Willman-Coup in Sudan.

TODAY'S MAGAZINE:
1. W. Metcalfe-Marketing Possibilities for Canada's Grain Crop.
2. R. Doucette-Air Canada Mediation Talks.
3. A. Allen-The Automobile and the Bicycle.

SPORTS, STOCKMARKET & NEWS HEADLINES:

WEDNESDAY

AFRO-EUROPE:

RADIO CANADA NEWS:
1. D. Sells-Profile of Sudan's New Leader, Major Atta.
2. M. Scheilifer-Arab Reaction to Sudan Coup.
3. H. Brileu-Roy Gordon Jenkins, British Deputy-Opposition Leader, Launches Scathing Attack on Australia
4. C. Godbold-U.S. Reassures Taiwan on Defence Agreements.

TODAY'S MAGAZINE:
1. A. Salem-Interviews Dr. Z. I. Zabrey, National Coordinator of the "Nutrition Canada" Survey.
2. A. Allen-The Automobile and the Bicycle.

SPORTS & NEWS HEADLINES:

SOUTH PACIFIC:

RADIO CANADA NEWS: Same as AFRO-EUROPE plus:
                            R. Inwood-Uncertainty Over Future
                            Administration of Montreal Port.

TODAY'S MAGAZINE:Same as AFRO-EUROPE.

FORUM:Foreign Aid.

CROSS CANADA NEWS:

SPORTS, STOCKMARKET & NEWS HEADLINES:

EUROPE AND NORTH AMERICA:

RADIO CANADA NEWS: 1. B. Cunningham-British Debate re ECM.
                            2. R. Inwood-Uncertainty Over Future
                               Administration of Montreal Port.
                            3. C. Godbold-U.S. Reassures Taiwan on
                               Defence Agreements.
                            4. Senior Armed Forces Officer-Cost of
                               Searches for Missing Aircraft.

TODAY'S MAGAZINE: 1. W. Metcalfe-Marketing Possibilities for
                               Canada's Grain Crop.
                            2. B. Neilson-Permanent Body Needed to
                               Protect Consumers' Interests.

FORUM:Same as SOUTH PACIFIC.

CROSS CANADA NEWS:

SPORTS & NEWS HEADLINES:

EUROPE II:

RADIO CANADA NEWS:General News for Europe.

AFRICA II:

RADIO CANADA NEWS: 1. R. Abra-Pakistanis on Situation for
                                 Them in Canada.
                              2. G. Mesley-Health Scandal Breaks in
                                 Montreal.
                              3. T. Jagninski-Montreal's Black People
                                 Supplying Their Own Summer Schools
                                 for Their Kids.

TODAY'S MAGAZINE: 1. R. Stone-Interviews Roger Jarvis Who
                                 Runs a Calgary Travel Agency
                                 Specializing in Tours of the Canadian
                                 North.
                              2. M. Zwelling-Federal Government Passes
                                 New Labour Bill.
                              3. B. Neilson-Permanent Body Needed to
                                 Protect Consumers' Interests.

SPORTS, STOCKMARKET & NEWS HEADLINES:

EUROPE III:

RADIO CANADA NEWS: 1. S. Rosenfeld-President Nixon's Proposed
                                 Visit to China.
                              2. PRESS REVIEW: Strategic Arms
                                 Limitation Talks in Finland.
                              3. J. Blake-Recent Report of the Standing
                                 Committee on Indian Affairs and
                                 Northern Development.
                              4. R. Abra-Pakistanis on Situation for
                                 Them in Canada.
                              5. G. Mesley-Health Scandal Breaks.
                              6. T. Jagninski-Black People Supplying
                                 Own Summer Schools for Their Kids.
                              7. D. Halton-China Ambassador to Visit
                                 Ottawa.

COMMENT: B. Nielson-Permanent Body Needed to
                              Protect Consumers' Interests.

SPORTS, STOCKMARKET & NEWS HEADLINES:

CARIBBEAN AND AMERICAN:

RADIO CANADA NEWS:
1. R. Abra-Pakistanis on Situation for Them in Canada.
2. G. Mesley-Health Scandal Breaks.
3. T. Jagninski-Black People Supplying Own Summer Schools for Their Children.
4. D. Halton-China Ambassador to Visit Ottawa.

TODAY'S MAGAZINE:
1. J. Blake-Recent Report of the Standing Committee on Indian Affairs and Northern Development.
2. T. Jagninski-Interviews Gwen Lord on the Problems of West Indian School Children.
3. A. Salem-Interviews Dr. Z. I. Zabrey on "Nutrition Canada."

SPORTS, STOCKMARKET & NEWS HEADLINES:

THURSDAY

AFRO-EUROPE:

RADIO CANADA NEWS:
1. D. Halton-Chinese Ambassador on His Way to Ottawa.
2. J. Drewery-Pakistani Supporters Say Situation Exaggerated.
3. D. Willman-Arabs Hate King Hussein.
4. PM Trudeau-No Election This Fall. (ACTUALITY)

TODAY'S MAGAZINE:
1. PRESS REVIEW: President Nixon's Forthcoming Visit to Peking.
2. J. Blake-Recent Report of the Standing Committee on Indian Affairs and Northern Development.

SPORTS & NEWS HEADLINES:

SOUTH PACIFIC:

RADIO CANADA NEWS:	Same as AFRO-EUROPE.
TODAY'S MAGAZINE:	Same as AFRO-EUROPE plus: B. Whitehead-Diamonds.
CROSSTALK:	
FOLK SONG TIME:	With Daphne Stanford and Gordon Redding.
CROSS CANADA NEWS:	

SPORTS, STOCKMARKET & NEWS HEADLINES:

EUROPE AND NORTH AMERICA:

RADIO CANADA NEWS:
1. B. Cunningham-BOAC Airliner Forcer to Land in Libya.
2. J. Chadwick-Egypt Trial re Anti-Sadat Plotters.
3. B. Cunningham- Parliamentary War Looms Over ECM.
4. PM Trudeau-No Election This Fall. (ACTUALITY)
5. Lorne Mystrom, Canadian MP-Misleading Advertising. (ACTUALITY)
6. D. Delmage-Chicken and Egg War May Be Over Soon.

TODAY'S MAGAZINE:
1. J. Merrit-Interviews Les Montashaw on the Nanaimo Bathtub Race.
2. R. Stone-Interviews Roger Jarvis on Tours of the Canadian North.
3. M. Sheldon-Creating Patriotism Through Advertising.

FOLK SONG TIME:

CROSS CANADA NEWS:

SPORTS & NEWS HEADLINES:

EUROPE II:

RADIO CANADA NEWS: General News for Europe.

AFRICA II:

RADIO CANADA NEWS: 1. B. Cunningham-BOAC Airliner Forced
                               to Land in Libya.
                            2. M. Littlejohns-U.N. Mission to
                               Portuguese Africa.
                            3. R. Abra-French Foreign Minister to
                               Visit Ottawa.
                            4. D. Delmage-Chicken and Egg War Over.

TODAY'S MAGAZINE: 1. M. Sheldon-Creating Patriotism
                               Through Advertising.
                            2. T. Weiss-Interviews Doug Sinclair on
                               Canadian Films.
                            3. R. MacInnes-A Visit to an
                               Oceanographic Laboratory in
                               Dartmouth, Nova Scotia.

CROSS CANADA NEWS:

SPORTS, STOCKMARKET & NEWS HEADLINES:

EUROPE III:

TODAY'S MAGAZINE: 1. A. Salem-Interviews Dr. Z. I. Zabrey on
                               "Nutrition Canada."
                            2. J. Merrit-Interviews Les Montashaw on
                               the Nanaimo Bathtub Race.
                            3. T. Weiss-Interviews Doug Sinclair on
                               Canadian Films.

RADIO CANADA NEWS: 1. B. Cunningham-BOAC Airliner Forced
                               to Land in Libya.
                            2. George Ignatieff, Canadian
                               Representative at Disarmament Talks in
                               Geneva-Canada's Plan for Nuclear
                               Disarmament. (ACTUALITY)
                            3. R. Abra-French Foreign Minister to
                               Visit Ottawa.

COMMENT:M. Sheldon-Creating Patriotism Through Advertising.

SPORTS, STOCKMARKET & NEWS HEADLINES

CARIBBEAN AND AMERICAN:

RADIO CANADA NEWS:
1. D. Willman-Situation in the Sudan.
2. R. Abra-French Foreign Minister to Visit Ottawa.
3. George Ignatieff-Canada's Plan for Nuclear Disarmament. (ACTUALITY)

TODAY'S MAGAZINE:
1. M. Sheldon-Creating Patriotism Through Advertising.
2. M. Zwelling-Federal Government Passes New Labour Bill.
3. J. Merrit-Interviews Les Montashaw on the Nanaimo Bathtub Race.

SPORTS, STOCKMARKET & NEWS HEADLINES:

FRIDAY

AFRO-EUROPE:

RADIO CANADA NEWS:

TODAY'S MAGAZINE:
1. M. Sheldon-Creating Patriotism Through Advertising.
2. G. Atkins-Interviews Chris Armstrong on Killing Sea Lampreys in the Great Lakes.

SPORTS & NEWS HEADLINES:

SOUTH PACIFIC:

RADIO CANADA NEWS:Same as AFRO-EUROPE.

TODAY'S MAGAZINE:
Same as AFRO-EUROPE plus:
W. Metcalfe-Marketing Possibilities for Canada's Wheat Crop.

CROSSTALK:

WORLD OF SCIENCE: 1. We've Got Rhythm.
                           2. Fume Danger Overstated.

CROSS CANADA NEWS:

SPORTS, STOCKMARKET & NEWS HEADLINES:

EUROPE AND NORTH AMERICA:

RADIO CANADA NEWS: 1. E. Condo-Saving Elm Trees.
                           2. Robert Stanfield, PC Leader-Comments
                              on His Recent Trip to Japan and His
                              Findings There. (ACTUALITY)
                           3. K. McDooel-Troops and Police Raid
                              Homes in Northern Ireland in IRA Hunt.
                           4. B. Cunningham-BOAC Plane Forced to
                              Land in Libya.
                           5. D. Delmage-Alberta Provincial Election.
                           6. P. Daniels-Dog Insurance.
                           7. A. Lewis-Peking Trade Group to Hold
                              Talks with Canadian Wheat Board
                              Officials.

TODAY'S MAGAZINE: 1. P. Keatley-Repercussions of
                              Counter-Coup in Sudan.
                           2. G. Atkins-Ox-pulling Competition in
                              Bridgewater, Nova Scotia.
                           3. R. Marven-Interviews Michael Marsden
                              on His Life in the North.

WORLD OF SCIENCE:Same as SOUTH PACIFIC.

CROSS CANADA NEWS:

SPORTS & NEWS HEADLINES:

EUROPE II:

RADIO CANADA NEWS:General News for Europe.

AFRICA II:

RADIO CANADA NEWS: 1. A. Lewis-Arrival of Chinese Trade
                             Mission.
                          2. G. Mesley-QuebecGovernment to Boost
                             Health Care for School Children.
                          3. T. Jagninski-Trials Underway for
                             Canada's Newest and Fastest Train.
                          4. D. Willman-Sudanese Counter-Coup
                             Not a Guarantee of Stability.

TODAY'S MAGAZINE: 1. P. Keatley-Repercussions of
                             Counter-Coup in Sudan.
                          2. D. Bazay-Interviews Paul Gerin-Lajoie
                             on the Development of an African
                             Development Fund.
                          3. J. Zeriski-RCMP and Its Use of Teenage
                             Spies.

CROSS CANADA NEWS:

SPORTS, STOCKMARKET & NEWS HEADLINES:

EUROPE III:

TODAY'S MAGAZINE: 1. B. Cobbin-Interviews Richard Rohmer
                             of Ontario's Royal Commission on
                             Book Publishing.
                          2. P. Holting-Interviews Steve Heagan
                             onWaste Disposal.
                          3. R. MacInnis-Interviews Dr. Murray
                             Mou-Young on Conversion of Oil into
                             Edible Proteins.

RADIO CANADA NEWS: 1. D. Willman-Sudanese Counter-Coup
                             Not a Guarantee of Stability.
                          2. G. Mesley-Quebec Government to Boost
                             Health Care.
                          3. T. Jagninski-Trials Underway for
                             Canada's Newest and Fastest Train.

COMMENT: D. Struthers-Air Canada Machinists' Strike.

SPORTS, STOCKMARKET & NEWS HEADLINES:

CARIBBEAN AND AMERICAN:

RADIO CANADA NEWS:
1. G. Mesley-Ouebec Government to Boost Health Care.
2. T. Jagninski-Trials Underway for Canada's Newest and Fastest Train.

TODAY'S MAGAZINE:
1. D. Struthers-Air Canada Machinists' Strike.
2. R. MacInnis-Interviews Dr. Murray Mou-Young on Converting Oil into Edible Proteins.

SPORTS, STOCKMARKET & NEWS HEADLINES:

SATURDAY

AFRO-EUROPE:

RADIO CANADA NEWS:

FOCUS: B. Whitehead-The Loon.

SHORTWAVE CLUB: With Basil Duke.

SPORTS & NEWS HEADLINES:

SOUTH PACIFIC:

RADIO CANADA NEWS:

FOCUS: Same as AFRO-EUROPE.

SHORTWAVE CLUB:

COUNTRY STYLE: With Ron Scott and Syd Davison.

L'ATTITUDE: 1. Ethnic Festival.
                                 2. Vive La Difference.
                                 3. Where Men Are Men.

SPORTS, STOCKMARKET & NEWS HEADLINES:

EUROPE AND NORTH AMERICA:

RADIO CANADA NEWS:

FOCUS: Same as AFRO-EUROPE.

SHORTWAVE CLUB:

COUNTRY STYLE:

L'ATTITUDE: Same as SOUTH PACIFIC.

SPORTS & NEWS HEADLINES:

EUROPE II:

RADIO CANADA NEWS: General News for Europe.

AFRICA II:

RADIO CANADA NEWS:

THE IN BIT:

SHORTWAVE CLUB:

COUNTRY STYLE:

SPORTS & NEWS HEADLINES:

EUROPE III:

RADIO CANADA NEWS:

SPORTS REVIEW:

RENDEZ-VOUS:D. Finkleman-A Visit to a French School in Toronto.

SHORTWAVE CLUB:

COUNTRY STYLE:

SPORTS & NEWS HEADLINES:

CARIBBEAN AND AMERICAN:

RADIO CANADA NEWS:

FOCUS: Same as AFRO-EUROPE.

SHORTWAVE CLUB:

SPORTS & NEWS HEADLINES:

CBC INTERNATIONAL SERVICE WEEKLY REPORT

LANGUAGE SECTION: English II
DATE: July 18, 1971 to July 24, 1971

A. CANADIAN PRESS REVIEW: a) Nixon Visit to Peking.
b) Resumption of SALT Talks.
(1/4 hour weekly)c) The James Bay Project.

TAPE:
1. WAMU, Washington, D.C.
2. North American Broadcasting Corporation, Monte Rio, California.
3. NABC Regional Centre, Northfield, Minnesota.
4. Radio CFN, Germany.
5. Malawi Broadcasting Corporation, Blantyre, Malawi.

FEED:
1: WNYC, New York City.
2. Broadcasting Foundation of America, New York City.

B. THE WORLD OF SCIENCE: a) Farewell Gonorrhea (4:01)
                             b) Hello Slowpoke(3:13)
                             c) Seabed Research Capsule (2:53)
                             d) Once Upon a Time There Was a Grizzly
                                Bear (2:22)

TAPE: 1. BFA program: *International Science
                               Report*—Distribution to 27 US stations.
                             2. 7 US independent stations.
                             3. 47 Overseas stations.

C. L'ATTITUDE: a) The Daily Whodunit (0:05)+ (3:40)
                             b) There's Something About an Island(3:53)
                             c) How Much Is a Queen Worth (4:32)

TAPE: 1. BFA programs: *International Literary
                               Report, Panorama of the Lively Arts*
                               and Features of the Week—Distribution
                               to 87 U.S. stations (frequent use of items).
                             2. 7 U.S. independent stations.
                             3. 43 Overseas stations.

FEED: 1. Australian Broadcasting Commission,
                               New York City.
                             2. WNYC, New York City.
                             3. Broadcasting Foundation of America,
                               New York City.

D.FORUM:a) Youth and Development (24:55)

TAPE: 1. North American Broadcasting
                               Corporation, Monte Rio,
                               California—Distribution to 169 stations
                               weekly).
                             2. BFA program: *New Dimensions of
                               Education*—Distribution to 70 U.S.
                               stations.
                             3. 6 U.S. independent stations.
                             4. 43 Overseas stations.

E. COMMENTARY ON AFRICAN AFFAIRS:
Four minutes weekly. Sent to 15 African stations: Patrick Keatley assesses the possibility of British warships purchase by one of South Africa's most important military figures.

F. SPECIAL ITEMS BY TAPE:
July 20—"Use of Wood in Housing" (1:27) by Gordon Mesley: Sent to Peter Hendry, Senior Information Officer, FAO (UN), Washington, D.C.

G. SPECIAL ITEMS BY SHORTWAVE AND/OR CABLE:

Nil.

CBC INTERNATIONAL SERVICE WEEKLY REPORT

TRANSCRIPTION AND RELAY PROGRAMS
DATE: July 18, 1971 to July 24, 1971

A. SPOKEN WORD TRANSCRIPTIONS:

FOLK SONG	A SONG HISTORY OFCANADA	4x1/4-hr:	1 Overseas: Radio Newspaper, Panama 1, R. P.
TALK	CANADIANECDOTES E-618-620	4x1/4-hr:	1 Overseas: Hong King Broadcasting Co.Ltd., Hong Kong
TALK	CANADIANECDOTES II E-618-620	3x1/4-hr:	1 Overseas: Hong Kong Broadcasting Co. Ltd., Hong Kong
LITERATURE	MORLEY CALLAGHAN SHORT STORIES E-662-674	13x1/2-hr:	1 Overseas: Rediffusion (M) Sdn. Bhn. Kuala Lumpur, Malaysia
HUMOUR	THE RUM RUNNERS	13x1/2-hr:	1 U.S. Educational
TALK	CANADIANECDOTES III E-780-785	6x1/4-hr:	1 Overseas: Hong Kong Broadcasting Co. Ltd., Hong Kong

DRAMA   KLONDIKE   5x1/2-hr: 1 Miscellaneous
                 E-912-916

POETRY   POEMS FOR VOICES   6x1/2-hr: 3 U.S. Educational
                 E-917-922   1 U.S. Commercial
                                      2 Overseas:
                                      - University of New South Wales,
                                      Kensington, N.S.W., Australia
                                      - Education Dept. (Radio), Island
                                      of St. Helena

TALK   THEREFORE CHOOSE   6x1/2-hr: 2 U.S. Educational
                 LIFE E-923-928   1 U.S. Commercial
                                      1 Overseas:
                                      - University of New South Wales,
                                      Kensington, N.S.W., Australia

DOCUMENTARY SEARCHING   13x1/2-hr: 40 U.S. Educational
                 E-929-941   7 U.S. Commercial
                                      16 Overseas:
                                      - Forces Radio Sharjah (RAF),
                                      Arabian Gulf
                                      - Radio Malaysia, Kuala Lumpur,
                                      Malaysia
                                      - ELWA, Monrovia, Liberia
                                      - Radio Brunei, Borneo
                                      - Radio Zambia, Lusaka, Zambia
                                      - DZHP Radio, Manila, Philippines
                                      - Rediffusion Singapore, Singapore
                                      - Antigua Broadcasting Service,
                                      St. John's, Antigua
                                      - Radio Veritas, Manila, P. I.
                                      - Rediffusion (M) Sdn. Bhd.,
                                      Kuala Lumpur, Malaysia
                                      - WSZO, Majuro, Marshall Islands
                                      - Radio Belize, Belize City,
                                      British Honduras
                                      - Rediffusion (Malta) Ltd.,
                                      Guaradmangia, Malta
                                      - Radio Newspaper, Panama, R. P.
                                      - Hong Kong Comm. Broadcasting,
                                      Hong Kong
                                      - Radio Gambia, Bathurst, Gambia
                                      - 1 Miscellaneous

FOLK ROCK	THE MUSIC FROM SEARCHING E-942	2x1/2-hr:	35 U.S. Educational 7 U.S. Commercial

2x1/2-hr: 35 U.S. Educational
                  7 U.S. Commercial
   17 Overseas:
- Forces Radio Sharjah (RAF),
  Arabian Gulf
- Radio Malaysia, Kuala Lumpur,
  Malaysia
- ELWA, Monrovia, Liberia
- Radio Brunei, Brunei, Borneo
- Radio Zambia, Lusaka, Zambia
- DZHP, Manila, Philippines
- Rediffusion (Singapore) Pte. Ltd.,
  Singapore
- Antigua Broadcasting Service,
  St. John's, Antigua
- Radio Veritas, Manila, P. I.
- Rediffusion (M) Sdn. Bhd.,
  Kuala Lumpur, Malaysia
- WSZO, Majuro, Marshall Islands
- Radio Belize, Belize City,
  British Honduras
- Rediffusion (Malta) Ltd.,
  Guardamangia, Malta
- Radio Voice of the Gospel,
  Addis Ababa, Ethiopia
- Hong Kong Comm. Broadcasting
  Co. Ltd., Hong Kong
- Radio Newspaper, Panama 1, R.P.
- Radio Gambia, Bathurst, Gambia
- 1 Miscellaneous

DOCUMENTARY   NASHAN-ESEN
                           E-943

2x1/2-hr: 30 U.S. Educational
                  5 U.S. Commercial
                  2 Miscellaneous
   15 Overseas:
- Forces Radio Sharjah (RAF),
  Arabian Gulf
- Radio Malaysia, Kuala Lumpur
- Awali Broadcasting Service,
  BAPCO, Bahrain
- DZHP, Manila, Philippines
- Antigua Broadcasting Service St.
  John's, Antigua
- Radio Veritas, Manila, P.I.
- Rediffusion (M) Sdn. Bhd.,
  Kuala Lumpur, Malaysia

- WSZO, Majuro, Marshall Islands
-Radio Belize, Belize City,
  British Honduras
- Rhodesia Broadcasting Corp.,
  Salisbury, Rhodesia
-Rediffusion Malta) Ltd.,
  Guardamangia, Malta
-Radio Voice of the Gospel,
  Addis Ababa, Ethiopia
-Malawi Broadcasting Corp.
  Blantyre, Malawi
-Radio Newspaper, Panama 1, R.P.
-Radio Gambia, Bathurst, Gambia

DOCUMENTARY   NORTH BY SEA   13x1/2-hr: 1 U.S. Educational
              E-944-950

B. MUSIC TRANSCRIPTIONS:

        COUNTERPOINT   13xl-hr: 1 U.S. Educational

C. QUOTES FROM CORRESPONDENCE:

"COUNTERPOINT" looks like a fine series and I am making plans for its use
sometime in the future. I must add my personal thanks for the high quality of the
other programs we have received from you, especially the JEUNESSES MUSI-
CALES series. These recordings are both technically and aesthetically pleasing.

                              Gordon Wildman, Music Director,
                                    WAUS, Andrews University,
                              Berrien Springs, Michigan, U.S.A.

I acknowledge, with gratitude, the records sent to me by air under the auspices of
your English Language Transcription Service. I have enjoyed the poems and lectures tremendously. . . . Thank you very much for your services in the field of educational broadcasting.

                                    Professor S. H. O. Tomori,
                                    Head of the Dept. of Adult
                              Education, University of Ibadan,
                                            Ibadan, Nigeria

CBC International Service Weekly Report

LANGUAGE SECTION: Française
DATE: 19 juillet 1971 au 26 juillet 1971
DAILY TRANSMISSIONS:

lière émission:
    AFRIQUE via BBC,
    EUROPE   07:45-08:00 GMT - 03:45-04:00 HAE
2ième émission:
    ANTILLES, USA,
    EUROPE   13:15-13:43 GMT - 08:15-09:43 HAE
3ième émission:
    AFRIQUE   19:15-19:58 GMT - 15:15-15:58 HAE
4ième émission:
    EUROPE   20:00-20:44 GMT - 16:00-16:44 HAE

EXPORTATIONS:

CANADA '71:
    Cameroun, Tchad, Saint-Pierre et Miquelon, Burundi, Nouvelle Guinée,
    Repé Khmère, CAE Allemange, Gabon
    HAITI; Radio Haiti, Radio Métropole, Radio
    Nouveaumonde, Radio Port-au-Prince.

    1. Chronique scientifique avec Jacques Michel et Bernard Daudier sur la
       météorologie au Canada.
    2. Géralde Lachance et Bernard Daudier: les voitures au Canada et le
       prix de l'essence.

LE MONDE PARLE AU CANADA: (reseau national)

    Émission réalisée par M. H. Auzat en collaboration avec la radio
    tchèque-visite de la capitale de la Tchécoslovaquie, Prague.

TUNISIE:

    1. Ent. de Huguette Pilon avec René Ferron-roman de Michèle Jacob,
       Feuilles de Thym et Fleur d'amour un nouveau recueil de poème de
       Claude Péloquin "Pour la grandeur de l'home."
    2. Chronique scientifique avec B. Daudier et J. Michel: satellite canadien
       pour les ressources naturelles.

  3. Ent. de Ch. Temerson à Paris avec Jean Marie Leger, lauréat du prix Léopold Senghot.
  4. Ent. de B. Halaou avec Jean Paul l'Aklier, de retour de Dakar où se tenait la conférence des ministres de la jeunesse des pays francophones.
  5. Reportage de Maryse Reicher sur le 7e concoùrs international de musique.

Lundi 19 juillet 1971:

lière émission:

NOUVELLES:

  1. Dossier CHINE:
Nixon voyage Pékin; GB annonce appui; candidature Chine ONU; Canada appuie pour 2e année candidature Pékin et votera résolution demandant que demande Albanie soit considérée comme question importante; Chou en Lai annonce visite minist. haut niveau de France; délégation francaise en Chine; Stanfield part pour Pékin.
  2. Reprise négociations à Air Canada.
  3. Fin congrès des Indiens du Canada-sonore Bringué.
  4. Situation des réfugiés palestineins en Jordanie.
  5. Reunion du parlement maro Musique: cian pour créer cour de su Ouverture from Tommy rete de l'état.
  6. Leaders religieux d'Af. du Sud comparent dirigeant aux nazis.
  7. Humour: directrice école de jeunes filles bannit les arachides qui sont à son avis des situmlants sexuels.
  8. Sports: baseball, natation cyclisme, course automobile athlétisme.

2ième émission:

NOUVELLES:

  1. Situation à Air Canada.
  2. Satisfaction de tout le monde dans la nationalisation de la Demerara.
  3. Défaite candidat du gouv Allende au Chili.
  4. Appui do parti socialiste de gauche national à Juan Peron (élections prés. en Argentine).

ENT. ET REPORTAGES:

1. Revue de presse de J. C. Daigle.
2. Ent. de B. Daudier avec J. L. Doudeau-la Can-Am.

3ième émission:

NOUVELLES: Chrétien part pour URSS entrevue de Millet.

ENT. ET REPORTAGES:

1. Revue de presse de J. C. Daigle.
2. Ent. de Baba Halaou avec Léon Damas, écrivain et poète antillais.
3. Chronique littéraire avec René Ferron et Huguette Pilon Encycl. antiquités.

MUSIQUE: R. Charlebois: Californie.

4ième émission:

NOUVELLES: Idem.

ENT. ET REPORTAGES: Idem.

1. Ent. avec Henri Legaré par Yvan Leclerc-ICNAF les pecheries au Canada.
2. Ent. de B. Daudier avec G. Lachance-les marché d'alimentation no. 1.
3. Courrier des auditeurs avec Judith Gay.

MUSIQUE: Raoul Roy: Greenland Fisheries.

Mardi 20 juillet 1971:

1ière émission:

NOUVELLES:

1. DOSSIER CHINE:
   URSS: afirme que si Pékin reconnu à ONU et Formose retranchée, ONU seront intern.; Wash.: refus de mommenter programme en 8 pts de Chou en Lai pour nor maliser relations Chine USA; Diplomate chinois, Huang Hua au Canada dans q.q. jours.

2. Ambass. Algérie au Canada arrivé-nominations autre diplomates par Sharp-sur la participation Decelles paour Algérie Can. du canada à l'Organisa.
3. 3 parlem. can. sont revetion pay américaine de la nus Pakistan-ent. Milletsanté. Lachance.
4. Conf. mins. prov. de Agriculture-sonore Bringué.
5. Anniversaire C. B. présentation totem de cette prov. au N. Brunswick sonore Duguay.
6. Soudan: virage à gauche de nouvelle administration-coup état heir.
7. OUA: forme commission pays chargés de libérer régions colonisées.
8. Compte à Rebours commence à Cap Kennedy-sonore Sauvé.

2ième emission:

NOUVELLES:

1. Grèves aux USA.
2. Grève en argentine.
3. Au Mexique: général Lara démos de ses fonctions.

ENT. ET REPORTAGES:

Ent. de Lucile Horner avec M. Jose Herrera Pena direct. du pavillon mexicain à T. des Hommes.

3ième émission:

NOUVELLES: Aucune nouvelle specifique.

ENT. ET REPORTAGES:

1. Chronique économique avec Idem avec Maryse Reicher et Henri Mhun: accords commerciaux avec Canada dansle livre blanc déposé par M. Heath pour entree de la G. B. dans le Marché commun.
2. Comm. de Louise Decelles Idem sur l'accréditation de 1' ambassadeur de l'Algéie au près du gouv. canadien.
3. Annonce concours J. Ouvrad.
4. Chron. Ouvrard/Horner: Nord est canadien.
5. Ent. avec L. H. Desjardins la Haute volta-visite
6. Ruban sur l'Unesco

MUSIQUE: A. Gagnon: Format 30.

4ième émission:

NOUVELLES: Idem.

ENT. ET REPORTAGES:

1. Ent. de J. Sarrazin avec G. Lefebvre sur les jeunesses musicales du Mont Orford.
2. Ent. de B. Daudier avec G. Lachance: less marchés d'ailmentation au Canada no. 2.

MUSIQUE: Lee Gagnon: Summertime.

Mercredi 21 juillet 1971:

lière émission:

NOUVELLES:
1. DOSSIER CHINE:
   Huang Hua à Ott. vendredi; Globe & Mail parle conditions posées par Chou en Lai pour normalisation des relations sinoamericaines; réactions de Washington; réactions prudentes Moscouves; Voyage Nixon en Chine; réactions france; Japon intéressé à normali ser relations avec Pékin; Stanfield à Tokyo vers Hong Kong et Pékin sonore Grenier.
2. Rumeurs élections générales à Ottawa et Regina sonore Bringué.
3. Conf. minist. prov. agriculture et preparation conf. des prem. mins. de Victoria.
4. Chrétien en URSS.
5. Situation Jourdan.
6. Mission apollo 15-lein Jacques Michel.
7. Debut débat à Londres sur projet présenté par Heath entrée GB marché commun.

2ième émission:

NOUVELLES:

1. Arrestations Mexico.
2. Premier anniversaire de la guérilla à Teoponte, en Bolivie sept bombes déposées.

3. Canadien et six philippin disparus sont retrou.
4. Sports.

ENT. ET REPORTAGES:

1. Ent. d'Y. Leclerc avec le consul gén. Haiti à Montreal centrale hydro
   électrique.
2. Ent. avec M. Enrico Franco- conf. sur industrie du bois à Vancouver.

MUSIQUE: G. Reno: L'amour carend jeureux.

3ième émission:

NOUVELLES: Aucune nouvelle spécifique.

ENT. ET REPORTAGES:

1. Chronique scientifique avec Jacques Michel et B. Daudier: Apollo 15.
2. Ent. avec M. Pouliot du centre québécois des relations internationales.
3. Ent. de M. Reicher avec M. A. Lamy de l'ONF: pavillon à Terre des
   Hommes.
4. Ent. avec L. H. Desjardins: visite du Niger.

4ième émission:

NOUVELLES: Idem.

ENT. ET REPORTAGES: Idem.

1. Chronique littéraire avec H. Pilon et R. Ferron encyclopédie antiquités.
2. Ent. de L. Horner avec M. M. Crépeau et Saumur congrès des témoins
   de Jehovah.
3. Courrier des auditeurs avec Judith Gay.

Jeudi 22 juillet 1971:

lière émission:

NOUVELLES:

1. Soudan: nimeiry reprend pouvoir-fil des événements depuis 24 heures.
2. Guinée: craitne coup état.
3. Ghana: expulsion attaché commercial soviétique.
4. Tanzanie: propose jour férié international.
5. Trudeau: pas d'élection avant 1972.
6. Trudeau: itinéraire voyage cote est.
7. Conf. mins. prov. agriculture à Edmonton-sonore Bringué.
8. Air Can: situation normale accord de principe.
9. Chretien en URSS: propose équipe URSS Can. exploration arctique.
10. Huang Hua arrive à Ott. demain.
11. Stanfield au Japon vers Pékin-sonore Grenier sur reactions japonaises voyage Nixon à Pékin.
12. Vice prem. mins. chinois dit volonte de son gouv. de libérer Taiwan devant délégation algérienne conduite par Bouteflika.
13. M. Jayakumar nommé haut comm. de Singapour au Can.
14. Compte rebours normal Cap Kennedy.

2ième émission:

NOUVELLES:

1. Avions can. au Pérou.
2. Nouvelle loi sur partis politiques au Brésil.
3. Aide de France à Haiti.
4. Récolte canae à sucre à Cuba.

ENT. ET REPORTAGES:

1. Chronique économique avec Mhun-et M. Reicher: accords avec le Canada dans livre blanc de M. Heath au sujet de entrée de la G. B. dans Marché commun.
2. Chronique sciéntifique avec J. Michel et B. Daudier.

3ième émission:

NOUVELLES:

Schuman en visite au Canada en septembre, au Québec également.

ENT. ET REPORTAGES:

1. Ent. de Louise Decelles avec M. Lachance qui revient du Pakistan.

2. Ent. de Lucile Horner avec M. Godin-l'U. Queen's de Toronto.
3. Ent. de Lucile Horner avec un participants de SECOM.
4. Ent. avec L. H. Desjardins visite du Dahomey.

MUSIQUE: I. Pierre: Un instant.

4ième émission:

NOUVELLES:

ENT. ET REPORTAGES: Idem.

1.Concours Ouvrard.
2.Chronique Ouvrard/Horner-Jours du Klondike.
3.Ent. de M. Reicher avec M. Hochart-emploi dubois dans construction de maisons.
4.Courrier des auditeurs avec Judith Gay.

MUSIQUE: Le Coeur d'une génération Vivre.

1. Ent. de B. Halaou avec Dr. Bourget-centre de recher ches agronomique de Québec.
2. Ent. avec Jacques N'Joya Tourisme et développement en Afrique noire.

4ième émission:

NOUVELLES: Idem.

ENT. ET REPORTAGES: Idem.

1. Ent. de B. Daudier avec G. Lachance-cuisine et accessoires.
2. Ent. de M. Reicher avec Monique Leyrac.

MUSIQUE:

1. M. Leyrac: Fugues de Back.
2. " : La Veuve.
3. Lee Gagnon: Summertime.
4. " : Take five.

Samedi 24 juillet 1971:

lière émission:

NOUVELLES:

1. Arrivée de ambassadeur de rep. pop. de Chine saluée avec enthousiasme par de nmbreux canadiens de'Origine chinoise.
2. Trudeau avec membres d'une délégation chinoise en visite depuis une semaine au Canada.
3. Stanfield à entrepris visite de 6 jours en Chine.
4. Mme Trudeau donnera nais sance à un enfant en décembre prochain. Première fois qu'un ler minst. can. deviendra père dans l'exercice de son mandat.
5. Situation au Soudan.
6. Spiro Agnew au Maroc pour visite de 24 heures.

2ième émission:

NOUVELLES: aucune nouvelle spécifique.

ENT. ET REPORTAGES:

1. Semaine parlementaire avec Louise Decelles et Maryse Reicher.
2. Ent. de Lucile Horner avec M. Biyd, comm. à L'Hydro Québec problème du systèméme trique au Canada.

Vendredi 23 juillet 1971:

lière émission:

NOUVELLES:

1. Déc: es de Ross Tatcher réactions sonore Bringué.
2. Trudeau dit à nouveau pas elections en 1971, Baldwin pc dit à son tour que Trudeau à peur de perdre.
3. Elections Alba fin aout.
4. Huang Hua arrivé en fin journée à Ottawa hier.
5. Sharp dit que visite Schumann au Can. en sept. té moigne amélioration des relations entre France et Canada.
6. Chrétien à rencontré à Moscou direct. domité planification Maibakov pour parler pipelines consturctions de maisons, etc.
7. Stanfield quitte Hong Kong ce soir pour Pékin.
8. M. Bryce conseiller de Trudeau devient direct. can. au fonds monétaire international.
9. Canada prete au Malawi pour achat 4 locomotives.

10. Situation Soudan: coups de feu à Khartoum, éxécution des putschistes et obsèques pour soldats morts en devoir.
11. Maroc: parlement refuse de creer cour de sureté de l'etat.
12. Ass. nat. Sénégal adopte motion condamnant violations systématiques du territoire par Portugal.

2ième émission:

NOUVELLES: aucune nouvelle specifique.

ENT. ET REPORTAGES:

1. Ent. de Lucile Horner avec M. M. Crépeau et Saumur-congrès des temoins de Jehovah.
2. Concours Ouvrard.
3. Chron. Ouvrard/Horner-Territoires du Nord Ouest.

3ième émission:

NOUVELLES:

1. Huang Hua est arrivé à Ottawa en fin de journée.
2. Stanfield quitte Hong Kong ce soir pour Pékin.

ENT. ET REPORTAGES:

1. Semaine parlementaire avec Louise Decelles et Maryse Reicher.
2. Ent. de Lucile Horner avec un participant de SECOM ent. no. 2.
3. Ent. de Michel Gélinaspar A. Vaisocky-théatre québécois à Toronto.

3ième émission:

NOUVELLES: Idem.

ENT. ET REPORTAGES:

AU CLUB DES AMIS DE RADIO CANADA: Avec B. Daudier, L. Horner et Judith Gay; Chronique de philatélie.

MUSIQUE:

1. C. Renaud: Chason sentimentale pour une fille sentimentale.
2. Les Scarabées: Viva la buena viva.
3. The Bells: Blanc petit oiseau blanc.

ALLO DX:Avec J. L. Huard et Yvan Leclerc: réponses aux questions techniques des auditeurs.

4ième émission:

NOUVELLES: Idem.

ENT. ET REPORTAGES:

IMAGES DU CANADA: Avec Maryse Reicher: Jim Johnson et Haay Aoki: 10,000 miles away, Foggy Dew, Sally Brown, Samson.

MUSIQUE du Corps d'Aviation Royal Canadien:

1. Brass Tactics.
2. Songs along the trail.
3. Step lively.

Dimanche 25 juillet 1971:

1ière émission:

ALLO DX: Avec J. L. Huard et Y. Leclerc: résponses aux questions techniques des auditeurs.

2ième émission:

NOUVELLES:

1. Entretien Allende-Lanusse.
2. Rétablissement des relations Chili-bolivie.
3. Fermes occupées en Bolivie par des guerillros.

ENT. ET REPORTAGES:

AU CLUB DES AMIS DE RADIO CANADA: Avec Judith Gay, Lucile Horner et Bernard Daudier: Chronique de philatélie.

MUSIQUE: D. Dufresne: Le monde commence au jour d'hui.

ALLO DX.

3ième émission:

NOUVELLES:

1. Situation au Soudan: conf. sentences de mort contre.
2. Tout est pret pour départ Apollo 15.
3. Opération grèffe cardiaque et pulmonaire Barnard à Groote Schuur.
4. Liberia: situation après mort de Tubman.
5. Visite ht-comm. zambien au Nigeria.
6. L'Allier, CRTC lien.
7. Caucus UN 17 et 18-8-71.
8. Création program. serv. soc. et de santé pour é coliers zones défavorisées.
9. Cargo DC8 Air Can. quitte Mont. vers Douala pour transport de 50 tonnes médicaments ouevres Lévger.
10. Recommandations conseil supérieur de Education sur nombre élèves en classe élémentaires.
11. Selon AEIPR, P.Q. n'a pas encore subi infiltration des communistes.
12. Sports.

REGARDS SUR LE CANADA:

1. Ent. avec Pierre Juneau de CRTC-politique de la cablovision.
2. Ent. de C. Piché avec 2 fr. et 2 anglophones-francais et anglais à l'U. de C.B.
3. Ent. avec Marc Laurendeau des Cyniques: film canadien IXE 13.

4ième émission:

NOURELLES:

1. De presse de Nimeiry El Nour.
2. Programme de Huang Hua au cours de semaine qui vient.
3. Ouverture demain à Halifax de conf. association des parlementaires du Commonwealth, sect. canadienne.
4. Opinion de Ronning sur visées americaines au Vietnam en regard de l'ouverture des relations avec Pékin.
5. Funétailles de Tatcher demain.

6. Visite premier ministre de Fidji cette semaine à Ottawa.
7. Mlle Georgina Rizk du liban élue Miss Univers.

AU CLUB DES AMIS DE RADIO CANADA: Voir troisième émission de samedi.

ALLO DX: Avec J. L. Huard et Yvan Leclerc.

MUSIQUE DE REGARDS:

1. R. Charlebois: le violent seul.
2. Léveillée: Rendez-vous.
3. Lightfoot: nous vi-8; vons ensemble.

CBC INTERNATIONAL SERVICE WEEKLY REPORT

LANGUAGE: German
DATE: July 18, 1971 to July 24, 1971
TRANSMISSION: 13:45-14:15 EDT-17:45-18:15 GMT
B.B.C. RELAY: 18:30-19:00 GMT

SUNDAY

NEWS BULLETIN:

NEWS COMMENTARY: Visit to China. (Maclean Hunter Business Pub.)

TALK: Pedal Power.

TALK: Radio Canada Shortwave Club No. 439.

MONDAY

NEWS BULLETIN:

TALK: British Columbia Marches Forward.
                            (From *Canadian Scene*)

TALK: Mountain Holiday in British Columbia.

TALK: Attractive Toys for Children.

SCIENTIFIC TALK   :New Artificial Kidney Offers Hope for
                                   Faster Treatment. (From *Montreal Star*,
                                   12.7.71)

STOCK MARKET REPORT:

TUESDAY

NEWS BULLETIN:

NEWS
COMMENTARY: Packing for Peking. (From *Gazette*)

TALK: Opportunity for Youth Programme.

TALK: Young Canadians Travel and Learn.
                                   (From *Canadian Scene*)

TALK: Life in Isolated Village Faces Industry
                                   Change. (From *Gazette*, 15.7.71)

STOCK MARKET REPORT:

WEDNESDAY

NEWS BULLETIN:

INTERVIEW/TALK: Felix Slavik, Mayor of Vienna, Elected
                                   President of IULA.

INTERVIEW: With F. P. Decker on Summer Programme
                                   of Montreal Symphony Orchestra.

TALK: Crown Assets Disposal Corporation.
                                   (From *Weekend Magazine*)

TALK: Jasper National Park. (From *Canadian
                                   Scene*)
STOCK MARKET REPORT:

THURSDAY

NEWS BULLETIN:

NEWS COMMENTARY: Prospect for Canadian Wheat Crop.

INTERVIEW: With Armenians on Armenian Week.

INTERVIEW: With H. J. Vogel on IULA Conference

TALK: Sightseeing Tours Through Old Montreal.
                            (From Canadian Scene)

STOCK MARKET REPORT:

FRIDAY

NEWS BULLETIN:

PRESS REVIEW: The Prospects for Arab Unity.

MUSIC: Hit Parade.

SCIENTIFIC TALK: Slow Poke: Reacteur Nucleaire.

STOCK MARKET REPORT:

SATURDAY

NEWS BULLETIN:

LETTER BOX:

MUSIC: Country Music.

RELAY FOR LIVE TRANSMISSION OVERSEAS

20.7.   2-WAY TALK   IATA Conference and Air Fare to Canada
                            b/c: Hallo Twens

DESTINATION: 17'15 Europawelle Saar

RELAY FOR LIVE TRANSMISSION OVERSEAS

23.7.   INTERVIEW/TALK   Mayor Slavik of Vienna as President of IULA

DESTINATION: 4'05 Austrian Radio

CBC INTERNATIONAL SERVICE WEEKLY REPORT

SECTION: Czech and Slovak
LANGUAGE: Czech
DATE: July 18, 1971 to July 24, 1971

1ST TRANSMISSION:

NEWS BULLETIN NO. 1
PRESS REVIEW: Looking Through the Canadian Newspapers:
                               Poland-Old Problems Confront the New
                               Leadership. By: R. Olynyk

TALK: Canadian Cities Series:
                                  Stratford, Ontario. By: G. Finstad

TALK: CBC Stamp Corner:
                               1. Summer Maple Leaf.
                               2. World's Fastest Postal Service Coming
                                  to Canada.
                               3. Listeners' Questions.
                               4. New Issues. By: G. P. Pick

MUSIC: Instrumental

2ND TRANSMISSION:

NEWS BULLETIN NO. 2
PRESS REVIEW: Looking Through the Canadian Newspapers:
                               Poland-Old Problems Confront the New
                               Leadership. By: R. Olynyk

TALK: Canadian Cities Series:
                               Stratford, Ontario. By: G. Finstad

TALK: CBC Stamp Corner:
                                   1. Summer Maple Leaf.
                                   2. World's Fastest Postal Service Coming
                                      to Canada.
                                   3. Listeners' Questions.
                                   4. New Issues. By: G. P. Pick

MUSIC: Instrumental

MONDAY

1ST TRANSMISSION:

NEWS BULLETIN NO. 1:
PRESS REVIEW: Looking Through the Canadian Newspapers:
                                   President Nixon's Speech on China: First
                                   Canadian Press Reaction. By R. Olynyk

ECONOMIC TALK: Canadian Industry Series:
                                   Canadian Oil Industry. (Based on *The
                                   Petro-chemical Journal.*)

CULTURAL TALK: Cultural Life in Canada:
                                   1. "Figaro" at The National Arts Center
                                      in Ottawa.
                                   2. Spanish Guitarists with the Montreal
                                      Symphony Orchestra.
                                   3. An Interesting Exhibition at the
                                      National Gallery.
                                   4. A New Magazine about Canadian
                                      Books. (Based on *The Gazette* and *The
                                      Montreal Star.*)

2ND TRANSMISSION:

NEWS BULLETIN NO. 2:
PRESS REVIEW: Looking Through the Canadian Newspapers:
                                   President Nixon's Speech on China: First
                                   Canadian Press Reaction. By: R. Olynyk

ECONOMIC TALK: Canadian Industry Series:
                                   Canadian Oil Industry. (Based on *The
                                   Petro-chemical Journal.*)

CULTURAL TALK: Cultural Life in Canada:
                                   1. "Figaro" at the National Arts Center
                                      in Ottawa.
                                   2. Spanish Guitarists with the Montreal
                                      Symphony Orchestra.
                                   3. An Interesting Exhibition at the
                                      National Gallery.
                                   4. A New Magazine about Canadian
                                      Books. (Based on *The Gazette* and *The
                                      Montreal Star.*)

                                   TUESDAY

1ST TRANSMISSION:

NEWS BULLETIN NO. 1:
NEWS COMMENTARY: Soviet Views of Mr. Nixon's China Visit.
                                   By: A. Krause, *Business Week* Magazine
                                   Correspondent, Moscow.

PRESS REVIEW: Looking Through the Canadian Newspapers:
                                   Canada and the East Pakistan Tragedy. By:
                                   R. Olynyk

SPORTS TALK: Sports Review:
                                   1. The Women's British Amateur Athletic
                                      Association Championship in London.
                                   2. Inglesias Captures Swim.
                                   3. Atlanta Chiefs Win Over Montreal
                                      Olympics.
                                   4. Thieves Take Olympic Gift.
                                   5. Tour de la Nouvelle France.
                                   By M. Vitek

2ND TRANSMISSION:

NEWS BULLETIN NO. 2:

NEWS COMMENTARY: Soviet Views of Mr. Nixon's China Visit. By: A. Krause, *Business Week* Magazine Correspondent, Moscow.

PRESS REVIEW: Looking Through the Canadian Newspapers: Canada and the East Pakistan Tragedy. By: R. Olynyk

SPORTS TALK: Sports Review:
1. The Women's British Amateur Athletic Association Championship in London.
2. Inglesais Captures Swim.
3. Atlanta Chiefs Win Over Montreal Olympics.
4. Thieves Take Olympic Gift.
5. Tour de la Nouvelle France.
By: M. Vitek

WEDNESDAY

1ST TRANSMISSION:

NEWS BULLETIN NO. 1

NEWS COMMENTARY: Canada and the United Western Europe. By: R. Olynyk

AGRICULTURAL TALK: Prospects for Canadian Wheat Crop. (Based on B. Metcalfe, *The Ottawa Journal*.)

MUSIC: Canadian Hit Parade. By: H. Zuber

2ND TRANSMISSION:

NEWS BULLETIN NO. 2:

NEWS COMMENTARY: Canada and the United Western Europe. By: R. Olynyk

AGRICULTURAL TALK: Prospects for Canadian Wheat Crop.
                              (Based on B. Metcalfe, *The Ottawa
                              Journal*.)

MUSIC: Canadian Hit Parade. By: H. Zuber

THURSDAY

1ST TRANSMISSION:

NEWS BULLETIN NO. 1:
PRESS REVIEW: Looking Through the Canadian Newspapers:
                              President Nixon's Visit to Peking.
                              By: D. Legate

TALK: Developing Countries: Economic Problems
                              and Need for New Technology-Part I.
                              (By: W. A. Wilson, *The Montreal Star*.)

ACTUALITY BROADCAST: Visit to the Arts Pavilion at "Man and His
                              World." By: H. Zuber

MUSIC: Popular.

2ND TRANSMISSION:

NEWS BULLETIN NO. 2:
PRESS REVIEW: Looking Through the Canadian Newspapers:
                              President Nixon's Visit to Peking.
                              By: D. Legate

TALK: Developing Countries: Economic Problems
                              and Need for New Technology-Part I.
                              (By: W. A. Wilson, *The Montreal Star*.)

ACTUALITY BROADCAST: Visit to the Arts Pavilion at "Man and His
                              World." By: H. Zuber

MUSIC: Popular.

FRIDAY

1ST TRANSMISSION:

NEWS BULLETIN NO. 1:
PRESS REVIEW: Looking Through the Canadian Newspapers:
                                 The Prospects for Arab Unity.
                                 By: V. Rajewsky

NEWS REVIEW: Canadian Round-up:
                                 1. Alcoa's Sale to China.
                                 2. Mr. Stanfield's Visit to China.
                                 3. Chinese Mission in Canada.
                                 4. Calgary Stampede 1971. By: A. Siegel

ACTUALITY BROADCAST: Visit to the U.S. Pavilion at "Man and His
                                 World." By: H. Zuber

2ND TRANSMISSION:

NEWS BULLETIN NO. 2:
PRESS REVIEW: Looking Through the Canadian Newspapers:
                                 The Prospects for Arab Unity.
                                 By: V. Rajewsky

NEWS REVIEW: Canadian Round-up:
                                 1. Alcoa's Sale to China.
                                 2. Mr. Stanfield's Visit to China.
                                 3. Chinese Mission in Canada.
                                 4. Calgary Stampede 1971. By: A. Siegel

ACTUALITY BROADCAST: Visit to the U.S. Pavilion at "Man and His
                                 World." By: H. Zuber

SATURDAY

1ST TRANSMISSION:

NEWS BULLETIN NO. 1:
PRESS REVIEW: Looking Through the Canadian Newspapers:
                                 The Government's Youth Programme in
                                 Action. By: R. Olynyk

MUSIC: Jazz Parade. By: H. Zuber

2ND TRANSMISSION:

NEWS BULLETIN NO. 2:
PRESS REVIEW: Looking Through the Canadian Newspapers:
                                    The Government's Youth Programme in
                                    Action. By: R. Olynyk

MUSIC: Jazz Parade. By: H. Zuber

CBC INTERNATIONAL SERVICE WEEKLY REPORT

SECTION: Czech and Slovak
LANGUAGE: Slovak
DATE: July 18, 1971 to July 24, 1971
TRANSMISSION: 12:15-12:30 P.M.-16:15-16:30 GMT
BBC Relay 19:00-19:15 GMT

SUNDAY:

MUSIC: Music on Request. By: I. Trebichavsky

MONDAY

NEWS   BULLETIN:

FEATURE: The World of Science:
                                    Pot Through the Ages. By: T. Paskal

MUSIC: Hit Parade.

TUESDAY

NEWS BULLETIN:

PRESS REVIEW: President Nixon's Planned Visit to China.
                                    By: V. Rajewsky

FEATURE:

Glimpses of Canada:
1. Oxfam Aid to Canadian Indians and Eskimos.
2. Four Day Work Week in British Columbia. By: Ellison, Bennet

WEDNESDAY

NEWS BULLETIN:

COMMENTARY:

Review of the Federal Labour Code. By: W. List

SPORTS TALK:

Sports Review:
1. Women's Track and Field Meeting in London. Success of Canadian Team.
2. Week at the North American Soccer League.
3. Marathon Swim Race on the Saguenay River.
4. Pele Retires from Brazilian National Team.
5. Tour de la Nouvelle France.
   By: M. Mares

THURSDAY

NEWS BULLETIN:

PRESS REVIEW:

Review of the Canadian Press: Resumption of SALT Talks. By: D. Legate

MUSIC:

Popular.

FRIDAY

NEWS BULLETIN:

PRESS REVIEW:

Islam's Vanishing Dream. (Based on *Montreal Gazette*.)
Review of the Canadian Press: James Bay Project. By: D. Legate

SATURDAY

LETTER-BOX: Answering Listeners' Questions on:
                               Canadian Dollar and the Development of
                               Canada's Currency. By: I. Trebichavsky

TALK: International Stamp Corner:
                               1. British Columbia Centennial Stamp.
                               2. Philatelic Contest. By: I. Trebichavsky

CBC INTERNATIONAL SERVICE WEEKLY REPORT

LANGUAGE: Hungarian
DATE: July 18, 1971 to July 24, 1971
DAILY TRANSMISSIONS:14:15-14:30 EDT-18:15-18:30 GMT
B.B.C. RELAY:19:45-20:00 GMT

SUNDAY

INTERVIEW: L. Volgyi, Vice-President of Synetics
                               Foundation Speaks of the Problems of
                               Pollution in General and "Food Pollution"
                               in Particular.

MONDAY

NEWS BULLETINS:

COMMENTARY: Ramifications of Mr. Nixon's China
                               Announcement. By: A. MacKenzie

LETTER BOX: The Caribou Road and Barkerville in
                               British Columbia.

SCIENTIFIC TALK: Milking Northern Animals.

TUUESDAY

NEWS BULLETINS:

FEATURE: The British Columbia Centennial

INTERVIEW: Mrs. O. Koerner Speaks about How Future Generations Learn Music. (Vancouver)

WEDNESDAY

NEWS BULLETINS:

NEWS REPORT: Chou En-lai's Eight Point Plan for Better Relations with the U.S.

SPORTS TALK: The Soccer Season in Canada. Women Athletes Prepare for the Pan-American Games.

THURSDAY

NEWS BULLETINS:

NEWS REPORT: The Situation in Sudan.

TALKS:
1. Victoria Archeologists to Hawaii-In a Canoe.
2. The Late MacKenzie King's Strange "Medieval" Ruins Near Ottawa.

FEATURE: The Chicken Dance of the Prairie Indian.

FRIDAY

NEWS BULLETINS:

NEWS TALK: Sudanese President Back in Control.

REPORTS: A Day of Art and Music at "MAHW"

SATURDAY

PRESS REVIEW: Nixon's Visit to Peking.

LETTER BOX: The Legendary Saguenay Kingdom
                               Roberval.

TALK: Provincial and National Parks in British
                               Columbia.

CBC INTERNATIONAL SERVICE WEEKLY REPORT

LANGUAGE: Polish
DATE: July 18, 1971 to July 24, 1971
TRANSMISSION:1st Transmission: 11:30-12:00 EDT-15:30-16:00 GMT
2nd Transmission: 13:00-13:15 EDT-17:00-17:15 GMT

SUNDAY

1ST TRANSMISSION:

NEWS BULLETIN:

LETTER BOX: Replies to Listeners in Poland.
                               By: M. Sangowicz

TALK: "Man and His World, 1971."
                               Topics:
                               1. "Man the Collector."
                               2. The Pavilion of Mexico.
                               3. Humor Pavilion.
                               4. Exposition in the Former Pavilion of
                                  France.

2ND TRANSMISSION:

TALK: Youth Chronicle:
                               Problem of Professors from U.S.A. at
                               Canadian Universities. By: Mary Plater
                               and W. Zoltowski

MONDAY

1ST TRANSMISSION:

NEWS BULLETIN:

COMMENTARY: The Ramifications of Mr. Nixon's China Announcement. By: Arch MacKenzie

TALK: Meeting of the Polish Section Shortwave Club.
Topics:
1. Notes and Announcements.
2. Technical Mailbag, Part II. From Mr. J. Bogdanski, Poland Certificate No. 1405: Longwave Transmitters of Extremely High Power; Practical Uses of Very Low Frequencies.
3. The Managements of the Radio Spectrum, Part XV. From Radio-Canada Shortwave Club Script 421 by D. Duke.

2ND TRANSMISSION:

MUSIC: Jazz Review.

TUESDAY

1ST TRANSMISSION:

NEWS BULLETIN:

COMMENTARY: Soviet Views on Mr. Nixon's China Visit. By: A. Krause

SPORTS REVIEW: Topics:
1. Pele, the "King of Soccer", Retires.
2. Preparation for 1976 Olympics: Quebec's Swimming Records Broken. By: M. Serwacki

2ND TRANSMISSION:

CULTURAL TALK: Quebec's Book Publishing Policy. By:
                                    R. Olynyk

SPORTS REVIEW: Topics:
                                    1. An Argentinian Wins the Saguenay
                                       Marathon Swim.
                                    2. Eddy Merckx of Belgium Wins His
                                       Third Consecutive Tour de France.
                                    3. Donohue Triumphs in Can-Am and the
                                       Michigan Twin 200. By: M. Serwacki

WEDNESDAY

1ST TRANSMISSION:

NEWS BULLETIN:

TALK: The Mariposa Folk Festival.
                                    By: M. Schweykowski

FEATURE: The Mariposa Folk Festival. By: L. Halyk

TALK: Canadian Chronicle:
                                    1. Canada-Peking Air Link.
                                    2. Ants May Help Fight Forests' Pests.
                                       By: V. Rajewsky

2ND TRANSMISSION:

INTERVIEW: Alleviation of Stress in Artificial
                                    Surroundings. Interview with Dr. Hans
                                    Selye, University of Montreal.
                                    By: George Atkins

TALK: The Thin Green Line: Canada's
                                    Non-Fighting Forces Around the World.
                                    By: R. Serafinowicz

THURDAY

1ST TRANSMISSION:

NEWS BULLETIN:

CANADIAN PRESS
REVIEW: Nixon's Visit to Peking. By: D. Legate

LETTER BOX: Mailbag. Acknowledgement of Receipt of
                                Our Audience Mail.

2ND TRANSMISSION:

TALK: "Man and His World, 1971."
                                Topics:
                                1. Few General Remarks on This Year's
                                Exhibition.
                                2. "Man the Collector."
                                3. The Pavilion of Mexico.
                                4. Humor Pavilion.
                                5. Exposition in the Former Pavilion of
                                France. By: F. Lubinski

FRIDAY

1ST TRANSMISSION:

NEWS BULLETIN:

NEWS REPORT: The French Foreign Minister, Maurice
                                Schumann, Visits Canada. By: D. Bazay

NEWS REPORT: French Foreign Minister To Visit Ottawa.
                                By: R. Abra

SPORTS REVIEW: Topics:
                                1. Panamerican Games Begin Next Friday.
                                2. Alpine Skiers Not Guilty but the
                                Problem of the Olympic Amateurism is
                                Not Resolved.

3.Annual Commonwealth Shooting
Contest. (Canadians Very Good.)
4. Soccer.
5. Car Racing. By: M. Sangowicz.

2ND TRANSMISSION:

NEWS BULLETIN:

LETTER BOX: Mailbag. Acknowledgement of Receipt of
Our Audience Mail.

SATURDAY

1ST TRANSMISSION:

NEWS BULLETIN:

INTERVIEW: With Mr. A. W. Zbik.
Topic: His Tour of Europe, Part I.

SCIENTIFIC TALK: "Slow Poke"-Nuclear Reactor.
By: A. Vaisocky

2ND TRANSMISSION:

TALK: Meeting of the Polish Section Shortwave
Club. By: M. Serwacki
Topics:
1. Notes and Announcements.
2. The Managements of the Radio
Spectrum, Part XVI. From the
Radio-Canada Short wave Club Script
No. 422, by D. Duke.

CBC International Service Weekly Report

LANGUAGE: Russian
DATE: July 18, 1971 to July 24, 1971
TRANSMISSIONS:
Transmission A:10:15-10:45-14:15-14:45 GMT Relay
Transmission B:12:00-12:15-03:15-03:30 GMT) Delayed
03:30-03:45 GMT) Relay.

Sunday

Program A:

NEWS BULLETIN:

FEATURE: 1. Listeners' Forum No. 259.
     2. Listeners' Comments on Mrs.
       Liberovsky's Trip to U.S.S.R.

FEATURE: Visit to Iran Pavilion.

Program B:

FEATURE: Listeners' Forum No. 259.
     (Repeat from "A")

Monday

Program A:

NEWS BULLETIN:

NEWS TALK: Visit to China. By: Maurice Cutler

FEATURE: Canadian Music Journal No. 172.
     Zola Chaulis at International Piano
     Competition in Montreal.

Program B:
FEATURE: Canadian Music Journal No. 172.
     (Repeat from "A")

TUESDAY

Program A:

NEWS BULLETIN:

NEWS TALK: The Plight of the East Pakistani Refugees.
                                    By: Bill Cunningham

FEATURE: Canadian Encyclopedia: Coins.

Program B:

FEATURE: Salade a la Canadienne:
                                    1. Canada to Ban Cigarette Ads.
                                       By: Robert Abra
                                    2. America's Immigrants of the West
                                       Coast. By: Gordon Mesley
                                    3. It's "Best Seller" Reading in
                                       Newspaper Ads.

WEDNESDAY

Program A:

NEWS BULLETIN:

NEWS TALK: President Nixon's Planned Visit to China.
                                    By: V. Rajewsky

FEATURE: Salade a la Canadienne. (Repeat from
                                    20.7.71)

Program B:

FEATURE: Canadian Science and Technology
                                    Kaleidoscope, No. 61:
                                    1. Canadian STOL Airplanes.
                                    2. Ultra-sound Against Birds. (Repeat from
                                       17.7.71)

Thursday

Program A:

NEWS BULLETIN:

NEWS TALK: The Future of King Hassan and Morocco.
                             By: William Hampshire

FEATURE: 1. Day by Day No. 80.
                             2. Stamp Corner.
                             3. Cruise on Bulgarian Ship "Varna"; Part II.

Program B:

FEATURE: Day by Day No. 80. (Repeat from "A")

Friday

Program A:

NEWS BULLETIN:

NEWS TALK: Chou En-lai's Eight-Point Plan for Better
                             Relations with U.S.A. By: Colin Godbold

FEATURE: 1. Ideas and Action No. 127.
                             2. Slavic Conference in Montreal.
                             3. Prof. G. Ivask on Russian Poetry.

Program B:

FEATURE: Ideas and Action No. 127.
                             (Repeat from "A")

Saturday

Program A:

NEWS BULLETIN:

NEWS TALK:	Press Review: 1. Resumption of SALT Talks. 2. The James Bay Project. By: D. Legate
FEATURE:	1. Apollo 15. 2. French Canadian Dances.
	Program B:
FEATURE:	1. Apollo 15. 2. French Canadian Dances. (Repeat from "A")

CBC INTERNATIONAL SERVICE WEEKLY REPORT

LANGUAGE SECTION: Ukrainian
DATE: July 18, 1971 to July 24, 1971
TRANSMISSIONS: 9:45-10:15 A.M. EST-13:45-14:15 GMT
B.B.C. RELAY: 16:15-16:30 GMT

SUNDAY

LETTER BOX:	International Letter Box: 1. Sunday's Prayer. 2. Our Mail Bag. 3. Protocol on Consultations Between Canada and USSR 4. Harvesting in Canada. 5. Travel Regulations Canada-U.S.A.
TALK:	CBC International Stamp Corner: New Seven Cents Stamp. From *Canada and Transportation.*
NEWS REPORT:	U.S. Reaction to Nixon's Peking Visit.
NEWS BULLETIN:	

MONDAY

FEATURE: A Survey of Ethnic Folkmusic Across
                            Western Canada.

NEWS BULLETIN:

TUESDAY

PRESS REVIEW: Review of the Canadian Press:
                            1. Canada and the United Western Europe.
                            2. President Nixon's Speech on China.

NEWS BULLETIN:

WEDNESDAY

PRESS REVIEW: Review of the Canadian Press:
                            President Nixon's Planned Visit to China.

TALK: The Oriental Pavilion at "Man and His
                            World."

NEWS BULLETIN:

THURSDAY

TALK: The Ethnic Mosaic Pavilion at "Man and
                            His World" Exhibition in Montreal.

COMMENTARY: The Plight of the East Pakistani Refugees.
                            By: Cunningham

NEWS BULLETIN:

FRIDAY

COMMENTARY: Poland: Old Problems Confront the New
                            Leadership. By: Olynyk

CULTURAL TALK: Metropolitan Toronto "International
                            Caravan 71" a Big Success.

NEWS BULLETIN:

SATURDAY

INTERVIEW:With Toronto Composer Z. Lawryshyn.

NEWS REPORT:Ukrainian Canadian Chronicle.

NEWS BULLETIN:

CBC INTERNATIONAL SERVICE WEEKLY REPORT

LANGUAGE: Spanish
DATE: July 18, 1971 to July 24, 1971
TRANSMISSION: Latin America (Spanish)
Daily from 8:00 p.m.-8:45 p.m. EDT-0000-0045 GMT

SUNDAY

SCIENTIFIC TALK: "Origin of Aspirin." By: Helen Hutchinson

CULTURAL TALK: "Canadian Portraits"-William Lyon
                            Mackenzie King. By: J. J. Rodriguez

LITERARY FEATURE: Latine American Legends-Cubanacan

MONDAY

NEWS BULLETIN: National and International News for the
                            Spanish-Speaking Audience.

NEWS COMMENTARY: "The Future of King Hassan and
                            Morocco." By: William Hampshire

LETTER BOX: Review of Weekly Audience Mail and
                            Answers to Listeners' Queries. By: Pablo
                            Bravo

TUESDAY

NEWS BULLETIN: National and International News for the
                               Spanish-Speaking Audience.

NEWS COMMENTARY: "Soviet Views of Mr. Nixon's China Visit."
                               By: Axel Krause

NEWS REPORT:"   Canadian Radio Gazette"
                               1. Interviews with Indio Pascual de la Cruz
                                  TDH (Mexico) and with Mr. Rossete
                                  McGregor. By: J. J. Rodriguez
                               2. "Access to University in Canada." By:
                                  Michael Sheldon
                               3. "Farewell to Mr. Alberto Genis Avila,
                                  Consul of Mexico at Press Club."
                                  Interview by Pablo Bravo.
                               4. Mention of XX International Congress
                                  of Local Authorities, Toronto; and
                                  Announcement of Special Program for
                                  Week of Worldwide Friendship,
                                  Organized by Paraguay.

WEDNESDAY

NEWS BULLETIN: National and International News for the
                               Spanish-Speaking Audience.

NEWS COMMENTARY: "The Review of the Federal Labour
                               Code." By: Wilfred List

CULTURAL TALK: "Philately"-A Series of Programmes on
                               New Stamps, with Contest. By: Carlos
                               Davila

INFORMATION TALK: "Canadian Cities"-Yellowknife. By: Jose
                               Barrio

MUSICAL INTERLUDE: Pete Fountain, Clarinet Solo.

THURSDAY

NEWS BULLETIN: National and International News for the
                                  Spanish-Speaking Audience.

NEWS COMMENTARY: "The Coup in the Sudan". By: Patrick
                                  Keatley

DOCUMENTARY: "Visiting Canada"-The Metropolis.
                                  By: Pedro Bilbao

FRIDAY

NEWS BULLETIN: National and International News for the
                                  Spanish-Speaking Audience.

NEWS COMMENTARY: "Canadian Aid to Africa." Interview with
                                  Paul Gerin-Lajoie.

PRESS REVIEW: 1. Nixon Visit to Peking.
                                  2. Resumption of Salt Talks.
                                  3. The James Bay Project. By: David Legate

SPORTS REVIEW: "The World of Sports." Summary of
                                  Sports Events in Canada and Around the
                                  World. By: Gerardo Mosquera

SATURDAY

NEWS BULLETIN: National and International News for the
                                  Spanish-Speaking udience.

COMMERCIAL REVIEW: "Canadian Expertise in Plants, Seeds
                                  Export of Same. Dairy Live Stock in
                                  Canada," from *Foreign Trade* Magazine.

MUSIC: "Musical Antenna"-Hugo Montenegro's
                                  Orchestra. By: Pablo Bravo

CBC International Service Weekly Report

LANGUAGE: Brazilian
DATE: July 18, 1971 to July 24, 1971
TRANSMISSION:Latin America (Brazil)
Daily from 7:30-8:00 p.m. EDT-23:30-00:00 GMT

SUNDAY

TALK: "Canadian Literature"-Stephen Leacock.

MUSIC: "Canadian Concerts"-Beethoven , Trio lp.
                         70 no. 1. (By: H. Schneeberger, Guy Fallot,
                         Karl Engel)

MONDAY

NEWS BULLETIN:

NEWS REPORT: 1. "The Future of King Hassan and
                            Morocco" By: William Hampshire
                         2. "Mr. Wilson and the Common Market"
                            By: Andre Manderstam

TALK: 1."Electoral Reforms." From *The Gazette*.
                         2."La Tour de las Paix, Une Des Plus
                            Populaires Attractions d'Ottawa."
                            From *La Presse*.

TALK: "Putting Life on Ice." By: Paskal

TUESDAY

NEWS BULLETIN:

NEWS REPORT: 1."Chou En-lai's Eight Point Plan For
                            Better Relations With the United
                            States." By: C. Godbold
                         2 ."The Sudan Coup." By: Diane Wilman

TALK:

1. "Up in the Air, Senior Birdman."
   By: Tom Alderman
2. "La Visite Prochaine de M. Chretien
   Dan l'Artique Sovietique."
   (Communique: Ministere des Affaires
   Indiennes)

TALK:

1. "Trade Union Educational
   Programmes." By: W. List
2. "The Review of the Federal Labour
   Code." By: W. List

WEDNESDAY

NEWS BULLETIN:

NEWS REPORT:

"The James Bay Project."
By: David Legate

TALK:

1. "Mine Sold for $12.50." From *Canada
   Dateline*.
2. "Youth in Canada." By: Gordon Mesley

TALK:

1. "Ants May Help Fight Forest Pests."
   By: V. Rajewsky
2. "Visit to China." By: Maurice Cutler,
   MacLeans

THURSDAY

NEWS BULLETIN:

NEWS REPORT:

1. "The Situation in Sudan." From the
   News Room.
2. "New Soviet Demands for Chinese
   Admission To U.N.." By: Colin Godbold

TALK:

"Audience Mail." By: Carlos Ceneviva

TALK:

"Elected Prisoner's Committees in
Canadian Prisons." By: Peter Louckes

FRIDAY

NEWS BULLETIN:

NEWS REPORT: 1. "Preparatifs pour Apollo 15."
By: Norman Lester
2. "Another Russian Attack on China, But No Mention of Nixon Visit."
By: Chris Kaplin

TALK: 1. "Information Canada." By: V. Rajewsky
2. "Bureau Celebrates 100th Anniversary."
By: J. Snikker

TALK: 1. "The Mariposa Folk Festival."
By: M. Schweykowsky
2. "Canadian Scene." From the Department of the Secretary of State.

SATURDAY

NEWS BULLETIN:

TALK: "CBC Shortwave Club." By: Basil Duke

MUSIC: "Folk Songs"-Tom Kines and Jean Price; Jacques Labrecque; Charles Jordan and Joyce Sullivan

BIBLIOGRAPHY

I. BOOKS

Abshire, David. *International Broadcasting: A New Dimension of Western Diplomacy.* Beverly Hills: Sage Publishers, 1976.

Anderson, James E. *Public Policy Making,* 2d ed. New York: Holt, Rinehart and Winston, 1979.

Babe, Robert E. *Telecommunications in Canada: Technology, Industry, and Government.* Toronto: University of Toronto Press, 1990.

Barnouw, Erik. *A Tower in Babel: A History of Broadcasting in the United States, Volume I—to 1933.* New York: Oxford University Press, 1966.

Bird, Roger, ed. *Documents of Canadian Broadcasting.* Ottawa: Carleton University Press, 1988.

Brebner, J. Bartlett. *Canada: A Modern History.* Ann Arbor: University of Michigan Press, 1960.

Briggs, Asa. *The History of Broadcasting in the United Kingdom.* Vol. 1, *The Golden Age of Wireless.* London: Oxford University Press, 1965.

_____. *The History of Broadcasting in the United Kingdom.* Vol. 2, *The War of Words.* London: Oxford University Press, 1965.

Browne, Don R. *International Shortwave Radio Broadcasting: The Limits of the Limitless Medium.* New York: Praeger Publishers, 1982.

Careless, J. M. S. *Canada: A Story of Challenge.* Toronto: Macmillan of Canada, 1963.

Childs, H. S., and J. B. Whitton, eds. *Propaganda by Shortwave.* Princeton, N.J.: Oxford University Press, 1942.

Clark, Gerald. *Canada: The Uneasy Neighbor.* New York: David McKay Co., 1965.

Cottrell, Alvin J., and James E. Dougherty. *The Politics of the Atlantic Alliance.* New York: Frederik A. Praeger, Publisher, 1964.

Dawson, Robert M. *The Government of Canada*, 3d ed., rev. Toronto: University of Toronto Press, 1957.

Eayrs, James. *The Art of the Possible: Government and Foreign Policy in Canada*. Toronto: University of Toronto Press, 1961.

Eccles, W. J. *The Ordeal of New France: The French Colonial Period*. Montreal: Pierre Des Marais, Inc., for the Canadian Broadcasting Corporation International Service, 1966.

Emery, Walter B. *National and International Systems of Broadcasting: Their History, Operation and Control*. East Lansing: Michigan State University Press, 1969.

Farrell, R. Barry. *The Making of Canadian Foreign Policy*. Scarborough, Ont.: Prentice-Hall of Canada, Ltd., 1969.

Fraser, Blair. *The Search for Identity: Canada, 1945-1967*. Toronto: Doubleday Canada Ltd., 1967.

Frost, J. M., ed. *World Radio-TV Handbook 1970*. 24th ed. Hvidovre, Denmark: World Radio-TV Handbook, 1970.

Granatstein, J. J., ed. *Canadian Foreign Policy Since 1945: Middle Power or Satellite*. Toronto: Copp Clark Publishing Co., 1969.

Grindrod, Muriel. *The Rebuilding of Italy: Politics and Economics, 1945-1955*. London: Oxford University Press for the Royal Institute of International Affairs, 1955.

Hale, Julian. *Radio Power: Propaganda and International Broadcasting*. Philadelphia: Temple University Press, 1975.

Hicks, John D., and George E. Mowry. *A Short History of American Democracy*. 2d ed. Boston: Houghton Mifflin Co., 1956.

Holt, Robert T. *Radio Free Europe*. Minneapolis: University of Minnesota Press, 1958.

Jackson, Robert J., Doreen Jackson, and Nicolas Baxter-Moore. *Politics in Canada: Culture, Institutions, Behavior and Public Policy*. Scarborough, Ont.: Prentice-Hall Canada, Inc., 1986.

LaPierre, Laurier. *Genesis of a Nation: The British Colonial Period*. Montreal: Pierre Des Marais, Inc., for the Canadian Broadcasting Corporation International Service, 1966.

_____. *The Apprenticeship: The Dominion of Canada's First Half Century*. Montreal: Pierre Des Marais, Inc., for the Canadian Broadcasting Corporation International Service, 1967.

Lasswell, H. D. *Propaganda Techniques in the World War*. New York: Alfred A. Knopf, 1927.

Levin, Harvey J. *The Invisible Resource: Use and Regulation of the Radio Spectrum*. Baltimore: The Johns Hopkins University Press, 1971.

Mammarella, Guiseppe. *Italy After Fascism: A Political History*. Montreal: Mario Casalini, Ltd., 1964.

Mandell, Eli, and David Toras. *A Passion for Identity: An Introduction to Canadian Studies*. Toronto: Methuen Publications, 1987.

Mansell, Gerard. *Let Truth Be Told: 50 Years of BBC External Broadcasting* London: Weidenfeld and Nicolson, 1982.

Masters, D. C. *The Coming of Age: The Modern Era: 1914-1967*. Montreal: Pierre Des Marais, Inc., for the Canadian Broadcasting Corporation International Service, 1967.

McNaught, Kenneth. *The Pelican History of Canada*. Baltimore, MD: Penguin Books, Inc., 1969.

Morton, Desmond. *A Short History of Canada*. Edmonton: Hurtig Publishers, Ltd., 1983.

Newman, Peter C. *Renegade in Power: The Diefenbaker Years*. Toronto: McClelland and Stewart Ltd., 1963.

Organski, A. F. K. *World Politics*. New York: Alfred A. Knopf, Inc., 1968.

Park, Julian. *The Culture of Contemporary Canada*. Ithaca, N.Y.: Cornell University Press, 1957.

Peers, Frank W. *The Politics of Canadian Broadcasting: 1920-1951*. Toronto: University of Toronto Press, 1969.

Raboy, Marc. *Missed Opportunities: The Story of Canada's Broadcasting Policy*. Montreal & Kingston: McGill-Queen's University Press, 1993.

Rosen, Philip T., ed. *International Handbook of Broadcasting Systems*. New York: Greenwood Press, Inc., 1988.

Schramm, W. ed. *The Process and Effects of Communication*. (Urbana: University of Illinois Press, 1970).

Shea, Albert A. *Broadcasting the Canadian Way*. Montreal: Harvest House, 1963.

Short, K. R. M., ed. *Western Broadcasting Over the Iron Curtain*. New York: St. Martin's Press, 1986.

Sington, Derrick, and Arthur Weidenfeld. *The Goebbels Experiment: A Study of the Nazi Propaganda Machine*. New Haven: Yale University Press, 1946.

Smith, B. L., H. D. Lasswell, and R. D Casey. *Propaganda, Communication, and Public Opinion*. Princeton, N.J.: Princeton University Press, 1943.

Sorensen, Thomas C. *The Word War: The Story of American Propaganda*. New York: Harper & Row, Publishers, 1968.

Soward, F. H. *Canada in World Affairs*. Toronto: Oxford University Press, 1950.

_____. and Edgar McInnis, and with the assistance of Walter O'Hearn. *Canada and the United Nations*. National Studies on International Organization. New York: Manhattan Publishing Company for the Canadian Institute of International Peace, 1956.

Stafford, David. *Camp X*. New York: Pocket Books, a Division of Simon & Shuster Inc., 1988.

Stevenson, William. *Intrepid's Last Case*. New York: Villard Books, Inc., 1984.

Strausez-Hupe, Robert, James E. Dougherty, and William R. Kintner. *Building the Atlantic World*. New York: Harper & Row, Publishers, 1963.

Talman, James J. *Basic Documents in Canadian History*. Princeton, N.J.: D. Van Nostrand Co., 1959.

II. PUBLIC DOCUMENTS

A. COMMISSIONS

Canada. Royal Commission on Radio Broadcasting. *Report*. Commission chairman was Sir John Aird. Ottawa: King's Printer, 1929.

_____. Royal Commission on Broadcasting. *Report*. Commission chairman was Robert Fowler. Ottawa: Queen's Printer, 1957.

_____. Royal Commission on Bilingualism and Biculturalism. *Report*. Commission chairmen were André Laurendeau and Davidson Dunton. Ottawa: Queen's Printer, 1969.

_____. *Report of the Task Force on Broadcasting Policy*. Commission Co-chairmen were Gerald Lewis Caplan and Florian Sauvageau. September 1986. Ottawa: Minister of Supply and Services, 1986.

B. COMMITTEES

Canada. Special committee on Radio Broadcasting. *Minutes of Proceedings and Evidence*. 1932, 1938, 1942.

_____. Special Committee on the Operations of the Commission under the Canadian Radio Broadcasting Act (1932). *Minutes of Proceedings and Evidence*, 1934.

_____. Special Committee on the Canadian Radio Commission. *Minutes of Proceedings and Evidence*. 1936.

_____. House of Commons. Standing Committee on Radio Broadcasting. *Minutes of Proceedings and Evidence*. 20 May 1938, 17 May 1951, 30 May 1951, 26 February 1953, 2 March 1953, 12 March 1953, 17 March 1953, 26 March 1953, 17 May 1953, 10 June 1954, 5 May 1955.

_____. House of Commons. Special Committee on Broadcasting. *Minutes of Proceedings and Evidence*. 1942.

_____. House of Commons. Standing Committee on External Affairs. *Minutes of Proceedings and Evidence*. 10 May 1955.

_____. Advisory Committee on Broadcasting. *Report*. Committee chairman was Robert Fowler. Ottawa: Queen's Printer, 1965.

_____. *Report of the Federal Cultural Policy Review Committee*. Commission chairman was Louis Applebaum and Co-chairman was Jacques Hébert. November 1982. Ottawa: Information Services, Department of Communications, Government of Canada, 1982.

C. DEBATES

Canada. Parliament. House of Commons. *Debates*. 1945 -79.

D. ORDERS IN COUNCIL

_____. Orders in Council P.C. 8168, 18 September 1942; P.C. 156/8855, 17 November 1943; P.C. 97/1983, 21 March 1944; P.C. 140/2247 of 4 April 1945; P.C. 128/4848, 27 November 1947; P.C. 13/2400 of 28 May 1948; P.C. 1955-56/488, 6 April 1955; P.C. 168-525, 19 March 1968 P.C. 168-525, 19 March 1968.

E. STATUTES

Great Britain. *The British North America Act, 1867*, 30 Victoria, c.3.
Canada. *The Wireless Telegraphy Act, 1905*. 4-5 Edw. 7, c. 49.

_____. *An Act to Create a Department of External Affairs*. 8-9 Edw. 7. 1909. c. 13.

_____. *The Radiotelegraph Act, 1913.* 3-4 Geo. 5, c. 43.
_____. *An Act Respecting Radio Broadcasting, 1932.* 22-23 Geo. 5, c.
51.
_____. *The Canadian Broadcasting Act, 1936.* 1 Edw. 8, c. 24.
_____. *Broadcasting Act, 1958.* 7 Eliz. 2, c. 22.
_____. *Broadcasting Act, 1968.* 16-17 Eliz. 2, c. 25.

                              F. MISCELLANEOUS

Canada. *Supreme Court.* "In the matter of a reference as to the jurisdic-
tion of Parliament to regulate and control radio communication." 30
June 1931. *Supreme Court Reports* 541 (1931).
_____. Dominion Bureau of Statistics, *Canada 1971: The Annual
Handbook of Present Conditions and Recent Progress.* Ottawa:
Information Canada, 1971.
_____. LaMarsh, Judy. Secretary of State. *White Paper on
Broadcasting.* Ottawa: Queen's Printer and Controller of Stationery,
1966.
_____. Public Archives. Orders-in-Council. 16 September - 18
September, 1942. Reference Group 2,1, Volume 2154.

                III. CANADIAN BROADCASTING CORPORATION

                      A. REPORTS AND SUBMISSIONS

Canadian Broadcasting Corporation. "International Service: Information
Prepared on the Desirability of Its Establishment, 1938-1942."
Ottawa, n.d. (Mimeographed.)
_____. *Annual Report.* 1945 through 1985.
_____. *CBC Desk Reference Manual.* Ottawa: Canadian Broadcasting
Corporation, 1946.
_____. "The International Service of the Canadian Broadcasting
Corporation: 1945-1950." Montreal, 1 October 1950.
_____. "Report on International Service." Montreal, October 1956.
_____. "CBC International Service: A Joint Submission of the
Department of External Affairs and of the Canadian Broadcasting
Corporation." Montreal, August 1960. (Mimeographed.)
_____. *Broadcasting in Canada: History and Development of the
National System.* Ottawa: Information Services, Canadian

Broadcasting Corporation, 1960.

_____. "International Service: Policies and Practices." Montreal, January 1963. (Mimeographed.)

_____. "The International Service of the Canadian Broadcasting Corporation." Montreal, December 1967. (Mimeographed.)

_____. *CBC - A Brief History and Background.* Ottawa: Information Services, Canadian Broadcasting Corporation, 1968.

_____. "International Service." Montreal, January 1968. (Mimeographed.)

_____. "General Information." CBC Northern Service. 15 December 1971.

_____. "International Broadcasting Service, 1971-72 Program Memorandum." n.d. (Mimeographed.)

_____. "Report on Organization and Job Classification in the International Service." July 1971. (Mimeographed.)

Radio Canada International. "Highlights: 15 Years of the Hungarian Section." 12 November 1972. (Mimeographed.)

_____. "Report of the Radio Canada International Task Force." 9 May 1973.

_____. Hall, James L., and Drew O. McDaniel, "The United States Shortwave Listener Audience for International Broadcasts." October 1973. (Mimeographed.)

_____. Yates, Alan. "Radio Canada International and Japan: A Survey of the Broadcasting Scene in Japan and as Assessment of Potential RCI Service in and to that Country." March 1975. (Mimeographed.)

_____. "Radio Canada International: An Efficiency Formula and It's Consequences." 1977.

_____. "The CBC - A Perspective." Vols. 1-3. Submission to the Canadian Radio-television and Telecommunications Commission in Support of Applications for Renewal of Network Licenses. May 1978.

_____."RCI Program Evaluation Form," Montreal, 1984.

B. CONFIDENTIAL FILES

Canadian Broadcasting Corporation. Montreal. Central Registry File numbers: IS54-5-1; IS4-5-1, vol. 1; IS4-2-6, vol. 1; C14-12-29; IS-2-25, vol. 1.

C. PROGRAM SCHEDULES AND WEEKLY REPORTS

Canadian Broadcasting Corporation International Service. *Program Schedules.* 1946 through 1971.

_____. "Weekly Report: English Section," 18-24 July 1971.

_____. "Weekly Report: French Section," 19-23 July 1971.

_____. "Weekly Report: Current Affairs Officer," 19-23 July 1971.

_____. "Weekly Report: Czechoslovakian, German, Hungarian, Polish, Portuguese, Russian, Slovak, Spanish, Ukrainian Sections," 18-24 July 1971.

IV. PERSONAL INTERVIEWS AND CORRESPONDENCE WITH PERSONNEL OF THE CANADIAN BROADCASTING CORPORATION INTERNATIONAL SERVICE, RADIO CANADA INTERNATIONAL, AND DEPARTMENT OF EXTERNAL AFFAIRS

Personal Interviews in Montreal, 1971:

Butcher, E. O., Head, Portuguese Section
Chipman, C., Head, Russian Section
Coté, L., Director, Information Programming
Delafield, C. R., Director
Mezai, J., Head, Hungarian Section
Pick, G. P., Head, German Section
Svedman, J., Current Affairs Officer
Rodriguez, J., Head Latin American Section
Schmolka, W., Head, Czechoslovakian Section
Stewart, E. C., Engineering Services
Tallman, P., Head, English Section
Townsley, B., Supervisor, Publicity and Audience Relations
Wesolowsky, J. B., Head, Ukrainian Section

Personal Interviews in Ottawa, 1971:

Hicks, A. L., Information Division, External Affairs
Pidgeon, A. L., Manager, CBC-IS Office

Personal Interviews in Montreal, 1987:

Familiant, A., Information Programming
Randall, K., Supervisor, Publicity and Audience Relations

Zimmerman, B., Director

Personal Interview in Ottawa, 1987:

Barban, G., Information Division, External Affairs

Correspondence

Letter from Daniel R. Proteau, Assistant Supervisor, Publicity and Audience Relations, 2 May 1972.
Letter from Brian Townsley, Supervisor, Publicity and Audience Relations, 18 December 1973.

V. Miscellaneous

Statement, Paul Martin. Secretary of State for External Affairs. 24 January 1964.
Telegram from Yvon Cherrier to Lester B. Pearson. 30 November 1967.
Telex PST102 from Department of External Affairs to C. R. Delafield. 8 December 1967.
Memorandum from Guy Coderre to President, C.B.C. 15 January 1968.

VI. Articles

Black, Gordon. "Shortwave Survives at RCI." *Broadcaster*, March 1980.
Blume, Helmut. "Barbed Wire Broadcasts." *Radio* 1 (April 1946), Staff Magazine, Canadian Broadcasting Corporation.
Careless, James. "Making Waves Abroad." *Maclean's*, 19 October 1987.
Dilworth, Ira. "The Voice of Canada: The International Service of the Canadian Broadcasting Corporation." *External Affairs* 1 (July 1949).
Fraser, Blair. "Last Chance for the CBC's $2-million Voice of Canada." *Maclean's*, 22 February 1964.
Hall, James L., and Drew O. McDaniel. "The United States' Shortwave Listener Audience for International Broadcasts." *Journal of Broadcasting*, Summer 1975.
Laver, Ross. "How We Differ." *Maclean's*, 3 January 1994.
Mackay, Gillian. "CBC Faces the Music." *Maclean's*, 24 December 1984.
Prang, Margaret. "The Origins of Public Broadcasting in Canada." *The Canadian Historical Review* 46 (March 1965).

VII. NEWSPAPERS

Daily Star (Toronto), 6 July 1965; 4, 6 December 1967.

Editorial, *Daily Times* (Victoria, B.C.),10 March 1964.

Globe and Mail (Toronto), 4 March 1964; 7 July 1965; 4 December 1967.

La Press (Montreal), 7 July 1965.

Montreal Gazette, 21 January 1951; 30 November, 2,5,6 December 1967.

Montreal Star, 1, 4, 5, 7, 22 December 1967.

New York Times, 26 February 1945; 23 January, 28 April, 1 May 1967;

Ottawa Citizen, 2 December 1967.

Editorial, *Toronto Telegram*, 19 July 1948.

Wallaceburg Ontario News, 19 December 1967.

VIII. UNPUBLISHED DISSERTATIONS AND THESES

Hall, James L. "The History and Policies of the Canadian Broadcasting Corporation's International Service." Ph.D. diss., Ohio University, 1972.

Hamilton, John E. III. "We Know They're Out There Somewhere: Evaluating the Audience Research Methods of International Radio Broadcasters: A Case Study of Radio Canada International." Master's thesis, University of Windsor (Ontario), 1987.

Toogood, Alexander F. "The Canadian Broadcasting Corporation: A Question of Control." Ph.D. diss., Ohio State University, 1969.

INDEX

ABC Alliance, 11;
abolishment, 102; see also, crisis and consolidation
Agence France Presse, 78;
Aird, Sir John, 6;
Aird Commission: 1; financing of and report, 6; see also, Royal Commission on Radio Broadcasting (1928)
Akor, John, 165;
austerity, a call for, 97;
Aylen, Peter: first director of CBC-IS, 19-20, 28, 46;

Balfour, Earl of; Committee; Declaration, 10;
Barban, Gaston, 173;
BBC: carries Canadian French programs, 21; coincides with CBC-IS first daily transmissions to USSR, 83; conducts public opinion surveys with CBC-IS, 90; forty languages and eighty transmitters, 174; Gallup Survey, 167-168; jamming, 91; joint audience research with CBC-IS, 170; relationship with CBC-IS, 67; scheduling coordination with CBC-IS, 68; size of shortwave service,167; transmitter rental, 127, 129; see also, British Broadcasting Corporation
Blume, Helmut, 29, 116-7;
Board of Broadcast Governors, 104;
Boyd, Hugh, 39;

Braithwaite, Dennis, 114;
Brewin, Andrew, 113, 115;
Britannia Heights, shortwave receiving station location, 12;
British North America Act, 7; provisions, 9;
British Broadcasting Corporation: broadcasting operations of, 158; relaying programs of, 8; see also, BBC
British United Press, 78;
British Security Cooperation, 11;
Broadcasting Act (1958), 104;
Broadcasting Act (1968), 118;
Brockington, L.W., 12-13, 188;
Brown, Alan, 158; appointed RCI Director, 164; 174, 176;
Bryce, Robert, 114, 115;
budget problems, 173-76;
Bushnell, E.L., 14, 20, 27, 32, 188;
Butcher, E.O., 153;
Butler, B.C., 32;

Camp X, 11;
Canadian Armed Forces, 107, 113, 115;
Canadian Broadcasting Corporation: establishment of, 8; Ford Hotel purchase, 75;
Canadian Radio Broadcasting Act (1932), 7;
Canadian Radio-television Telecommunications Commission, 172-3;

291

Canadian Radio Broadcasting
    Company, 6;
Canadian Radio Broadcasting
    Commission, 7;
Canadian Press, 78;
Caron, Jean-Lucien, 158;
CBA, Sackville, 17;
CBC Research, 168;
CFCF,Montreal, 3; see also, XWA
Cherrier, Yvon, 113
Chevrier, C.B., 101;
Chipman, Carroll, 150-1, 171;
Christian and Military Alliance, 5;
Citizenship and Immmigration,
    Department of, 109;
CJAD-AM, Montreal, 56;
CJYC, 5; see also, Universal Radio of
    Canada
CKCX, 5; see also, International Bible
    Student's Association
CKNC, 21;
Coderre, Guy, 123-4;
constitutionality question, 108;
Cossitt, Tom, 170-1;
Coté, Lucian, 141, 154;
crisis and consolidation, 111;

Delafield, Charles R.: appointed, testi-
    mony, 65, 69, 72; biographical
    data, 75-6, 90-1, 112, 114, 117;
    memorandum of 1969,157; on
    External Affairs advice, 138-9;
    retirement, 164, 176;
Désy, Jean: administrative relation-
    ships, 60-61; controversy, 183;
    coordination with VOA and BBC,
    68; effectiveness issue, 90; employ-
    ment, 109; liaison with External
    Affairs, 61-62; managerial style,
    not CBC employee, 89; resigned,
    77; seconded to Director, CBC-IS,
    59; testimony, aims of CBC-IS
    operations, 71-2; Villa Lobos con-
    cert, 63-65;

Deutsche Welle, 158, 163;
Diefenbaker, John G., 97-8;
Dilworth, Ira: appointed director,
    CBC-IS, 30; Keyserlingk charges,
    59; operational policy, 35-6;
Douglas, T.C., 114;
Drew, George, 49, 57, 93;
Dumbarton Oaks Conference, 42;
Dunton, Davidson: chairman of the
    board,CBC, 32, 39, 59, 68; general
    manager, Wartime Information
    Board and member, Shortwave
    Joint Commmittee, 20; jamming,
    92

European Broadcasting Union, 166;
Expo '67, 111, 133; see also, Man
    and His World
External Affairs, Department of: 1960
    policy request received, 97; and
    shortwave broadcasts, 15; CBC
    liaison ,17, 55, 89; creation, 9;
    Kerserlingk attacks, 56, 57;policy
    coordinator, 58;

Familiant, Alan, 169;
Federal Cultural Policy Review
    Committee (Applebaum-Herbert),
    175;
Fowler, Robert M., 105;
Fowler Committee: CBC-IS relation-
    ship with CBC and External
    Affairs, 117; purpose, 105; recom-
    mendations, 106-110, 112; recom-
    mends transmitters for Northern
    Service, 98;
Frajkor, George, 113;
Fraser, Blair, 103, 107;
Free French, 15; see also, WRUL
Frigon, Augustin, 15; shortwave joint
    committee, 19, 32;

Gallup Associates, 167;
Glazebrook, G., 32;

Good Neighbor Policy, 10; see also, Roosevelt
Goodale, Ralf, 172;
Gotlieb, A.E., 173;
Gould, Jack, 39;
Graydon, Gordon, 70;
Group of Four, 165-6;

Heeney, A.D.P., 32;
Holowach, Ambrose, 74-5;

Information Abroad Committee, 69;
International Bible Students Association, 5-6; see also, Jehovah's Witnesses
International Frequency Registration Board, 37;
International Telecommunications Conference (1932), 12;
International Telecommunications Union, 36, 37;

jamming: caused by negative Soviet reactions, 91; Dunton testimony, 92; problematic across Eastern Europe, 99; VOA, BBC, CBC-IS coordination to minimize effect, 68; see also, VOA, BBC
Jehovah's Witnesses, 5;
Johnson, A.W., 171;
Joint Report (1960), 99;

Keyserlingk, Robert, 56, 58-9, 183;
King, Mackenzie, 11, 12, 15, 18, 27;
King George VI, royal visit of, 14;
Korean Conflict, 53;

LaMarsh, Judy, 110;
Lamontagne,Maurice, 105;

MacBride Commission, 166;
Man and His World, 111; management, 30, 75; consequences of, 164-66;

Manson, Donald, 13, 188;
Martin, Paul, 102, 113-4;
Marven, Ralph, 47;
McCann, J.J., 48, 73-4;
McCarthy, Joseph M., 182, 183;
Mogilansky, M., 171;
Morin, Rene, 14, 188;
Morrison, H.W., 58-9;
Morton, Desmond, 111;

National Film Board of Canada, 109, 181, 183;
National Research Council, 109;
Newark News Radio Club, 167;
NHK, 164;
North Atlantic Treaty Organization (NATO), 33-5, 70;
Northern Service of CBC: establishment of 98; operations after proposed abolishment, 115; shared time, 107, 113; sharing time with CBC-IS, 100; transmission time, 101; transmitters dedicated for, 176; use of Sackville transmitters, 99;

Office of War Information (U.S.), CBC broadcasts used by, 21;
Official Languages Act, 2;
Order in Council P.C. 1968-525, 118;
Order in Council P.C. 8168, 32, 60, 75, 109;
organization: after integration, 123-26; status and financing, 100; structure, 19, 31; 1971 example, 139
ORTF, 158, 163

Paris Peace Conference (1919), 10;
Pearson, Lester B.: ambassador to U.S. and CBC-IS transmitter procurement, 18-9; comments on abolishment, 115-17; explains liaison between External Affairs and CBC-IS, 57-8, 61; receives wire

requesting comments on abolish-
ment, 113; secretary of state and
comments on Czechoslovakian ser-
vice, 48; testimony on program-
ming, 71, 81;
Permanent Joint Board on Defense,
11;
Phelps, Arthur: appointed director,
CBC-IS, 30;
Pick, Gerd, 146-8;
Pidgeon, Arthur L., 76-8; policy:
defined, 54-6; 1960 statement,
120;
Presbyterian Church, 5;
Programming Patterns: 1947-50:
Europe, 42-44; 1951-59:
Australasia, 85 Latin American,
85; Russian, 80-83; Western
Europe, 84; Summary, 86; 1960-
69, 127-132; 1971: Caribbean-
U.S.A., Africa, and S. Pacific, 153
Eastern Europe, 148-52; Latin
America, 152-53; Western Europe,
145-48;
propaganda, definition of, 34-5;
psychological warfare: definition of,
34, war use of, 28-9; 182;

QSL card, 169;

Radio Australia, 168;
Radio Belgrade, 159, 163;
Radio Canada International, name
change, 157; Task Force, 186;
Radio-Canada Shortwave Club estab-
lished, 135, 143;
Radio Corporation of America
(RCA): 18, 19; RCA Victor
Company, 133;
Radio Havana, 106, 167;
Radio Italiana, 87; see also, RAI
Radio Japan, 159, 163;
Radio Moscow, 106, 167;
Radio Nederland, 163, 165, 167-68;

Radio Sweden, 163, 165;
Radio Tanpa, 175;
Radio Vaticana, 87; see also, Vatican
Radio
Radiotelegraph Act (1913), 5;
Rae, S.F., 33;
RAI, 87;
Reuters, 78;
Robertson, Norman, 19, 32;
Rodriquez, J.J., 153;
Roosevelt, Franklin D., 10, 11;
Royal Commission on Bilingualism
and Biculturalism, 2;
Royal Commmission on Radio
Broadcasting (1928), 6; see also,
Aird Commission
Sackville, New Brunswick: CBC-IS
transmitter site cost, 16; effective
range, 162; efficiency rating, 174;
established, 79; Fowler Report,
107; recommendation for site mod-
ernization, 104 supervisor of engi-
neering, 104, 113;

Schmolka, Walter, 148;
Screening, CBC-IS personnel, 49;
Shaw, Robert, 111;
Shortwave Joint Commmittee, 69;
Soward, F.H., 32;
Special Training School 103: 111; see
also, Camp X
Special Committee on the Canadian
Radio Commission (1936), 8;
Standing Committee on Radio
Broadcasting (1938), 13;
Standing Committee on Radio
Broadcasting (1942), 15, 16;
Starr, Michael, 115;
Statute of Westminster, 10;
Stephenson, William, 11;
Stewart, E.C., 18;
Stone, T.A., 19;
Svizzero Italiana Diffusione, 87;
Swiss Radio, 87, 165;

Tantramar Marshes, 17;
Task Force on Broadcasting Policy (Caplan-Sauvegeau), 176;
Taylor, Deems, 39;
Thornton, Sir Henry, 4;
Townsley, Brian, 158;
Trade and Commerce, Department of, 32, 109;
Trans-Canada Network, CBC-IS, inaugural address carried on, 27;
Tyler, Keith, 39;

UNESCO, 166; see also, MacBride Commission
United Nations: Aylen joins staff of, 30;
United Church of Canada, 5;
United Nations, 36, 42, 53;
Universal Radio of Canada, 5; see also, CJYC

Vatican Radio, 87;
VE-Day, 30;
Voice of America: categorized large service, 163; coincided transmissions, 83; Cold War broadcasting, 182-83; comment from American listener, 116; compared with CBC-IS, 30; coordination with CBC-IS, 68; counter-propaganda, 65; jamming, 9; languages broadcast, 101-102; languages and hours

broadcast, 107; participation with RCI research, 170; RCI Task Force participation in, 158; "war of ideas" campaign, 67;
Voice of West Germany, 167;

WARC, 37;
Wartime Information Board, 20; see also, Dunton
Wesolowsky, J.B., 151-2;
White Paper on Broadcasting (1966), 110, 112-13, 117;
Wilgress, Dana, 54, 60, 70;
World Allocation Radio Conferences, 37; see also, WARC
World Service of the BBC, 65; see also, BBC
WRUL, Boston, 15, 21;

XWA, Montreal, 3; see also, CFCF

Yaroshevsky, F., 170-1;
Yates, Alan, 164-5;

Zimmerman, Betty: appointed director, RCI and member MacBride Commission, 166; clarification of RCI relationship with External Affairs, 173; program review process, 169; RCI Task Force Chair, 157; weathering economic difficulties, 176.